GEORGE SZELL'S REIGN

MUSIC IN AMERICAN LIFE

*A list of books in the series appears
at the end of this book.*

GEORGE SZELL'S REIGN

Behind the Scenes
with the Cleveland Orchestra

MARCIA HANSEN KRAUS

UNIVERSITY OF ILLINOIS PRESS
Urbana, Chicago, and Springfield

Library of Congress Control Number: 2017949934
ISBN 978-0-252-04131-0 (hardcover)
ISBN 978-0-252-09991-5 (e-book)

In memory of Felix Kraus and Carl Beecher

"The chief ability of a genius consists in pursuing his objective with a far greater intensity than average people can even imagine."
—Klaus Eidam, "The True Life of Bach"

Contents

Illustrations follow page 132.

Introduction

THIS IS AN ACCOUNT OF symphony conductor George Szell's quarter-century reign as music director of the Cleveland Orchestra. Hired in 1946 to create a fine symphony orchestra, he built that institution into what many considered the world's best.

From his beginning as a child prodigy in Vienna, Szell knew his potential. He was finally able to achieve it in Cleveland, inspiring his musicians with his vision of great symphonic performances. The players put up with his tyranny, recognizing that they and he were united in a magnificent undertaking. This book details how he bent them and others to his will, forging an orchestra that put Cleveland on the international cultural map.

As the wife of oboist Felix Kraus, who played under Szell for seven dramatic years, I was privileged to hear behind-the-scenes stories that illuminated Szell's authoritarian methods and personality. A musician myself, I vividly recall the April morning in 1963 when I first heard the orchestra rehearsing with Szell in Severance Hall. The brilliance and clarity of the sound was astounding. I couldn't help but know that I was in the presence of musical greatness.

Five years ago I began contacting retired Szell-era Cleveland Orchestra members with a view to writing about them and their difficult taskmaster. Many of these musicians were octogenarians, and their recollections needed to be captured before the opportunity passed. Seeking to explain such a complex person as Szell, I have, in some instances, employed speculation as a way of vivifying his life.

Without Szell's insistence and leadership, it is doubtful that the spectacular Blossom Pavilion would exist. Interviews with its designers and builders convinced me of its place among the world's great structures. My chapters and illustrations dealing with its construction will, I hope, encourage readers to go see for themselves.

While talking to people who were involved with Szell, I became aware that most of them considered him a musical genius. And many of his musicians said that playing in the Cleveland Orchestra under his autocratic leadership was the high point of their lives. Brilliant, controversial, and driven, Szell was in thrall to a demanding muse.

Will there ever be another like him? Probably not.

Marcia Hansen Kraus, 2016

GEORGE SZELL'S REIGN

CHAPTER 1

A Prodigy's Apprenticeship

AT AGE TWO AND A HALF George Szell had strong musical opinions. One day his mother, noticing that her precocious son seemed musical, had put him on her lap and played a tune on the piano. She hadn't gone very far when he slapped her wrist.[1] He didn't like the mistake she had made and wouldn't tolerate it. That was the beginning of his years as a prodigy.

If that slap had been administered to an uneducated hausfrau in a remote village, George would have received a paddling and that would have been the end of the incident. But in a random stroke of luck, he was born in 1897 to upper-class parents who lived in a fine neighborhood in Budapest, cultivated the arts, and had left their Jewish roots behind when they converted to Catholicism. The elements necessary for George's future success were therefore present, including even the right city, because in 1900 his parents moved to Vienna, a center of amateur and professional music making.[2]

George was fortunate to have a music-loving father. Kalman doted on his only child and, realizing his son was exceptional, determined to do everything in his power to foster the boy's talent. He wasn't wrong in his assessment of his son's superiority because the child soon began composing. Kalman had sired a wunderkind.

Six-year-old George was taken to Richard Robert, one of the city's foremost piano teachers, where he joined a class of other talented children, among them young Rudolf Serkin.[3] That wasn't enough for the proud father. He regularly brought the child with him to opera and orchestra concerts, hired tutors so there would be no time wasted in public schools, provided a fine piano for lengthy practice sessions, and agreed with the teacher that there should also be music theory and composition lessons. In this nurturing environment George flourished, eagerly competing with his fellow students, memorizing great chunks of piano literature and giving frequent recitals. He soaked up music like a sponge, retaining it all.

At nine years of age George was a sturdy lad with regular features, blond hair, blue eyes, a sense of humor, and a fondness for pranks. At eleven he made his public debut playing his own compositions, and critics hailed him as the new child Mozart. A year later, in 1909, the Emil Gutman concert agency put out an eight-page brochure extolling George's accomplishments as a pianist and composer, affirming that he was "not a conventional prodigy but a genuine artist in the person of a child."[4]

Like the young Wolfgang Mozart, who listened to a Miserere by Giorgio Allegri and then wrote it down note for note, young George could listen to an orchestral piece and then transcribe it. Few musicians in the world can duplicate such a feat.

His parents wisely refused to exploit him, limiting his public appearances despite lucrative offers from concert managers. With no need for money, they consented to only a single concert tour of major European cities including London, where George dazzled critics and audiences alike. It would be wrong to conclude that George, thus shielded by his parents, was unaware of his exceptional abilities, because his adoring father kept proofs of George's musical achievements in glass display cases in the family's parlor.[5] Such exhibits contributed to George's growing sense of his own superiority; modesty was not one of his virtues. As the young boy demonstrated his improvisational abilities on the piano, he would announce to admiring listeners what instruments should be playing certain passages. He even predicted his own future, saying that he would become a conductor.

Vienna's newspapers were filled with accounts of what had transpired the night before at the Staatsoper, the city's world-famous opera house. In coffeehouses people gossiped about the latest opera productions, the latest piano and orchestral concerts, which conductor hewed closest to Beethoven's intentions, which divas were good or mediocre, and which string quartet was worth listening to.[6]

Viennese weren't content with merely listening to music. Many of those in the middle and upper classes also played an instrument, either in amateur orchestras or chamber music groups. A favorite pastime consisted of playing string quartets in each other's homes, their friends listening intently to a Beethoven or Haydn composition and then everyone enjoying a delicious assortment of strudels and tortes. All were expected to authoritatively discuss the music. The tone-deaf boned up on musical facts and composers' lives, not letting it slip that they were congenitally unfit for music. In Vienna that was tantamount to revealing you were illiterate.

The paths of prodigies aren't all strewn with roses. After the initial acclaim, they have to weather puberty when they are no longer cute and their minds begin to register things theretofore ignored. It is then that many of them fade from public view, unable to cope with approaching adulthood and the loss of youthful appeal. When George was fourteen and already a finished musician, he went through a difficult period. One of his friends, Hans Gal, recalled that George began shirking piano practice, indulging in sadistic pranks and becoming physically violent with his teachers and the household servants.[7]

He became so impossible that his parents, unable to control their young tyrant, packed him off to Carl Jung in Switzerland. Although there is no evidence George's behavior was caused by any mental aberration, psychoanalysis was becoming acceptable in Vienna—it was actually a fad in certain social circles—and the Szells were well able to pay for treatment. Whatever treatment he received in Switzerland, however, seems not to have changed him much. After a couple of months he returned to his parents barely improved, though his already extensive vocabulary now contained bits of psychological jargon.[8]

Neglecting his musical work, he began frequenting bookstores, cramming into his head the classics of German literature and indulging his taste for fine food and clothing, proclivities he shared with his father. He soaked up books, his retentive memory enabling him to fill gaps in his knowledge caused by years of total immersion in music, and emerged with a fairly well rounded education. He picked up what remained to be learned by listening to the Viennese intelligentsia in coffeehouses where they traded critical remarks about art, music, literature, philosophy, and each other. Soon, however, he collected himself, returning to playing and conducting.[9]

George fit right into the musical hothouse that was Vienna. At sixteen the tall, strapping musical whiz began accompanying the Staatsoper singers and pestering the pit musicians with questions about their instruments. This paid off two years later when the composer Richard Strauss was late for a recording session of his tone poem *Don Juan*. Confidently stepping onto the podium, George conducted the first part of the sixteen-minute piece.

Arriving soon after, Strauss was greatly impressed by what he heard. Here was an eighteen-year-old conducting more than competently—brilliantly in fact. When George relinquished the podium to the great composer, Strauss declined to start over from the beginning, saying that young Szell's interpretation was good enough to go out on the record as Strauss's own.[10]

By then George had composed more than three hundred works, and his proud father hired an orchestra to perform several of them so George could hear what he had written. Composing, however, fell by the wayside. When Rudolf Serkin surprised him on his sixteenth birthday with a performance of a Szell piano composition, Szell admonished his friend, "Rudy, how can you play such trash?"[11] This realistic estimation of his own compositions when measured against those of the great composers drove his conviction that his genius was to be fulfilled through conducting.

In an effort to understand one of the most important instruments of the orchestra, George took up the French horn. It's possible he chose it because of his admiration for Richard Strauss, who had written two horn concertos and prominent horn parts in his tone poems. Under the influence of those beautiful solos, he began practicing the instrument. Here he had limitations. The horn was much more difficult to play than the piano, and his great intelligence seemed of little avail in trying to bring it to heel. The slightest tension of facial muscles could cause cracked notes, and theoretical knowledge was fairly useless.[12]

Chagrined that the capricious horn wasn't yielding to his will, he gave it up, though the hours of practice hadn't been entirely wasted. He had learned enough about the intricacies of the instrument to enable him to impress hornists with his knowledge. What he had not been able to learn by himself he gleaned from other French horn players.[13]

Although he didn't have the time or inclination to learn to play the string and woodwind instruments, he impressed many violinists by watching their fingerings and then demanding different ones. Theoretical knowledge coupled with close observation enabled him to earn the respect of string sections. It was easy to see what was going on with violinists' moving fingers and arms. But woodwind and brass instruments were mysterious because they were played using the tongue, diaphragm, and muscles inside the mouth. Only puffed cheeks, pursed lips, and reddened faces indicated the effort involved in playing them. And the woodwind instruments in particular could be intractable because of their need for delicate reeds and perfectly adjusted mechanical parts.[14]

Szell prided himself on knowing a great deal about most orchestral instruments but paid scant attention to the percussion ones. In his experience, they were mostly just rhythmic devices. It would have surprised him to know that, many years in the future, choosing a triangle would confuse him and a problem with a drum would cause him public humiliation.

Among Richard Robert's advanced piano students was a talented young woman named Olga Band. She and twenty-three-year-old Szell began studying orchestral scores together and performing piano duet recitals. Perhaps sharing the same piano bench made it then seem logical to share their lives. So they married. But after six years Olga wearied of Szell's obvious superiority of mind and uncompromising nature. Their artistic differences and Olga's insecurities escalated into spats, and they stopped speaking to each other. This estrangement did not go unnoticed by Josef Wolfstahl, concertmaster of the Berlin State Opera, who was madly in love with Olga. He accidentally blurted out his feelings in a tearful confession. Gratified by this turn of events, Olga ran off with Josef, choosing a less talented musician who wasn't a hypercritical perfectionist preoccupied with his flourishing career.[15]

Not one to be defeated by rejection, Szell rallied and continued directing all his considerable energy toward conducting. His years of forays to Holland, Russia, and Great Britain, as well as St. Louis in the United States, gave him a chance to make many contacts and stay away from areas of Europe where right-wing politicians and anti-Semitism were making life dangerous for minorities. By 1937, at the age of forty, he was established in Glasgow as principal conductor of the Scottish National Orchestra with Polish violinist Henri Temianka as his concertmaster.

Looking for ways to enjoy himself and earn money, Szell teamed up with Temianka, also a former child prodigy. The pair quickly became successful, performing recitals and garnering favorable reviews, although one critic pointedly singled out Temianka for praise, taking exception to Szell's domination of the performance.[16]

There seemed to be nothing musical that Szell didn't know. Quick to notice anyone's musical abilities, he realized that Temianka's gorgeous tone and virtuoso technique made him a fit partner in their concert collaborations. What made them lifelong friends, however, was their mutual enjoyment of off-color jokes, pranks, and elaborate postconcert dinners. Afterward, primed by wine and admiring friends, Szell would sit down at the piano and perform entire operas from memory. Temianka was particularly impressed by Szell's flawless two-hour rendition of Mozart's *Magic Flute*, not a page of music in sight. He could do the same thing with orchestral scores or any other piece of music that crossed his path.[17]

British orchestras, unlike those in Europe, had women in their ranks, many of them the equal of their male counterparts. In Glasgow Szell was surprised to find that a woman, Evelyn Rothwell, was the first oboist. Intrigued, he began courting her and wrote a piano and oboe piece for the two of them. Such a display of his musical feathers would surely captivate her. Evelyn later reminisced about Szell's courtship: "The composition he wrote for me was very Straussian and romantic. He was quite a fine musician. Once I had only the oboe part to the Mozart *Oboe Quartet* and he sat down at the piano and played the other parts without the music. He treated me to expensive restaurant dinners. It was a little embarrassing."[18] She had another swain: the conductor John Barbirolli. When Barbirolli spotted Szell's composition on her music stand, he noted the name of the composer and, realizing that he had a rival, tore the piece to shreds. Years afterward, Rothwell spoke of Szell's typically impatient approach. "He asked me to marry him and gave me an ultimatum. If I didn't accept his proposal within three months he was going to marry someone else. But I was tangled up with John at the time."

Szell didn't waste time moping about his rejection because he had another woman in his life, beautiful, vivacious Helene Teltsch in Prague, who at twenty-four had sat for her oil portrait by a popular society artist. Although married, with two children, she was irresistibly drawn to Szell's verve and abilities. She manifested her interest in him with looks and teasing, and he, getting the message, reciprocated by throwing her into a swimming pool.[19]

That flirtatious dunking was more than mere high jinks. The incident marked the beginning of an enthrallment lasting eight years as he waited for Helene to make up her mind to marry him. It could not have been an easy decision for Helene. In marrying Szell she would be leaving her husband, two young sons, and a gracious lifestyle that included a large house with servants. But George was witty, enormously gifted, successful, and deeply in love with her. She gradually succumbed to the prospect of a life of glamour[20] with a man who was obviously a musical genius. Her mind made up, she divorced her husband, joining Szell in Scotland. Both were old enough to know what they wanted in a spouse—Szell was forty-two, Helene thirty-nine. Helene came from a well-to-do Prague family and had received the education and piano lessons of a properly brought up girl of that era.

In 1938 Helene and George were married in a courthouse ceremony in Glasgow witnessed by Temianka and his sister. A newspaper reported that the bride and groom were fashionable in fur-collared coats, while Helene also wore chic Russian boots and a fur hat. They proved well suited to each other and became inseparable. Szell privately addressed her with sentimental endearments: "Dear Mugele" and "Dear Mugi," and signed his letters "Pussi" and "Pussi Teddybear." Such verbal intimacies would have astonished all but a few of his closest friends who knew how much he adored her.[21]

Helene ably handled her brilliant husband. One reason for her success as Mrs. George Szell was her ability to tolerate her husband's ceaseless focus on conducting. Tactfully quelling him when he sometimes raged out of bounds, she stayed out of the line of fire when he got too wound up. She was an ideal wife for him, bringing him much-needed stability. They should have been able to enjoy Szell's rapid ascent in the musical world, but then the bottom fell out of their life. World War II began.

In the wake of the Nazis' rise to power, George and Helene joined the mass exodus of artists, musicians, scientists, writers, actors, and theater directors, all booking passage to the United States or South America. They reached New York City in 1939, prepared to stay in the United States for the war's duration.

Unlike many talented refugees who had difficulty acclimating themselves to a different culture and finding employment, George landed on his feet. In 1942 he was hired to conduct at the Metropolitan Opera and teach composition and advanced theory at Mannes School of Music, where he frequently dazzled students with his fabulous memory and ability to play piano transcriptions of complicated orchestral and string quartet scores.[22]

The Szells lived in a small apartment on Park Avenue. When he wasn't busy at the Met, he continued to guest-conduct. Hailed by audiences and critics alike, he impressed the orchestras he conducted as a great, though difficult, musician. At the Met he alienated manager Rudolf Bing, whom he considered incompetent, insulted singers and players who weren't up to snuff, and criticized the flimsy stage sets, one of which had fallen down in the middle of a performance. After two years he declared the Metropolitan Opera House an impossible mess, quitting in the middle of his contract.[23]

The New York Philharmonic was more than glad to have his services, as were other orchestras around the country. Critics lauded his intense dedication and thorough knowledge of the most intricate musical scores.

In 1945, however, he experienced a severe setback. He contracted measles with resulting mastoiditis. Before the introduction of measles vaccine, measles was a serious illness and one of the leading causes of death in children. It frequently spread to the brain, causing meningitis, facial paralysis, and partial or complete hearing loss. His temperature soared alarmingly, and the diagnosis was chilling. This serious malady threatened to cut short his career, if not his life.[24]

He confessed to his close friend, the conductor Max Rudolph, that he could no longer correctly identify notes, either singly or in chords, although to openly admit that would mean an end to his conducting. Only his doctor, Helene, and Max knew the truth. It must be kept secret. But how long could he pretend he still had the sensitive ears lauded by audiences, the press, and the musicians he conducted? His glory had been his hearing, enabling him to detect exact notes, who was playing them, and whether all were perfectly in tune. If that priceless possession was gone, how could he lead his players? But there was no recourse: submit to an operation or risk a permanent end to his career.

Fortunately the operation took place just in time. As weeks passed, his hearing slowly began to improve. After several months he regained full recovery of that precious faculty. The only clue to what he had endured was the scars behind both ears.[25]

The Met altercations and fight with Rudolph Bing had thrust him into the limelight, and wealthy music lovers took note. Here was a conductor with unusually high standards, a man who had led numerous performances of Richard Strauss's notorious opera *Salome*, a man who knew the classic symphonic literature by heart, a man who had graced podiums since the age of sixteen. Just the person needed to build a fine symphony orchestra that would bring honor to a city.

By 1946, with various symphony boards vying for him, Szell could pick and choose. Cannily, he chose the city most suitable for achieving his goal: creation of the finest symphony orchestra in the world. That city was Cleveland.

CHAPTER 2

The Orchestra's Beginnings

CLEVELAND AT THE BEGINNING of the twentieth century was busy and prosperous. Founded on the shore of Lake Erie, it had become one of the nation's largest manufacturing centers. Its coal-fueled factories turned iron into steel. Oil had been discovered in West Virginia and southern Ohio, and Standard Oil refineries joined the belching smokestacks of Republic Steel and other mills on the banks of the Cuyahoga River in a lowland dubbed "the flats." High on a bluff overlooking this industrial maelstrom was Public Square, flanked with buildings belonging to merchants and banks that catered to the newly rich. And stretching to the east up Euclid Avenue was "Millionaires' Row" lined with the elite's Victorian mansions.

Unfortunately that area suffered from stenches and smoke from the nearby factories. Houses and buildings were turning black, the air unbreathable, and businesses were expanding into the genteel neighborhood. So the privileged hundreds decamped to faraway Shaker Heights, Cleveland Heights, and Bratenahl. The exodus was a triumphant procession because the abandoned Victorian piles were exchanged for French chateaus, Italianate villas, and Tudor manor houses designed by local architects who quickly grasped that their wealthy clients wanted splendor and hang the expense.[1]

For all its wealth, however, it was evident to discerning minds that Cleveland lacked many of the finer things. It was among the largest, most prosperous cities in the country, yet where were its monuments? Where were its refinements? Where were the places to take visitors and feel proud? Those who had gone on the Grand Tour returned enthusiastic about what they had seen in Europe: the Parthenon, the Pantheon, the Louvre, Versailles, Bayreuth, paintings and statuary. They wanted similar things at home.

In Cleveland there should be libraries, concert halls, museums, parks, and universities. They had seen what money and taste could do in Europe, and they had the means to endow their own city with culture and beauty. Civic pride and altruism dictated these refinements not just for themselves but also for the masses, and radio had made available the strains of Beethoven and Sousa. Listeners began buying pianos,[2] joining music clubs, and singing the latest popular tunes. Enter a strong-willed female named Adella Prentiss Hughes.

It had taken a while for Hughes to burst full-blown onto the Cleveland scene. Born in 1869, she was bitten early by the piano bug. Indulged by her well-to-do parents, she spent the first two decades of her life practicing and getting an education at Vassar, further polished by study in Europe. Determined to make musical history, she returned to Cleveland convinced she was one of the enlightened with a mandate to lift culture to a higher plane in her hometown.

In 1897 she started her own booking agency and soon brought to Cleveland such concert artists as Fritz Kreisler, Ignacy Paderewski, and Pablo Casals. Her years of piano study paid off when she expertly accompanied Kreisler in one recital. On another occasion her musicianship enabled her to accompany from memory a famous basso when he appeared without his music.

Thinking it was not enough to bring soloists and various symphony orchestras for single engagements, Hughes resolved that Cleveland needed its own orchestra. In 1918 she started one with herself as manager.[3] Since this undertaking required significant financial backing, she enticed various wealthy civic leaders onto her board of trustees.

She and her trustees decided that Cleveland's brick Masonic Temple was totally unsuitable as a concert hall. Instead, there should be a beautiful edifice of stone with classic columns and a dome, sitting in dignity on a promontory—a sanctuary befitting the music of the great composers. They knew whom to hire: the Cleveland architectural firm of Walker and Weeks, which had designed many of the city's most important buildings. It could create a hall that would become known as the finest in the country.

Hughes's idea was more than a vision; it became a vocation. She cajoled philanthropist John L. Severance into donating a million dollars to build a proper home for her orchestra. When it became apparent that sum was not enough, he and other wealthy families, including the Blossoms, the Mathers, the Prentisses, and the Hannas, donated another two and a half million to produce, in 1931, the great Severance Hall.

Cleveland's new concert hall was satisfyingly opulent. Its lobby dazzled with pink marble staircases, Egyptian friezes, fluted jasper marble columns, and bronze art nouveau lamps that shed light on the lotus-blossomed terrazzo floor. And the ceiling over the auditorium was enhanced with silver tracery copied from the lace on one of Mrs. Severance's gowns. An impressive Georgian building, Severance Hall overlooked Euclid Avenue, a main thoroughfare, and incorporated a drive-through entrance for chauffeured limousines. In this sheltered passageway not a single satin-shod foot ever touched bare ground.

Aesthetics were only part of it.[4] The hall was equipped with the newest in lighting and acoustics, a pit in front of the stage for opera productions, a piano elevator in the stage apron, a huge Skinner organ, a cyclorama, programmable colored lights in the ceiling for preconcert entertainment, a four-hundred-seat theater for chamber music performances, "conditioned" air, a broadcast and recording room, elevators to the four levels, a chorus room, and a boardroom.

Hughes considered Severance Hall hers and herself its hostess. Each concert night she stationed herself at the main entrance, graciously welcoming members of the audience as they entered. The green room's appointments— silk velvet drapes, dainty floor lamps, artistically stippled walls, elegant Empire-style furniture, and a vitrine displaying orchestral scores and photographs of great composers—strongly hinted at a woman's refined touch.[5] While these interior decorations were being completed, Hughes occupied herself with ongoing conductor problems.

Years before, Hughes had hired conductor Nikolai Sokoloff, a tempestuous Russian émigré who proved to be brilliant but difficult. He was let go after fifteen tumultuous seasons and was succeeded by Artur Rodzinski, another temperamental artist who reputedly carried a pistol. Rodzinski, during his troublesome tenure, led the Cleveland Orchestra in a concert in Syracuse that garnered the headline "A Gale Blows in from Lake Erie." Oboist Bob Zupnik recalled that at this concert Rodzinski conducted every piece too fast[6] in order to catch an early train to New York City. Convinced that one of the players intended to murder him, he was taking no chances riding in a later train with all of them.

Having heard that the orchestra's trustees were dissatisfied with him— the Syracuse headline may have had something to do with that—Rodzinski arrived early for a meeting in the Severance Hall boardroom and ordered a janitor to bring him a stepladder. He climbed to the top of it and sat waiting for the trustees. As they filed in, he looked down on them, and when all were seated—including a horrified Hughes—he spoke from his high perch.[7] This bizarre action probably helped make his departure from the Cleveland Orchestra to the New York Philharmonic somewhat of a relief for the trustees.

The board next hired conductor Erich Leinsdorf. Socially adept, he cultivated Hughes, who thought him charming, not in the least like her former two prickly maestros. But he served only a short time because, with World War II underway, he was drafted into the army. After the war, the trustees resumed their search for a permanent conductor. In 1946, ignoring Hughes's preference for Leinsdorf, they hired George Szell to guest-conduct several concerts. It was immediately apparent to the local music critics, audiences, and the trustees that Szell was the one capable of lifting the Cleveland Orchestra to unprecedented heights.[8] It only remained to sign him.

Hughes tried to undermine this effort by conspiring with a wealthy friend to put Leinsdorf, newly discharged from the army, back on the podium. Wary of Szell, an even more forceful person than herself and an obvious genius, she may have suspected he would be impossible to deal with. The orchestra's board of trustees, however, pronounced themselves unshakably in favor of Szell.[9]

Knowing how much they wanted him, Szell had the upper hand in his contract negotiations. He specified that the meeting between himself and four others—the manager, the president of the board, and two trustees— should be divided up. Rather than talk to the four of them at the same time, he insisted on meeting with each member separately.[10]

His strategy worked. He easily dominated the interviews and achieved a contract with no restrictions on his powers, including a clause that he could leave at any time if his powers were challenged.[11] This stipulation—actually a flagrant threat—kept his employers anxious to do his bidding.

His terms—which included the number of subscription weeks, number of personnel, touring, scheduling, recording, broadcasting, soloists, guest conductors, and leaves of absence—would prove to be important factors in the orchestra's subsequent climb to world fame. Those terms also prove that he was a brilliant tactician, spelling out precisely how he intended to build a great orchestra.[12]

CHAPTER 3

Szell's Improvements

CLEVELAND WAS A CITY with a fertile combination of things necessary to Szell's plan: a board of trustees willing to finance a costly cultural jewel, a musicians' union that ignored the plight of its symphony players, one of the wealthiest cities in the nation owing to its concentration of heavy industry, a well-designed concert hall containing luxurious amenities, and no other professional orchestra in the city.[1] Those things played a part in what was soon to transpire.

The orchestra Szell took over in 1946 was a good one. That was not enough for him. He had an ideal model in mind and intended to go even beyond it. Sometime before Szell was born, German conductor Hans von Bülow had electrified European audiences with his Meiningen Court Orchestra. Financed by Duke George II of Saxe-Meiningen, a small German duchy, this orchestra under Bülow didn't just play better than many other orchestras in Europe, it performed all nine Beethoven symphonies *from memory*.

Bülow divided up his sixty-five-piece orchestra into four sections—strings, woodwinds, brasses, and percussion—then whipped each into shape separately. Every bow stroke, nuance, and phrasing was dictated in exhaustive detail until each musician could play his part without recourse to printed notes. But his creation lasted only a few years because the musicians—exhausted and underpaid—dropped by the wayside. By the time that happened, Bülow, who couldn't be bothered with backsliding, was already off guest-conducting in greener international pastures where he was hailed as the world's greatest conductor.[2]

Decades later, aware of Bülow's achievements and inspired by some brilliant Toscanini concerts, Szell set about tearing the Cleveland Orchestra apart and putting it back together much improved. He began with a spate of firings in his first year.[3] He already had announced his intentions to the board of trustees, and so they weren't surprised. The musicians he fired included violinists who didn't play in tune or whose bows produced scratchy sounds, oboists who sounded thin and nasal, clarinetists whose instruments squeaked, French hornists who cracked their notes, and drummers with unsteady rhythm. This housecleaning served notice to the other players that no one was safe. Then he fired assistant conductor Rudolph Ringwall, who seems to have done his job adequately. Adequate was not good enough. His position was given to the young apprentice conductor Louis Lane, who quickly endeared himself through tact, talent, and unremitting diligence.[4]

Lane, a composer intelligent enough to realize his compositions weren't going to set the world on fire, had decided to audition for the newly created apprentice conductor post in Cleveland. He impressed Szell by demonstrating his knowledge of a rarely performed Mozart symphony. When he confessed he had chosen that particular piece because Szell probably wasn't familiar with it, the maestro realized he had a clever fellow in front of him. Lane soon became Szell's disciple and right-hand man.[5]

Unlike Lane, Lillian Baldwin, head of music education in the Cleveland public schools and responsible for planning the Cleveland Orchestra children's concerts, was spurned. Szell pronounced her ideas for school concerts "trash."[6] He was dismissive of her musical rhymes and cute drawings that accompanied her printed programs. His children's concerts were not to be sullied with nursery room twaddle, nor would his orchestra play down to its young audiences. It would perform, unabridged, the great masterpieces of symphonic literature. So Baldwin got the boot.

Baldwin's firing greatly upset Hughes. Jolly children's concerts of short light classics had been one of her priorities. Szell, who considered Hughes his nemesis, had already written off both her and her friend Lillian as out of touch and old fashioned. It was not that Szell was misogynistic; he would later accept highly qualified women into his orchestra.[7] He was pursuing a vision and didn't want anyone telling him how to run his show.

After assessing what he had left to work with, Szell went about stealing first-rate musicians from other orchestras, hiring young innocents freshly out of conservatories, and mercilessly rehearsing everyone. Anyone who didn't measure up was fired. For several seasons the turnover was dramatic;

he kept at it until he had the personnel he needed to achieve his goal. How could he get away with this? For a brief answer to that, one needs to look into the workings of the American Federation of Musicians' Union in the earliest decades of its existence.

In the Great Depression of the thirties, musicians were underpaid and frequently not paid at all. Then Chicago trumpeter James Petrillo decided to take matters into his own hands. He enrolled many musicians into a new union, the American Federation of Musicians. As its numbers grew, the union became more powerful, and Petrillo—now head of the organization—and his fellow officers drew up a set of bylaws detailing the rights of musicians.[8]

Each local union president had autonomy, and so in Cleveland the union president could administer the bylaws as he saw fit. As a result, Cleveland Orchestra musicians had protection only at their president's whim. Guarding their prerogatives, the Cleveland union officials decreed that contract negotiations would take place solely between the orchestra's management and themselves. They also ruled that Cleveland Orchestra musicians didn't have the right to ratify their own contract. Nor could they protest their working conditions.[9] Only the union officials could do that. These conditions allowed Szell to carry on relatively unhindered.

In the first year of his leadership, Szell fired sixteen musicians, and season after season saw the departure of musicians whose playing didn't please Szell. Some players left voluntarily, however, determined not to put up with Szell's tyranny.[10] Their places were promptly filled by other musicians who apparently thought they could handle the challenge.

Tearing things apart so that they could be put back together much improved entailed more than merely swapping musicians. Szell decided Severance Hall's acoustics also should be improved. Its luxurious velvet drapes and sound-absorbing carpets had to go. But after that was accomplished, there still wasn't enough resonance. The musicians couldn't adequately hear each other on stage, and the music wasn't properly projecting to the audience. To remedy these impediments, in 1958 Szell contacted Heinrich Keilholz, a European recording engineer and acoustician. Keilholz came, assessed the situation, and decreed that there should be a modern acoustical shell constructed of maple-veneered plywood, the vertical portion of it a sturdy box filled nine feet high with sand.[11] That renovation caused the orchestra to sound better than it ever had, and although the stage now presented a plain contemporary background, it served the music and that was what counted.

Szell in Cleveland was a fish out of water. Having fled Europe's Nazis, he found that anti-Semitism was also rife in his adopted country.[12] Just minutes away from Severance Hall was an attractive neighborhood of French Norman-style houses called Forest Hill that barred Jews and blacks from owning houses within its boundaries. The neighborhood was the former estate of John D. Rockefeller. A portion of it had been developed by him into a village of "character, beauty and permanence" governed by extensive deed restrictions. Neither Szell nor his Jewish musicians were allowed to live in restricted Forest Hill. Similarly, Szell couldn't join most Cleveland country clubs. Only Oakwood Country Club, in nearby Cleveland Heights, admitted Jews. It was therefore on Oakwood's enlightened greens that he worked on his golf game in his rare leisure moments.[13]

Szell's heavy Viennese accent and Teutonic appearance were decided drawbacks in a country that had just waged a war with Germany. With his Homburg hat, coat with high fur collar, and thick glasses that obscured his eyes, he could have been mistaken for someone out of a spy movie.[14] On the one hand, European conductors with their years of experience in historic concert halls were at a premium; symphony boards actively sought them out. On the other, their personalities set them apart from most Americans, who were busily putting the war years behind them and relaxing with movies, sports, and radio programs.

For Szell, U.S. popular culture was somewhat of a closed book, and one rehearsal at Severance Hall proved it. High from the previous night's baseball game during which the Cleveland Indians had captured the American League pennant, the musicians decided to play "Take Me Out to the Ball Game" to celebrate Cleveland's victory. When Szell lifted his baton, out came the familiar tune, familiar to everybody except Szell, who had never heard it and had certainly never attended a baseball game. "No, no, no," he protested. "It's supposed to be the Berlioz we rehearse first." Concertmaster Josef Gingold spoke up, explaining they were playing the song to celebrate the Indians' winning of the pennant. Szell was mystified. What Indians? What pennant? Then he quickly recovered his aplomb. "Oh, I see. A joke."[15]

Radio, however, helped Szell get a handle on national culture, and a few years later it was obvious that he had been influenced by comedian Jimmy Durante. Speaking to his favorite pianist, young Leon Fleisher, Szell affectionately called him "Schnozzola."[16] He also enthusiastically embraced American car worship, buying a Buick and proudly posing beside it for a photograph.

Recording engineer Vladimir Maleckar recalled once driving Szell in his wood-paneled station wagon. Maleckar's car had caught Szell's eye, and he wanted to know all about it. So this was a "Woodie," the capacious vehicle with large tailgate and fold-down seats that could accommodate eight people and ferry sports equipment, children, pets, camping gear, rowboats, bales of hay, and Christmas trees. There were certainly no vehicles like station wagons in any European city. Interesting. Most interesting.[17]

Szell's shepherding of his musical flock was urgent, constant, and often intrusive. His obsession to create the world's finest orchestra meant he had to have a reliable assembly of musicians, and so he ceaselessly monitored. He thought of himself as "Papa Szell,"[18] guiding his children. Many of his musicians, however, thought of him as an annoying mother hen.

A mother's watchfulness can be counted on to erupt just inside the front door. "You're not going out in *that* are you? You'll catch your death. Where are your mittens? Why aren't you wearing your hat?" Similarly, Szell was fixated on preventive clothing, especially galoshes. He was sure nobody in wintry Cleveland should go out without them, especially his musicians who had to slog through the snow-covered parking lot next to Severance Hall. Wet feet led to colds, which led to missed rehearsals and concerts. Galoshes warded off such disasters.

Cellist Lynn Harrell was seen wearing a cast on his leg.

"What's wrong?" Szell asked.

"I broke my ankle."

"How did that happen?"

"I fell on some ice. "

"But how did you do it?"

"My feet slipped when I stepped off the curb."

"Were you wearing galoshes?"

"No, just my shoes."

"Aha!" Szell was jubilant to get at the root of the problem. "No galoshes. You should always wear your galoshes on icy days in the winter."[19]

One rainy morning in the middle of a tour, Szell accosted cellist Teddy Baar as he left a hotel on his way to the concert hall for the rehearsal. Baar later repeated their conversation for the entertainment of oboist Felix Kraus.

"Why aren't you wearing galoshes?"

"I guess I forgot them."

"Where are they?"

"Up in my room."

"You go back and put them on."

"I'll be late to rehearsal."

"Go!"

Szell had waved him off with an imperious gesture.[20] Health was of paramount importance. How could there be a great orchestra if everybody in it was sniveling with colds? Szell kept himself in top physical shape by spending summer weeks at European resorts and staying out of contact with runny-nosed children.[21]

Fresh air was something to be cultivated. When the orchestra played in Switzerland, Szell roamed the train that was taking them through the mountains. Stopping at each row of seats, he urged his musicians to open their windows and breathe in the pure mountain air. Many complied and began sniffing as ordered. "No, no," Szell protested. "You must breathe deeply. Get the oxygen into your lungs like this." He demonstrated proper breathing technique. Everyone hastened to follow suit while he looked on with satisfaction. There would be no stale oxygen in his musicians' chests if he could help it.[22]

Szell's theories on proper diet included avoidance of rich and spicy foods just before concerts. Trumpeter Dick Smith recalled an incident with Szell at a Salzburg restaurant when the orchestra was on tour. He had sat down and waited to be given the menu. When the waiter approached, Smith asked for it but was told, "The gentleman over in the corner has already ordered for you." Smith turned and saw Szell sitting and smiling at him. The food he had ordered for Smith was suitably bland, guaranteed not to upset the stomach. At meal's end, Smith was presented with the check. Szell's solicitude didn't extend to paying for Smith's dinner.[23]

At some point, Szell's obsession with musical perfection began to take into account the personal lives of the people charged with creating it. Some of his players spoke of their gradually changing conductor. "He really mellowed in his later years. He realized he had succeeded in building a great orchestra and he could relax and be more friendly."[24]

The mellowing also was prompted by something else. At first, his constant surveillance had been motivated by cold calculation. There were countless things that could go wrong in a performance and they must be avoided by strict attention to detail. His overseeing of each thing—insistence on punctuality, warm winter clothing, proper diet, and avoidance of emotional upsets—had led inevitably to the players themselves. As their personalities, education, marriages, families, and financial concerns became known to him, he realized he was responsible for them. They were giving their lives to the thing he was creating.

If a musician's parent, spouse, or child was seriously ill, Szell gave immediate permission for the musician to be excused to tend to the emergency. The player's salary was not docked during his absence. Sickness and death were honored by Szell, who had experienced such things in his own life and quietly sympathized with the sufferer.[25] He monitored conditions at Severance Hall, from the chairs the players sat on to the temperature of the air. No detail was too insignificant to engage his attention because it could affect his players and therefore the music. He truly did become "Papa Szell," responsible for everything that went on.

Malingering among his "children" however, was sternly rebuked, and he looked askance at opportunism, although sometimes with humor. When his principal violist, Abe Skernick, asked for a small raise in his salary, explaining his wife was pregnant and they needed extra money, Szell granted his request. A year or two later Abe asked for another raise when his second child was due. Again Szell granted it. But a request for a third raise necessitated by yet another child on the way was too much for Szell. "Abe, haven't you ever heard of f—ing for pleasure?" he asked. He granted the raise, but Skernick never risked asking a fourth time.[26]

Beautiful Severance Hall was run with an efficiency that would have been the envy of any general who learned of it. Among themselves, the musicians joked that if Szell had been a German general during World War II the Germans would have won. Any new recruit into the orchestra was made to feel the military precision on his first day, when he was told which spot in the parking lot had been assigned to him. It was Szell who did the assigning and then monitored from his office window to be sure the musician drove his car into the designated place.[27]

Neatness and organization saved time, ensuring that more work could get done. Szell's secretary, Peggy Glove, was a model employee, and she and Szell worked well together. Tastefully dressed, poised, and efficient, she expertly took Szell's dictation, kept her desk free of clutter, stayed overtime when necessary, and handled her mercurial employer with tact. Glove had the energy and patience to put up with whatever problems Szell sent her way, routinely soft-pedaling some of his raw dictation in her typewritten letters that went out over his signature. Grateful for her loyalty and efficiency, Szell on one occasion presented her with a beautiful porcelain vase with a flower painting on its side. He had found it in Europe and knew it would please her.[28]

Her exact opposite was the orchestra's program annotator, Klaus George Roy. Viennese-born Roy was widely admired for his writing ability, his well-researched program notes, and his dignified radio interviews with soloists who appeared with the orchestra.

Szell liked Roy, his erudition, and his writing style. But he couldn't abide Roy's messy lair. One day he had to discuss a matter with his respected musicologist and, instead of summoning him to his own office as usual, he went to Roy's office. There he recoiled in disgust. "How can you work in such a pigsty?" he exclaimed.[29]

Roy was unperturbed. His research involved knowing where everything was, out in the open, ready to hand. Ready to foot also. Lots of his notes and books were stacked on the floor, forming mazes through which he thoughtfully trod, intent on musicological tidbits.[30] The musicians were grateful that Roy also tended a large collection of recordings they were entitled to borrow when they wished to study a work they'd soon be performing. Roy had to bend to one of Szell's pronouncements. He signed his program notes Klaus G. Roy—not Klaus George Roy—because Szell had magisterially said, "There is only one George here."[31]

Orchestra manager A. Beverly Barksdale was a courtly Southern gentleman who'd been a singer. His sense of humor enabled him to cope with his temperamental maestro, who often scathingly ordered him to do something immediately, take action, and not equivocate. Instead, perhaps remembering the Uncle Remus stories of his childhood—"Brer Fox say nuthin an' lay low"—he quietly withdrew into his office when Szell became difficult.[32] The players, convinced that Szell ran everything and everybody at the hall, mistakenly assumed that Barksdale followed only one step behind Szell and carried Szell's briefcase. In actuality, Barksdale moved efficiently behind the scenes.

Szell never interfered with one important member of the staff, Larry Pitcock, who ruled the box office. Pitcock carried in his head the entire seating chart of Severance Hall, the names of all the regular subscribers, and where they sat. He had a stern approach to his job and could alienate anyone who wanted special favors. It was he who answered the phone when someone called the box office.[33]

He and Szell agreed that any unsold tickets at Saturday night concerts should be available for fifty cents each in the last few minutes before the concert began. This gave students and other financially strapped music lovers a chance to hear concerts at a bargain price. Sometimes concerts were sold out. That was the case when Pitcock answered the phone one afternoon and heard a wealthy donor on the other end of the line.

"This is Mrs. X. I need another ticket for tonight's performance."

"Sorry. We're sold out."

"You don't seem to realize to whom you are speaking. This is Mrs. X."

"Madam, I don't care *who* you are. We're sold out!"[34] He slammed the receiver down.

There was a repercussion. Mrs. X informed the board of trustees that she had been treated shabbily and would no longer give any money to the orchestra. So be it. Pitcock ruled the box office, and Szell approved of how he did his job.[35]

This kind of incident made David Levinson's job more difficult. In charge of public relations, he had to make sure operations ran smoothly. He was partly aided by music critic Robert Finn, whose reviews in Akron's *Beacon Journal* and Cleveland's *Plain Dealer* were usually tactful and approving. It wasn't hard to write enthusiastic reviews, because the orchestra habitually gave stellar performances. If there were glitches, Finn usually reported them discreetly or not at all. As far as the public knew, everything emanating from Severance Hall was close to perfect. Even Szell's reputation as a controlling tyrant was admired. That must be what it took to turn a bunch of talented mavericks into a great orchestra.

There was one group at Severance Hall that Szell never tried to command: the stagehands. As members of the stagehands' union, they received higher salaries than the musicians and were virtually untouchable. To qualify for their jobs, the three stagehands had to do carpentry, work the complicated banks of lights, move large instruments on and off stage, drive the truck that transported all the equipment needed on tours, and handle the musicians' unwieldy wardrobe trunks. While positioning chairs and music stands on the stage prior to concerts, stagehand Jack Lynch insisted the musicians had to stay offstage until the job was done. This caused a few flaps with players, who wanted to sit down and warm up. Lynch always won in these encounters because his union was more powerful than the musicians' union. Lynch was not someone to tangle with.

Neither the musicians nor management attempted to cross the three men who did the physical labor at the hall. It was a case of the tail wagging the dog. They were more important than anyone else at Severance Hall excepting Szell.

Without them, the entire place would shut down. Probably because he knew this, Szell never challenged their methods or authority. He did, however, give a sweeping lesson to the janitor one day early in his reign. Stepping out of his office, he saw the fellow brooming up lint. A few moments of observation made it obvious to Szell there was a better way to sweep. The fellow's method was inefficient. It had to be corrected. The janitor never told anyone whether Szell actually took hold of his broom and swept, but the story got around that Szell had instructed him in proper sweeping technique.[36]

Szell's intrusions didn't stop at the exit door of Severance Hall. Oboist Kraus, who frequented nearby Di Vita's grocery store, recalled one day being in the meat section and pondering some lamb chops. He asked the advice of one of the butchers and, upon mentioning he was in the Cleveland Orchestra, got an earful about Szell.

"You play under that guy? He's some buttinsky.[37] You know, he buys all his meat here. Cooks it himself as far as I can tell. He comes around behind the counter and bosses me how I should cut and trim his meat. Me! A butcher for forty years! I know how to slice and trim. He wants to guide my knife and then he wants to do it himself. Every time he comes in it's the same thing. He comes back here where customers aren't allowed and fusses about the trimming, the thickness, the whatever, and I've got to be polite. It must be the same with you men in the orchestra. Him bossing every little thing. How do you live with someone like that?" The same question might have been put to Helene, who was used to Szell bringing home his meat and vegetable purchases and then elaborately preparing them in their cavernous white-tiled kitchen. On these occasions Helene exited, allowing him free rein.

Szell had a sensitive palate, loved good food, had memorized various recipes, and liked relaxing in the kitchen as he concocted sauces and marinades. His repertoire included tripe, liberally spiced, and tasty Hungarian stews. At the end of his cooking sprees, there was always a shambles of dirty pots and pans. Helene ignored that, gladly eating whatever he cooked. It was invariably delicious.[38]

Many other people have eaten one of Szell's specialties because his recipe for goulash is included in Irma Rombauer's famous book, *The Joy of Cooking*. Szell and Rombauer were good friends and liked nothing better than discussing recipes with each other.[39] Although Rombauer was a music lover and had been president of the Women's Committee of the St. Louis Symphony, when she and Szell got together music was secondary. Food and cooking were the main topics of their conversation. They would sit for hours trading culinary lore. It's probable that Szell gave her recipes for other dishes besides goulash. His food memory was almost on a par with his musical one.

Wine was another of his interests, dating from his late teen years when he was busy eating as many delicacies as possible and imbibing fine wines. The wife of a member of the orchestra's board of trustees recalled a postconcert party during which Szell was drawn aside and given a choice between two bottles of rare wine that the party's host had been saving for him. Szell chose one, took a sip, held it in his mouth for many seconds, looked thoughtful and then delighted, and finally nodded approval. Apparently this vintage was an excellent one and the two settled down alone to enjoy their bottle.[40]

Although Szell's interest in cooking and cleaning might seem to mark him as relatively domestic, he had little patience with one element of domesticity: children. Having been an only child and in later life rarely experiencing children up close, he viewed them as disruptive creatures who might benefit from music lessons but who otherwise should be strictly confined to their own quarters, out of the way of adults and their activities.

His lack of understanding of the child mind was manifested in his children's concerts. He insisted they should consist of the great classics played with no cuts. This, of course, made impossible demands on children's attention spans. Though recognizing that it was important to bring classical music to children who would be his future audiences, he preferred to leave the children's concerts to his conducting assistant and apprentices.[41]

One day he went to the home of lawyer Frank Joseph, who, as president of the board of trustees, was proving himself an able caretaker of the orchestra. While Szell and Joseph sat at a table discussing orchestra business, Joseph's small son cavorted about the room. The proud father smiled indulgently, amused by his son's antics. Szell was not amused. "Please remove your child," he ordered.

CHAPTER 4

The Woodwind Section

THE SOURCE OF MUCH TROUBLE in orchestral woodwind sections can be traced to the cane fields in southern France. It is there that farmers cultivate a species of cane called *Arundo donax*. A distant cousin to bamboo, it grows to fifteen feet and is fit for music making only after being cut and aged in the fields for several years.[1] Double-reed players—oboists, English hornists, and bassoonists—know a distressing fact: no two pieces of this cane are alike. They react differently when shaved to a delicate thinness on an expensive and unreliable gadget called a gouging machine, which requires constant, anguished tinkering. Cane is expensive, selling for two hundred dollars a pound. Frequently up to half that pound has to be discarded because it is either too dry, too wet, or wormy. The few reeds that can be successfully crafted are then subject to changing atmospheric conditions. And they are maddeningly unpredictable: One may last only a few minutes after being played on, although another may last for months if handled carefully.

That still leaves the unpredictable ebony instrument to be fussed over because there is yet another difficulty. No two pieces of ebony are the same. Their grain and density depends on age, moisture, and light conditions in the forests where the trees grow.

Matching cane to reed to instrument is what drives oboists to distraction and produces insomnia, bad tempers, and alienation from their fellow man. To play the oboe is to know periods of stress, depression, and contemplation of suicide. Lawns are left unmowed, children are neglected, and marriages come unglued as the hapless players drudge on. One oboist, who had climbed to the lofty position of principal oboist in a famous orchestra, confessed that many times on his way to a concert featuring an important oboe solo he prayed that a truck would drive over him so he wouldn't have to play on his undependable reeds and instrument.[2]

Why then do people put themselves through this torture? The music. Beautiful oboe solos in masterpieces by great composers. As impressionable teenagers, they hear those pieces and imagine how wonderful it would be to play in a symphony orchestra and actually get paid for it. Being young, they have no experience with indigestion, sleeplessness, psychiatrists' fees, divorce, humiliation, and unemployment.

In 1904 a talented young Frenchman's oboe playing caught the attention of U.S. conductor Walter Damrosch. He hired Marcel Tabuteau, fresh out of the Paris Conservatoire, to play in his New York Symphony.[3] Tabuteau went from there to the Metropolitan Opera Orchestra, and then in 1918 he landed the principal oboe position in the Philadelphia Orchestra and soon began teaching oboe at the Curtis Institute of Music in the same city.

At that august conservatory he berated his students while imparting valuable musical knowledge. "Damn fool" and "stoopeed" were Tabuteau's usual epithets when someone's playing violated musical integrity. He denigrated his students for the smallest musical infraction. "Why do you want to be a musician? Why don't you be a plumber or a dentist?" Entering his studio in fear of humiliation and exiting after verbal harassment, his students became convinced that they would never be able to play anything. One of them regularly threw up before his lesson. Within forty minutes healthy young males were reduced to limp noodles.[4] This psychological torture was purposeful. Tabuteau was convinced that he was doing them a favor because, in the harsh world of professional music, it was survival of the fittest.

Any musician's résumé containing the words "Curtis" and "Tabuteau" automatically guaranteed an applicant preferential treatment from personnel managers and conductors. But one of Tabuteau's most illustrious oboe students, Marc Lifschey, needed no résumé or recommendation. His playing said it all. It was inevitable Szell's frequent guest-conducting would bring him in contact with Lifschey, who had become principal oboist in the National Symphony of Washington, DC. When the maestro heard Lifschey spinning golden phrases, he instantly knew he had found his El Dorado. He must have him. Dangling a lucrative contract, he snatched Lifschey for Cleveland.[5]

What Szell didn't know at the time soon became abundantly clear: in Marc Lifschey he had a tiger by the tail. It was a small tiger—Lifschey was barely five feet tall—but he was nevertheless capable of damage. His temper made him a trial to the others in the woodwind section, especially second oboist Elden Gatwood, who sat next to him.

Szell made no secret of his fixation on Lifschey. Here was a musician with the very attributes he valued most: beauty of tone, mastery of phrasing, alertness to the playing around him, and total dedication to his art. When Lifschey played an important oboe passage, Szell held the rest of the orchestra in check so that his tone and phrasing could shine forth.[6] He even told various friends he had built his orchestra around Lifschey.

Lifschey wanted to play his own way. But Szell, convinced he could teach fine musicians to play even better, tried to micromanage Lifschey's playing with commanding gestures and piercing stares. This was more than Lifschey could bear. He thwarted Szell by looking down at the floor while playing his solos. The feisty tiger played instinctively, with little idea how he produced his wonderful tone. Nor had he ever bothered to learn the intricacies of cane and gouging machines. In this he was like his partner, second oboist Elden Gatwood, who was self-taught and knew little to nothing about reed making.[7] Somehow these omissions in his oboists had escaped Szell's notice.

Lifschey was constantly at the mercy of his balky materials. He sat down to make a new reed only as a last resort when his oboe wouldn't respond to his artistry. When occasionally his oboe—as is usual with most woodwind instruments—cracked from temperature or humidity changes, Lifschey would dash off to a repairman in Philadelphia, requiring his assistant Bob Zupnik to play his solos. This is what assistant players are hired to do, but they usually have enough forewarning to prepare. Every few months Lifschey skipped rehearsals and even concerts when he couldn't face playing. He would call in sick at the last minute and Zupnik had to pinch-hit.[8] No other musician in the orchestra who carried on like that would have been tolerated.

Whenever Lifschey managed to produce an adequate reed, he played gorgeously. But he criticized his fellow musicians while they played, stamping his feet and swearing. Sometimes he deliberately played out of tune to make fun of his colleagues' intonation. All this Szell reluctantly put up with, although the two frequently went toe to toe in Szell's office. These sessions accomplished nothing. Lifschey continued his prima donna ways. Such unprofessional behavior would have scandalized his teacher Tabuteau, who always counseled his students to keep on the good side of conductors.

Szell reveled in his top-notch woodwind section. Its stars were the four principal players: Marc Lifschey on oboe, Maurice Sharp on flute, Robert Marcellus on clarinet, and George Goslee on bassoon. Their instruments have the most individual solos within the symphonic literature and are easily identifiable.

Composers have long singled out woodwind instruments for important solo melodies, the cleverest use being Prokofiev's *Peter and the Wolf*, in which they each portray a different character in the fairytale. Prokofiev emphasized their highly individual sounds: the oboe's nasal quackiness for the duck, the clarinet's suavity for the cat, the flute's fluttery airiness for the bird, and the bassoon's buzzy humor for the grandfather. But in most other compositions, woodwind players try to smooth over their colorful characteristics so they can blend more seamlessly with their colleagues. With a few exceptions, like Beethoven's use of the clarinet to sound the call of a cuckoo in his *Pastorale Symphony*, most compositions in the classic symphonic repertoire require beauty of tone rather than exotic color.

Traditionally, if the first measures of a melody are played by the oboe and the flute takes over the rest of the melody, it's understood the two players will come to an agreement on volume and nuances, neither of them standing out inappropriately. In the Cleveland Orchestra, individual solos were left up to the players unless Szell didn't like an interpretation. Then he would dictate how the solo should be played. The principal players tried to match each other's ideas, and if the clarinetist played thirteen notes in his trill, the musician playing the trill after him would do the same.

Compounding the difficulties woodwind players have to cope with is the seating of players on stage. The string sections at the front of the stage occupy fully half of it. The woodwind section sits behind them in two straight rows, and the brasses in straight rows behind them. This linear positioning results in some players' inability to see each other unless they turn their heads, an action frowned upon as unprofessional if it's done while a colleague is playing a solo. So they have to rely on their hearing. Years of keen listening give them aural radar, telling them what their colleagues in the four lines are doing.

All the orchestra's principal woodwind players were concerned with beautiful phrasing. Szell accorded them preferential treatment, calling them by their first names and privately rehearsing them in his office. Their exalted positions and higher salaries gave the four a confidence not shared by most other members of the orchestra.

Principal flutist Maurice Sharp, affectionately called Moe by his colleagues, was a solid and expert player. A snappy dresser, he wore Countess Mara ties to rehearsals and lent further glamor to his person with a gold flute rather than the customary silver one played by most flutists. His decision to invest in such an expensive item wasn't based on mere glamor, however. The heavy density of gold makes for a warmer tone than can be achieved on a silver flute.

Some of Sharp's confidence may have stemmed from his custom of regularly downing two martinis prior to concerts.[9] Thus relaxed, suffering no nerve problems, he rarely made a mistake. Szell probably didn't know of Sharp's preconcert cocktails, considering him to be dependable and rock-solid.

Sitting behind Sharp was principal clarinetist Robert Marcellus, whose ability to seemingly lengthen a phrase while keeping with the beat was in a class by itself. Marcellus had studied with the famous French clarinet teacher Daniel Bonade and had developed into a clarinetist with few equals. He had an enormous record collection and stayed up late listening to interpretations and tone qualities of other musicians, selecting the attributes he most admired and then trying to incorporate them into his own playing.

Marcellus's obsession with beautiful sound turned bizarre when he asked his dentist to grind down the tips of his lower front teeth so he could improve his mouth's position on his mouthpiece. His students followed suit, sandpapering their own teeth.[10] There must have been some puzzled dentists in Cleveland. Szell knew little of how Marcellus achieved his wonderful tone and unusual phrasing. He only knew he was a fine clarinetist; there was no need to hector him. Marcellus was totally dedicated, attentive during rehearsals and impeccable in performances.

Principal bassoonist George Goslee was another of Szell's favorites in the woodwind section. He was unflappable, owing his composure to inherited wealth and success in the stock market. Goslee always had a smile on his face, frequently uttering witticisms having to do with what was emanating from the podium. His remarks were usually delivered *sotto voce*, but on one occasion he raised his voice enough to be heard by the entire orchestra.[11]

The morning's rehearsal had drifted past twelve o'clock and Szell, his head in the score, was attempting to dredge up a few more corrections. "Hungry!" Goslee called out.[12] Szell didn't look up but the plea registered. He genially declared that, since things seemed to be in good shape, the rehearsal was at an end. This concession was highly unusual. It was Szell's custom to use every last second of the five rehearsals each week. Twenty minutes still remained. Perhaps he had been hungry too.

So Szell had superb principal woodwind players that he could depend on. For a while. Then in 1959 Lifschey resigned in a fit of pique. Bent on working for a less controlling boss, he joined the Metropolitan Opera Orchestra, and Szell hired as his replacement another former Tabuteau student, Al Genovese. A fine oboist, Genovese had the distinction of having been hailed by the great Tabuteau during a Curtis woodwind class: "Young man, you play too well."[13] Coming from hypercritical Tabuteau, this accolade was so rare that it is still repeated by oboists. In contrast to Lifschey, Genovese got along with his colleagues and the atmosphere in the oboe section improved considerably. His only fault was that he wasn't Lifschey.

But Szell was inconsolable. He wanted his favorite back, the one he said he had built his orchestra around. Finally, after months of pining and unable to overcome his obsession, Szell tempted Lifschey with more money. It must have been a considerable sum because the tempestuous prodigal reluctantly returned.

Unchanged, Lifschey resumed his old ways, challenging Szell's orders. One of their confrontations on stage took place when Szell asked him to play a certain passage louder. "So you're asking me to honk it?" Lifschey asked, insinuating that his refined style was being rejected in favor of crudity. "Yes, Marc, HONK it!"[14] Szell replied. Lifschey then deliberately produced a loud, ugly sound that Szell chose to ignore.

Rather than endure the constant tension and eager to escape both of them, second oboist Elden Gatwood defected to the Pittsburgh Symphony. His position was filled by Felix Kraus, another Tabuteau disciple, who had been principal oboist in the National Symphony. He was thrilled to become a member of the Cleveland Orchestra under George Szell, who had hired him with the words "You are now joining the world's greatest orchestra."[15]

Kraus experienced an eye-opener soon after he took up his position next to Lifschey. He had come in brief contact with Lifschey at Curtis but was unaware of his temper. He soon discovered it. Every order from Szell to play louder was immediately countermanded by Lifschey, who insisted Kraus play softer. He emphasized his demand by swearing and stamping his feet. It seemed Lifschey wanted no oboist other than himself to be heard, even though various pieces called for the first and second oboists to be equally matched in volume. Called into Szell's office and reprimanded for his self-effacing playing, Kraus explained that he was carrying out Marc's orders.

"Marc isn't your boss. I am. I'm ordering you to play louder whenever I motion you up, and you are to ignore Marc," Szell said.[16] The countermanding went on month after month with Kraus knowing he would eventually be fired because he couldn't satisfy both of them at once.

But tectonic plates were grinding, slowly building up pressure. On January 4, 1965, the volcano erupted. During rehearsal on that morning, a prominent oboe solo in Prokofiev's *Fifth Symphony* gave Lifschey a chance to express his disdain for Szell, his colleagues, and whatever else bothered him that morning—probably a lousy reed. He deliberately played his solo a quarter-tone flat. Szell ignored him. Marc was, as usual, just being Marc. When the passage was repeated a few minutes later, however, Lifschey played it even more ferociously out of tune. This time Szell had to react. Continuing to put up with Lifschey's insubordination in front of one hundred musicians would be a significant loss of face, a humiliation not to be endured. He stopped the music and addressed his principal oboist.

"Now Marc what's wrong with the pitch?" he asked, likely aware that Lifschey was looking for a chance to be obstreperous.

"That's the pitch I play. If you don't like it, get yourself another boy," Lifschey answered.[17]

"Marc, if you can't behave yourself go upstairs and hand in your resignation," Szell said.

A hush fell over the orchestra as the players realized what was happening. In the silence that followed, Lifschey yanked the reed out of his oboe and held it aloft. Snapping it in two, he said, "I've taken s—t for fourteen years and that's enough." He then barged through the music stands, swearing under his breath, and stomped off stage. Szell called after him, "You leave now and you are never coming back."[18]

There were a hundred stunned faces in the ranks. None had ever witnessed such a public insult to their famous conductor. What kind of scene was about to occur? But Szell exhibited no emotion, only saying to his assistant principal oboist, "Bob, would you move over?"[19] This terse command indicated that Bob Zupnik should take Lifschey's place and play the principal oboe solos. The rehearsal continued.

Afterward there was pandemonium in the locker room. What was going to happen to Lifschey? If he didn't apologize to Szell, he would be permanently out. Then who would play the big first oboe solos in the Bartók *Concerto for Orchestra* due to be recorded in just eleven days? There also was the upcoming East Coast tour in the first weeks of February, culminating in a Carnegie Hall performance. They all knew Szell was counting on the virtuosic concerto to bring down the house.

In the midst of the turmoil, Zupnik remained outwardly calm. He had stepped into Lifschey's shoes many times, substituting at the last minute in pieces he'd never had a chance to rehearse. The difference now, however, was that he would have to play principal oboe in a recording going out to the world and then do the same thing again in the Carnegie Hall performance.

But that wasn't all. The longest and most important tour the orchestra would ever undertake was scheduled to start in the middle of April. It consisted of eleven weeks under the auspices of the U.S. State Department: six weeks in the Soviet Union and five in Scandinavia and Europe. Important critics would be poised to render judgment. Tempestuous Lifschey could hardly have chosen a worse time to quit. The musicians wondered what Szell would do. Was it possible he would call off the tour?

Several years of planning this tour had taken place between the State Department, Szell, manager Barksdale, and the orchestra's board of trustees. With a mandate to ease the Cold War, various officials hoped an exchange of cultural organizations might work. The United States would send orchestras to the Soviet Union; the Soviets would reciprocate with ballet companies. Nothing controversial or political. Fences would be mended.[20] The plan had come to fruition, with everyone set to go. Except for one hitch. The orchestra no longer had Lifschey.

Some of Lifschey's colleagues were aghast that he'd ruined himself by publicly insulting Szell. They agreed he had to be saved; someone should intercede on his behalf. More was at stake than just Lifschey's job. The orchestra needed its star player. Right after the Saturday night concert, a group of concerned musicians gathered at hornist Mike Bloom's house along with violist Abe Skernick, who enjoyed a warm relationship with Szell. They begged Skernick to phone their difficult maestro, explain that Marc hadn't really meant what he'd said, and ask that he be forgiven. All gathered close and waited anxiously as Skernick dialed the number and began his conciliatory speech.

"This is Abe. I'd like to talk to you as a friend."[21] The slam of the receiver on the other end of the line was clearly audible. So much for that.

Shortly afterward, Lifschey came to his senses. It was the middle of the concert season. He had no immediate prospects because all first oboe positions were filled. He would have to abase himself to get back into Szell's good graces. Gathering his courage, he picked up the phone. Later that same day he related to several friends what happened. Helene had answered, and when she told her husband who the caller was, strange animal sounds emanated from the background.[22] Usually the most articulate of men, Szell was so enraged he couldn't produce any words. The noise was that of a frenzied beast. "It's no use, Marc," Helene said. "He refuses to speak to you."

It was one of the worst times in Szell's life. He had spent years calculating, hiring, and firing until he had accumulated musicians able to carry out his every desire. Now, with international fame in the offing and a great musical edifice in place—superbly matched pairs of trumpets, horns, clarinets, bassoons, flutes, well-disciplined string sections, a fine percussion section—one of the pillars of his wonderful structure had crumbled.

Lesser souls would have despaired. Szell didn't. He lost no time, offering the principal oboe job to reliable Bob Zupnik, whose capable playing whenever he had to substitute for Lifschey had always saved the situation. Unfortunately, Zupnik didn't want to leave his comfortable assistant position for a higher-paid *un*comfortable one.[23] Not permanently anyway. But he consented, just for the tour, to play principal oboe half the time. Someone else would have to play the other half.

An immediate problem was the thirty-four-minute Bartók *Concerto for Orchestra* scheduled to be recorded in just eleven days. Composed in 1943, the work was intended to showcase the various sections of a symphony orchestra. It had entered the repertoire as a masterpiece of contemporary classical music. When Szell first heard it played by the Boston Symphony, he had set his sights on it immediately, quickly gaining access to the score.[24] He hardly had to study it to realize it was a perfect vehicle for the orchestra he hoped to eventually build. Further, it would silence some critics who claimed he avoided most contemporary music. He had bided his time until, two decades later, he had enough fine players to do the piece justice in a recording that would be part of his legacy. But the showdown with Lifschey had blasted a hole in his plan.

Hours after Szell confronted Lifschey and had been turned down by Zupnik, he began working the phone. His first call went to Elden Gatwood, his former second oboist who had left to play principal oboe in the Pittsburgh Symphony. Gatwood turned him down too. Having successfully jumped out of the frying pan, he didn't intend to jump back in. Szell also tried to contact a well-known oboe virtuoso, James Caldwell, who was a favorite of Pablo Casals. But Caldwell was off somewhere in the mountains of Spain playing in a music festival and couldn't be reached. Szell had to face reality. It was the middle of the concert season. No reputable musician would violate his contract to come play in Cleveland.[25]

Recalling that Harold Gomberg, principal oboist of the New York Philharmonic, had played when he guest-conducted that orchestra, Szell decided to ask Gomberg's advice. What he forgot—and this could have had a bearing on what followed—was how he had mistreated Gomberg on that occasion.

Gomberg, however, had not forgotten. After listening to Szell's tale of woe, he suggested one of his students who freelanced in New York. This young man might be just the person to help in the emergency. Gomberg didn't mention that the suggested oboist had been given short shrift by Tabuteau, who was scornful of the neophyte's incorrect way of tightening his lips while playing. Tabuteau used a technical word describing the player's facial muscles, coupling it with one of his famously colorful insults.

"Monsieur, let me tell you about your embouchure. You have the lips of a chicken and the jaw of a crocodile."[26] That epithet—later gleefully repeated in a French accent by the Tabuteau students who had witnessed the encounter—may not have reached Gomberg. Some gave him the benefit of a doubt.

Unaware of Tabuteau's chicken–crocodile pronouncement and desperately grasping at straws, Szell did something other conductors often did: he took someone's word that a certain musician was suitable. Without having heard a single note played by the unknown oboist, he called offering him a job. Flattered he was being singled out to step into the great Marc Lifschey's shoes, the young man assented at once to Szell's offer. A plum had fallen into his lap. Szell promised he would work with him in daily coaching sessions, the orchestra's second oboist would rehearse with him also, and he'd get a two-year contract specifying his position as principal oboe. With that settled, and confident he could quickly integrate the new player into the orchestra, Szell turned his attention to recording the Bartók.[27]

As the orchestra concentrated on polishing Bartók's masterpiece in readiness for the imminent two-day recording session, the intricate interplay between the sections coalesced, the woodwinds and brasses duetting flawlessly. The clarity and originality of the work were revealed in what was to become the definitive performance. With the Bartók recording completed, Szell began rehearsing the other compositions the orchestra would play on its East Coast tour. After they triumphed in Carnegie Hall—Zupnik courageously playing the principal oboe parts—everyone returned to Cleveland to prepare for the important international tour in April and May.

The first rehearsal with the young Gomberg-recommended oboist was a grim revelation. In less than a minute Szell realized his mistake. It was too late to do anything about it; the contract had been signed. Concealing his dismay while carefully choosing his words, he spoke to his perplexed troops. "We must now get used to a different kind of sound."[28]

The musicians traded furtive glances. This guy sounded awful. Where had he come from? Where had he played before? Was he really their new first oboist? This rank beginner was going to play the big oboe solos on the most important tour that the orchestra had ever undertaken? It didn't make sense. What had gotten into Szell?

Years later, second oboist Kraus recalled his consternation. "Szell asked me to take the new oboist under my wing. But I was shocked when I heard him play. It sounded more like a saxophone than an oboe. I guess he hadn't been playing for very long. I couldn't believe Szell had hired this fellow. We were supposed to be a matched pair, but it was ludicrous. Our tone quality and everything were miles apart. He'd never played any of those big first oboe solos either. What could *I* possibly do?" More important, with less than a month before the orchestra's departure, what could *Szell* possibly do?

CHAPTER 5

World Tour

AS PART OF THE ELABORATE PREPARATIONS for the orchestra's 1965 tour to the USSR, the musicians received booklets listing the locations where they would be staying and the names, addresses, and telephone numbers of hotels and concert halls. They were warned about things they shouldn't do: purchasing icons and photographing anything militarily important were illegal. Some of them who'd taken a crash course in Russian were eager to try out their phrases on Russians they would meet, and others were wary of doing anything that might be considered suspicious.

As they disembarked from airplanes, trains, and buses it seemed they were not only in a foreign country but also in stranger places than any had ever experienced. The major cities were uniformly drab although there were some exotic sights like the Kremlin, the Hermitage museum, and the domes of St. Basil's cathedral.[1]

As the orchestra made its way through Soviet cities and towns, sold-out concert halls marked its progress. The Russians' enthusiasm contrasted oddly with the official Cold War stance. The KGB were everywhere. The musicians were always accompanied by one or two of them, who forbade taking pictures of bridges, railroads, and airports and kept a watch for suspicious activities. Their usual answers to questions were a surly "Is possible" or "Nyet." Despite this surveillance, the players managed to sell their jeans, give American cigarettes to starry-eyed youths, buy antique tchotchkes with coveted U.S. dollars, and keep their stashes of American toilet paper safe from pillage. They'd been told Russian brands were stiff as wax paper and not up to the job.[2]

The food and hotels were dreadful, but the fervent audience applause, the Russian musicians who invited the Cleveland players to their apartments, and the obvious goodwill of the people made up for the lack of creature comforts. The musicians were charmed by their joyous reception, and the Russians could hardly do enough to show their appreciation, giving the players gifts, some of which were obviously cherished belongings.

One student who wanted to show his enthusiasm for the great Cleveland Orchestra pressed an antique ivory brooch into the hand of an orchestra member.[3] Such generosity was frequent, and the players were deeply moved as they saw the poverty of the people and their desperate yearning for beauty and a better life. They sympathized especially with the Russian musicians, whose instruments were in sorry shape, giving them reeds, extra strings, and other pieces of equipment. Principal trumpeter Bernie Adelstein even gave one of his trumpets to a needy student.[4]

The Clevelanders were heroes, Szell was treated like royalty, applause at the end of concerts was deafening, and the players were worshipfully followed in the streets by people smitten with the celebrities. At the end of each stay there was much lamentation from the crowds as the orchestra left for the next city.

The sights and the adulation were rarely witnessed by oboist Bob Zupnik, who spent every moment he wasn't sleeping or playing busily scraping reeds in his drab hotel rooms. Szell had specified that Zupnik had to perform most of the first oboe solos in the well-known classic symphonies. The new player was to be entrusted with the less familiar modern works. Second oboist Kraus wasn't in consideration as the substitute because he had to be the one playing the second oboe parts.

Zupnik knew his reed-making efforts were paying off because the audiences were ecstatic after concerts, clapped in rhythm, begged for encores, and refused to let Szell leave the stage. Zupnik didn't regret having to absent himself from after-concert celebrations because the food in restaurants was always dishearteningly the same: chicken Kiev drowned in butter. Tales of his colleagues' sightseeing forays reached him from time to time.[5]

Other tales circulated among the musicians, some of them involving surveillance. They'd been warned that hotel rooms were bugged, but many players discounted such warnings as fiction. Then flute-piccolo player Bill Hebert proved that at least some of the stories were true.

CHAPTER 5

The players had just come into a city and unpacked in their shabby hotel rooms. After hearing that Hebert's room was several grades better than theirs, some trooped down corridors to see it. Hebert opened the door, warningly put a finger to his lips, beckoned them inside, and pointed to the ceiling. One of them whispered he was just being paranoid. Why would Russians want to spy on orchestra players?

Hebert whispered back that he would prove there were hidden microphones. Raising his voice, he said, "This is a fine room, but you'd think they'd provide it with hand towels. There isn't a single one in the bathroom. I need some hand towels." Then, lowering his voice to a whisper, he said to his colleagues, "Wait a couple of minutes."

Soon there was a knock at the door. Hebert opened it, revealing a hotel employee proffering two hand towels.[6] Word spread. Thereafter the musicians took care to censor themselves.

But there was nothing they could do about the searches that took place in their rooms during their absence. Trumpeter Bernie Adelstein recalled encountering trombonist Al Kofsky in the hall of one hotel. "Al was hopping mad. He'd come back to his room to find that his new Remington battery-powered shaver had been dismantled, the pieces all laid out. The Russians must have thought it was some kind of spy device because they'd taken it completely apart and then hadn't been able to put it back together."[7]

Years later cellist Diane Mather recounted her tour memories. "Some of us women in the orchestra tried to help our new oboist. He'd been put in a really impossible situation. He was a nice young man, rather witty actually. We befriended him and tried to be encouraging. But can you imagine the pressure of having to play those concerts with no prior experience and Szell in front of him? He coped as well as he could.

"It was the first time anybody ever asked me for my autograph. It had always been that Szell was the important person and we musicians were nobodies. But in Russia we were treated like celebrities. At one concert the ovations went on for so long we finally all left the stage and started packing up our instruments. Still the applause continued, and Szell had to go back out and take a bow. More applause. He kept leaving and returning to bow some more. They went on clapping in unison. It was so different from our concerts in Cleveland where the audiences take us for granted and applaud minimally. We usually only got standing ovations at Carnegie Hall."[8]

The crowds pushing against the gates to get inside the halls, the audience members sitting often two to a seat, bunches sitting in the aisles and on the floor resembled nothing the Clevelanders had ever experienced. "Well, at least not for a concert of classical music," one musician said. "You expect that kind of thing at rock concerts. But for a symphony orchestra? People wall to wall? Not an inch to spare? Pretty unbelievable."[9]

Most of the players, aware that they were ambassadors of goodwill, were on their best behavior. In contrast, one trombonist couldn't resist the free-flowing vodka. On an inebriated night after a concert he showed his scorn for Russians by hitting one of them over the head with his trombone.

Angry officials sent word to Szell that he must immediately get rid of that player. Their demand got Szell's back up. He ordered manager Barksdale to say that if his musician didn't play, the orchestra wouldn't play either. This reply to their ultimatum gave the Russians pause. Then Szell, calming down and knowing the situation demanded utmost tact, summoned a translator to smooth things over with deep apologies and gracious statements conveying his admiration for their wonderful country. Days later some of his diplomacy was undone by the same player.

To show their hospitality, the Soviets threw a banquet lavishing quantities of food and vodka on their honored guests. Szell sat at the head table with Helene, a translator, various Russian dignitaries, and some musicians, among them the troublesome trombonist. Once again intoxicated, he began muttering some things that were on his mind. He especially didn't care for his hosts and wanted them to know it. Raising his volume, he shouted, "Goddamn Commies," and then topped his words by seizing hold of the tablecloth and dragging all the dishes onto the floor.

Instantly leaping up and grabbing a chair, Szell went after his drunken player. There was pandemonium as the musicians tried to restrain their infuriated conductor. While the perplexed Soviets looked on, several musicians hustled their colleague out the door. Much as they would have liked to throttle him themselves, he had to be spared for the good of the orchestra.[10]

The other horrified musicians sat frozen, their minds assailed by thoughts of an escalating Cold War. Did this scene jeopardize the entire goodwill venture? Trying to pretend nothing had happened while the crockery was swept off the floor, the Clevelanders went back to poking at their chicken Kievs. The banquet resumed with the Soviets smiling encouragingly. Apparently drunken scenes were the norm, and what were a few broken dishes among friends?

At the end of their six weeks in the Soviet Union, the orchestra crossed into Scandinavia and then went on to the rest of Europe. The contrast with

Russia was remarkable. The players happily went from one shop to another, reveling in Linzer tortes, Sacher tortes, Salzburger nockerl, Westphalian ham, German beer, and other enticements. The stores were full of gorgeous merchandise, and people on the streets of major cities sported gold jewelry and beautiful clothing.

European audiences were familiar with famous symphonic works, had opinions on how they should be played, and flocked to the concerts. The critics, though generous with praise, were on the lookout for anything less than perfect. One night their patience was rewarded. The new first oboist played a wrong note.[11] It was a mistake impossible to miss and was a shock to the players, Szell, and the audience. The critics pounced, gleefully writing it up in their reviews.[12]

Some of the players thought Szell had brought it on himself by hiring someone before hearing him play. Others blamed Lifschey for throwing a fit at a crucial time for the orchestra's reputation. There was agreement, however, that if Szell hadn't been so enamored of Lifschey's artistry he wouldn't have kept the temperamental prima donna for as many years as he had.[13]

Finally the eleven-week tour came to an end, and the exhausted players returned to Cleveland, where they were welcomed by a band at the airport, a red carpet, hundreds of enthusiastic fans, bouquets of flowers, and a mayoral proclamation. Each player's name was announced as he or she stepped out of the airplane while reporters crowded around, interviewing the musicians for colorful comments about the Soviet Union.

Szell wasn't there.[14] He was golfing in Switzerland, enjoying a much-needed rest. He could finally relax because he had planned ahead. Unbeknownst to the musicians, he had hired a new oboist for the principal position, someone solid and reliable, who would join the orchestra in September for the beginning of the new concert season.

The poor oboist who'd tried and failed was consigned to limbo. Because his contract ran for another year, he had to be retained and paid. But he never played another note with the Cleveland Orchestra.

CHAPTER 6

Szell's Dictates

THE TOP-PAYING POSITIONS in symphony orchestras are usually concertmaster and principal oboe. Of the two, the principal oboist's job is most
stressful because he must give the tuning A to the orchestra and play numerous solos for which he must prepare by spending countless hours crafting
undependable reeds. In the Cleveland Orchestra the position didn't pay as
much as it did in other major orchestras.

Even though the Cleveland Orchestra had become world-famous, its musicians' salaries were the lowest of any of the Big Five (the others were the New
York Philharmonic, the Boston Symphony Orchestra, the Chicago Symphony
Orchestra, and the Philadelphia Orchestra). Except for the concertmaster and
some key players, few of the musicians could afford to own homes, having
to supplement their orchestral earnings by giving music lessons or holding
part-time jobs. That didn't deter one former Tabuteau student who wanted
to leave the Washington DC National Symphony. He thought the Cleveland
Orchestra under George Szell was the pinnacle. At last Szell was lucky.

John Mack, the new principal oboist, was the opposite of Marc Lifschey.
He was reliable and adaptable, had soaked up every piece of information to
be gleaned from his teacher Tabuteau, knew most of the first oboe orchestral
solos from memory, and was willing to follow Szell's orders to the letter. He
considered the symphony orchestra one of mankind's greatest inventions
and often said so. His Curtis days had shown him his path, from which he
never deviated.[1]

Szell told Zupnik "Your new principal is very professional."[2] His statement implied there would be no more disruptions in the oboe section; Zupnik would no longer have to play solos on short notice with no rehearsal. Soon Lifschey's temperamental prima donna behavior was only a distant memory.

"John Oboe Mack" was how the new oboist listed himself in the Cleveland telephone book. That listing was no mere whim; he lived and breathed playing and teaching the oboe. He and Szell were alike in one important respect: no effort was too great where music was concerned.

Mack willingly submitted to coaching sessions in Szell's office. He wasn't the only one summoned to take instruction. Many of the other principal players regularly trod a path to that mecca, where they were bent into compliance with Szell's rules. These rules became implanted in everyone's brains, one of the most important being that they shouldn't relax during rests. They should be totally alert to what was going on around them, ears pricked up like rabbits and poised to run with the beat. That beat had four sixteenth notes inside it. Attention to rhythmic subdivisions was at the core of split-second precision.

Everyone was so tightly alert that it was well-nigh impossible to make a mistake. Occasionally, however, the human element crept in. Someone had eaten the wrong thing for dinner or his wife had left him, causing a cracked, out-of-tune, or misplaced note. Szell, busy directing musical traffic, wasn't too preoccupied to remember who had done what. Days afterward he would find a way to remind the culprit of his transgression.

Sometimes the severe discipline backfired. Szell saw his troops at one rehearsal tensed to spring at the slightest jab of his baton. Since the music being rehearsed was a jovial Haydn minuet, he realized fear wasn't setting the right mood. "Relax!" he commanded, manufacturing a smile.[3] Before concerts, principal players could be seen backstage getting last-minute instructions from Szell on the passages they had been drilled on previously. Such intense training week after week, month after month, produced high-strung musicians—as their wives frequently complained. Relaxation was rarely encountered at Severance Hall. Instead it was postponed until summer when Szell was gone.

Most symphony audiences don't realize that each orchestra has a music librarian who is just as important as any of the players. But Szell and manager Barksdale both knew this, as did Tom Brennand, one of the orchestra's violists, who filled the role of librarian.[4]

An unfortunate thing can happen with an orchestral part; it can be left forgotten at a player's home on concert nights. If a string player forgets his music it's not deadly serious. He is one of sixty others; he and his stand partner's playing won't be missed. But since each woodwind, brass, and percussion player has a separate part, his notes are crucial. And so Szell instituted a strict rule: No one could take music home after the Thursday morning rehearsal. Brennand gathered the music from the stands, taking it into the large room lined with shelves and cabinets that was the music library. He then doled it out a few hours later just before that evening's concert.

Parts and scores are sacrosanct. Many of them are rented from music publishers and they have to be returned within a certain time. In addition, they have to be returned in good shape. It is the librarian's duty to erase the musicians' jokes, pictures, ribald comments about the conductor, and messages to their counterparts in other orchestras. It's okay to pencil in eyeglasses to warn of a crucial place in the music; such a warning can be kept. But a few musicians fancy themselves cartoonists and wits. The comments and pictures they write on their parts cause hours expunging their graffiti.

Brennand had to cope with musicians determined to take their parts home because they had to practice a crucial passage on which their reputation depended. With the advent of photocopying machines, this problem largely disappeared; within seconds a performer can have a duplicate of his music for home use. But players take out their parts anyway, forget them, and then hold up rehearsals and concerts while they race home to get their music.

No wonder some librarians become testy. Their adversaries are players whose misdeeds necessitate constant wariness. Brennand never got to relax after a performance. He had to return to the cluttered back room and erase, tape, and search for mislaid pages. He'd been at it since 1942 and it would be understandable if he sometimes thought about the year when he could retire.

Mack never defaced his part with jokes or pictures. His penciled comments were straight from Szell and dealt strictly with musical matters. Szell and Tabuteau were his gods. Their words were gospel and he disseminated them to his students. Like most of Tabuteau's other protégés, Mack imitated his teacher's gravelly French accent, imbibed quantities of Scotch as Tabuteau did, surrounded himself with reed shavings as Tabuteau did, and gouged enormous quantities of cane as Tabuteau did. Mack had total dedication to Szell and the Cleveland Orchestra, coupled with a boundless enthusiasm for playing and teaching. He had a near-perfect attendance record at rehearsals and concerts; his teaching methods magnetically attracted students.

Mack was in total agreement with Szell on proper wardrobe. One should appear at rehearsals in jacket and tie, only removing the jacket if one became overheated. Underneath that jacket should be a respectable dress shirt. For concerts, socks had to be black and above-calf height to keep audience members from having to look at hairy male legs.[5] All the men carefully observed these sartorial strictures, and the women were similarly conservative. But when the fashions of the sixties got past Szell's portcullis, he erupted.

He informed manager Barksdale by letter that none of the female Severance Hall staff members were to ever cross the threshold wearing a miniskirt. If they did, he warned, he would "cause a scandal."[6] Also forbidden were beards and ponytails on males. But the worst—the very worst—was the sight of a bare female thigh. That was not to be tolerated. Mack was in agreement with Szell on that, warning his female students that they had to be suitably covered when in his presence. A minister's son, he knew where sin lurked. More and more girls were taking up the oboe, and he didn't want titillation distracting from serious musical matters.

With Mack present it was no longer necessary for Szell to hold back the orchestra's volume during an oboe solo. Mack cultivated a big sound that projected well into the farthest reaches of Severance Hall; it had heft and a satisfyingly dark quality.[7] His peers acknowledged that he was among the top orchestral oboists in the country. There was one thing that bothered Mack though. People still remembered the poignant playing of Marc Lifschey. In deference to this sensitivity, Szell never mentioned Lifschey's name in Mack's hearing.

CHAPTER 7

The String Section

MAJOR SYMPHONY ORCHESTRAS number approximately one hundred musicians, with more than sixty of them playing a stringed instrument. Of those sixty, more than half are violinists. And of that half, at least twenty are as high-strung as their instruments. On any given day of the orchestra season, one of them is probably in the personnel manager's office, complaining about something or someone.

It's not easy being a violinist. One has to play on a fingerboard little more than a foot long and place a note within a thirty-second of an inch to be perfectly in tune. That kind of precision requires hours of practice each day. At rehearsals and concerts one will have to play many more notes than one's colleagues in the woodwind, brass, and percussion sections.

This makes for animosity between the string sections and the other three sections of the orchestra. Why should a cymbal player who executes only three crashes in a concert be paid as much money as a violinist who plays three thousand notes? For that matter, why should the conductor get the highest salary when he doesn't play any notes at all? These complaints aren't usually voiced. But they hang in the air, straining relations onstage and off.

When a violinist says he needs a higher salary, it's because he frequently plays on an instrument that can cost several hundred thousand dollars—far more if it's a Stradivarius or Guarnerius or some other old Italian instrument he has gone into debt for. Even the bow he uses can cost thousands.

String players are irritated by the sight of assistant principal woodwind and brass players doing little at most rehearsals and concerts while they themselves play constantly and, as a result, suffer stiff necks and shoulders, carpal tunnel syndrome, and aching wrists. The most wear and tear is to their fingers. One violinist recounted her tribulations:

I have to stay in constant practice to maintain the calluses on my fingertips. A vacation away from the violin means that my calluses start to disappear. Getting them back is painful. To prevent losing them I keep my violin in my hands while I'm talking on the phone or reading. My left-hand fingers have to keep moving around on the fingerboard so their tips stay hard. One of the most painful things is playing high up on the G string. You have to press harder because up there the string is higher off the fingerboard. That metal G-string with its silver wrapping can be torture if you practice on it for very long. Cellists and bass players are worse off because their fingers have to press down much thicker strings to make contact with the fingerboard.[1]

A cellist confessed she sometimes suffers split calluses from hours of practice. Then she has to quit playing for a week while her fingers heal. Pianists aren't the only ones who get bloody fingers. We women have more finger problems than men because our fingers are more delicate.[2]

Seasonal weather changes can cause frustrating problems for cellists. One of them complained at length:

Bridges. I have several of them for when humidity changes cause the wood of my cello to expand or contract. I have to install a different bridge that changes the distance between strings and fingerboard, and put it on in exactly the same place so its left foot is in proper contact with the sound post. The monkeying around I have to do. Every spring. Every fall. And if I don't get the bridge in exactly the right position the instrument sounds terrible. You can take an Amati cello, install its bridge or sound post badly and its tone goes south. You could swear you were playing some Bavarian packing crate.[3]

All string players have to put up with the foibles of their stand partners because it's customary to seat two string players together, reading from the same piece of music. Such partnerships can be as fraught as a bad marriage. Bass players in particular need space for their huge instruments. Positioning themselves in relation to their stand partner's bass and their own is tricky, especially if they are playing on risers.

Marty Flowerman, who joined the Cleveland Orchestra's bass section in 1967, lamented the carnage that happens to basses because of their size and the dangers of climbing risers to the back of the orchestra.

Basses are jeopardized going through narrow doors and dodging the other players and their instruments. Most basses have nicks and scratches from accidents onstage. We need two basses, one to leave at the hall, because carrying one back and forth is dangerous. If you leave your instrument unattended during an intermission break somebody is going to stumble over it. Basses look big and sturdy, but they are really fragile. And many bass players have back problems from years of leaning over their instruments.[4]

Flowerman touched on the principal bassist's role in Mahler's *First Symphony*. Its funeral march movement begins with a lugubrious minor-key parody of the well-known *Frère Jacques* melody. "That solo is a big headache for bass players who try to give it beautiful tone quality and phrasing. It's just a simple tune, supposed to be played simply. But most players overthink it." Principal bass players lose sleep over this solo and suffer stage fright as they try to cope with Mahler's exposed melody, not realizing it is *supposed* to sound forlorn.[5]

All those problems and more Szell knew from his many years of conducting. So he had a grievance procedure in place consisting of two buffers. The first of these was the orchestra's personnel manager Olin Trogdon. If Trogdon couldn't calm the waters, the matter was referred to manager Barksdale. They were supposed to deal with players' complaints without bothering Szell. Nevertheless, Szell often got involved because it was in his nature to have a finger in every pie. Some situations ended up in Szell's sanctum, which was risky. A malcontent could end up worse off than before by the time Szell got through with him.

Szell usually handled salary negotiations, and they could be frightening. One modest request elicited the warning "I'm prepared to lose five good men over five dollars a week,"[6] effectively squelching any further conversation on the subject.

Violinists' peeves included something Szell couldn't do much about: overwork. Because brass and wind players can't play continuously—having to stop blowing to take in oxygen—the violins and the other string sections play the majority of the time in most of the pieces in the classic symphonic repertoire. Also, string sections blend well with each other; composers, recognizing that fact, keep them constantly busy.

In the seventeenth century Nicolò Amati, Joseph Guarneri, Antonio Stradivari, and other Italian violinmakers would have been amazed to know their instruments would eventually sell for millions of dollars.[7] The spruce and maple they used to fashion their violins, violas, and cellos were in common use, and the design was simple. What wasn't simple was the complicated way of applying varnish and the finicky measurements. Such details were supposedly secret, but the measurements themselves weren't hard to discover.[8]

As time went on, there was lots of money being made by violin dealers, who drove up the prices of Italian violins and French bows. This caused a minor art form to arise: the forgery of famous makers' labels. Any violinmaker with a finely calibrated measuring device could copy the dimensions of famous makers' violins. Labels rendered suitably aged were glued inside cheap instruments that were then circulated. Some labels were naïvely inscribed "Made by Stradivarius in Japan." Because violins found in attics and cellars with such labels were commonplace, violin repairers in Europe and the United States had to disappoint thousands of hopeful Stradivarius owners by explaining the label meant nothing. Antonio Stradivari had never lived in Japan.

The greatest of the famous violin virtuosos in the twentieth century was Jascha Heifetz, a Russian child prodigy who had matured into a consummate artist. The crystalline clarity of his technique and luscious tone quality, combined with rare good taste and musicianship, made him a fortune, some of which he invested in three Stradivarius and two Guarnerius violins. His fabulous playing of the monumental Bach D minor Chaconne on one of these glorious instruments could have been what German poet Rainer Maria Rilke had in mind when he wrote a poem containing the line "In the room a violin was giving itself to someone."[9] Within thirteen minutes, Bach's unaccompanied masterpiece erects a spine-tingling structure sounding like several violins playing at once. It builds up climax after climax, requiring incredible finger and bow technique. Probably no violinist in Bach's day was able to perform this solo the way Heifetz did. Bach was a virtuoso organist, and even though he also played the violin he could hardly have convincingly played the complicated *Chaconne*. It remained for Heifetz two centuries later to bring it astoundingly to life.[10]

Heifetz had an aloof stage presence coupled with the ability to face down any conductor, and he commanded some of the highest fees in the music business. Plainly he was the king. When it was announced in 1953 that he would perform a concerto with the Cleveland Orchestra, many of the players probably wondered how Szell and he would get along. Which of them would prevail?

At the greatly anticipated rehearsal, all the musicians were on the lookout for a colorful confrontation, but it never took place. The two formidable artists were on their best behavior. Near the end of the uneventful rehearsal, Szell said to Heifetz, "We should just go over a few places that need a bit more work." "I'd rather not," answered Heifetz, who then strode off the stage. He knew the audience was coming to hear him play his flashy encores, not the Cleveland Orchestra.[11]

No critic could fault him except New York composer-critic Virgil Thomson, who called Heifetz's encore specialties "silk underwear music."[12] Thomson was a thorn in the side of many performers. He wrote insulting words about Heifetz, whom he accused of being a cold and bloodless perfectionist, citing Heifetz's unexciting stage presence. Anyone hoping to see tortured grimaces, crouches, hair askew, and a sweaty forehead was in for disappointment. Heifetz simply stood immovable in one spot and, with a minimum of gestures, played superbly. His smooth features conveyed none of the passion of the music. But if one closed one's eyes, the magic was all there. In this he was very much like Szell, whose back conveyed nothing to audiences. Szell neither leapt, swayed, nor turned a tortured profile to onlookers. The drama was in the music itself.

Szell and Heifetz had many things in common. Both had been child prodigies, were Jewish, were close to the same age, were obsessed with creating musical perfection, and were composers and arrangers of numerous works. Heifetz had made nearly a hundred transcriptions of classical and popular melodies. The major difference between them was that Heifetz was worshipped and world famous, while Szell had yet to be internationally hailed as one of the world's greatest conductors.

In comparing these two artists, it should be realized that Heifetz had to master only one small instrument, whereas Szell had to rule over a hundred musicians in his orchestra. Molding disparate players into a unified whole takes much longer than it takes to conquer a violin. It would take forty-nine-year-old Szell a decade to create a fabulous orchestra and then a decade longer—through tours, recordings, and broadcasts—to make the world aware of what he had done.

Many violinists hope to become another Heifetz, joining an orchestra only as a last resort when they realize they will never have Heifetz's technique or the money to buy a great old Italian violin. But one first violinist in the Cleveland Orchestra, Sidney Weiss, was an exception because he already owned a Stradivarius. One day he decided to copy its measurements and make a reasonable facsimile. He got to work, producing what looked and sounded like the real thing. He then auditioned for a better position in the orchestra.

Greatly impressed by his technique and beautiful tone quality, Szell wanted to know what fine instrument he was playing. Sidney said it was a Weiss. Szell had never heard of that maker. Questioning Weiss further, he was astonished that his own violinist had actually made the instrument that had just been pouring forth beautiful sounds.[13] Weiss was promoted. He then carried out the rest of his plan. It consisted of selling the Stradivarius for a large sum and leaving the Cleveland Orchestra.[14]

Sidney was not the only fine violinist who left. Arnold Steinhardt, an assistant concertmaster, became increasingly impatient with being under Szell's thumb. Longing for independence, he resigned so he could form his own string quartet. And concertmaster Joseph Gingold preferred the calm of teaching violin at Indiana University.[15] Szell usually understood such departures, remaining friends with his favorites.

Szell had cultivated a kind of father-son relationship with young Steinhardt. Recognizing Steinhardt's talent, he arranged for a summer of violin lessons with famous violinist Joseph Szigetti and paid for the trip. He called Steinhardt into his office many times to tell him about music he should study, books he should read, and even showed him how to keep his socks up.

Instead of buying a better instrument, one violinist bought a new car. Taking note of that, Szell summoned its driver to his office for a sound berating.[16] What kind of musician would prefer a new car to a better violin? Fine-quality instruments produce fine sounds, and his orchestra needed as many of them as possible. He was sure violins bearing the labels of old Italian masters were superior to all others. (Except for the Weiss.)

New cars weren't the only things Szell was on the lookout for. Latecomers were anathema. He entered Severance Hall at nine on the dot each morning and expected his musicians to arrive at nine-thirty so they would be warmed up for the ten o'clock rehearsal. People who dashed in at the last minute were warned with baleful stares that their tardiness had been noticed. If they persisted in last-minute arrivals they were called into the lion's den for withering admonishment.[17]

One stringed instrument player who never needed to be told to appear earlier in the morning was Alice Chalifoux, the orchestra's diminutive and expert principal harpist. Chalifoux had to tune the forty-seven strings on her harp, and so she walked in the door even before Szell did. A convent-educated girl from Birmingham, Alabama, she sometimes used her harp case for a dressing room, could play all the harp music extant, and was always thoroughly prepared. Although she appeared to be a demure little thing, she had the interesting ability to swear like a stevedore when the mood was upon her. She had joined the orchestra in 1931 when she was only twenty-three, a recent graduate of Curtis, and was its first female musician. She held her own with the men, quickly picking up their salty language. Szell especially seemed to bring out her latent glee.

"He was a prude in some ways and wasn't used to having a woman telling off-color jokes," Chalifoux would later recall. "He said my jokes embarrassed him and made him blush.[18] Hah! I could handle him." Chalifoux was one of the few musicians in the orchestra who could get away with such behavior. She was a great harpist, knew it, and knew Szell knew it.

The harp is a very complicated instrument, having not only forty-seven strings but also seven pedals to change the pitch of those strings. Although Szell knew a lot about the harp and its mechanism, he never tried to tell Chalifoux how to play it. He probably knew how that would have ended.

Chalifoux occasionally practiced her harp in a large closet in the assistant personnel manager's office, knowing it wouldn't disturb the rest of the orchestra. She did her own harp repairs, sometimes putting the instrument flat on the floor and lying beside it to work on its interior mechanism.

Al Kofsky was used to seeing her prone with pliers and a screwdriver. He recalled that Alice once gave him a bad scare. "One morning I came into the room and saw her body partially concealed by a blanket as she lay stretched out next to her harp. All that was visible were her feet sticking out. I said, 'Alice?' but her feet didn't move. I thought she was lying there dead. I ran out and called for help, and people came running. Suddenly Alice appeared asking what all the fuss was about. She really read me out for that."[19]

Szell treasured Chalifoux's virtuosity, enduring her ribald jokes, maybe even savoring her spunkiness. But a fight between them arose when she absented herself from a rehearsal one morning because her husband had been hospitalized suddenly. Chalifoux chose to be with him rather than rehearse an important harp part scheduled for that week's concert.

Barksdale attempted to explain to Szell why Chalifoux wasn't there, but Szell was livid and refused to listen. He called her several hours later, raging that she had violated her contract. Chalifoux raged right back, telling him, in essence, to go fly a kite. She then telephoned Barksdale and said she intended to publicize Szell's callous treatment of her at a time when her husband was critically ill.

Accustomed to frayed tempers, Barksdale immediately got hold of a lawyer sometimes used by management to calm waters. This diplomat hastened to Chalifoux's home to convince her that she would only be hurting herself by inflating the spat into a cause célèbre. In the meantime, Szell came out of his dudgeon and regretted he had let his intolerance of absenteeism ruin a friend-ship with one of his best players. He needed her more than she needed him.

Later that same day, Chalifoux answered her doorbell and was startled to see Szell standing on her front steps with an enormous bouquet of choice blooms. This costly offering plus his abject apology did the trick. The two reconciled, Chalifoux's husband recovered, and the public never found out that the spunky little harpist had won a victory over her world-famous boss.[20]

Chalifoux graced the Cleveland Orchestra for forty-three years. She be-came one of the country's finest harpists and teachers, her students welcomed into major orchestras. She was never a problem like many of the violinists, who were in a habitual state of discontent.

Those string players who start out as prodigies expect to become concert artists. When fame doesn't materialize, they resign themselves to membership in an orchestra where they must play in unison with other similarly frustrated players. This fate is so hard to take that some never get over it. They teach on the side and in their free evenings get together with other string players to play quartets for fun. Theoretically the fun should never come to an end because of the vast and wonderful string quartet literature written by some of the greatest composers. But personalities can clash, causing beautiful musical evenings to end in heated arguments. Such altercations frequently take place between the first and second violinists and partly stem from their thwarted soloist ambitions.

Some orchestral string players become convinced their talents are squelched by playing symphony music under a controlling conductor and leave to form string quartets. Although this allows them to express them-selves musically, the downside to such freedom is that every note they play can be clearly heard. The first violinist of the quartet is frequently the leader, making for dissension. "Who are you to tell me how to play? I went to Curtis too." Just as many string quartets disband as are formed. It's a hard life going from city to city playing difficult music for small audiences, and the pay is low. Only the beauty of musical masterpieces keeps them at it.

In general, however, musical disagreements among quartet players are fairly civilized. Felix Freilich, one of the musicians who had fled the war in Europe, was hired by Szell and stayed to become one of his valued violin-ists. During one amiable string quartet evening, Freilich listened patiently while violist Vitold Kushleika summoned up impressive technical terms to explain why a certain phrase had to be played a certain way. He then asked Freilich, "Do you understand what I'm saying?" "Yes, I understand perfectly," answered Freilich, "and I choose not to do it like that."[21] This polite rejoinder ended Kushleika's speech. The music resumed.

Szell had to deal with underlying currents of discontent among the prima donna prodigies and didn't always come out on top. Cathleen Dalschaert played in the first violin section of the orchestra, and when Szell had been riding the firsts for some minor infraction Cathleen took it into her head that he was specifically insulting her. At the end of the rehearsal she stormed into his office to give him a piece of her mind. She had been a soloist in Australia before joining the Cleveland Orchestra and had a soloist's temperament. Informing him that she would soon be giving a recital, she said he'd "damn well better be there." Szell meekly accepted her invitation, perhaps relieved that he hadn't been physically assaulted.[22]

One concert violinist became anathema to Szell: the famous Polish violinist Henryk Szeryng, who soloed with the orchestra during his 1961 tour of the United States. A player in the violin section recalled that

> Instead of starting to play his concerto at the rehearsal, Szeryng began by lecturing us. He talked on and on for maybe ten minutes. It was pretty arrogant of him to act as if we were all amateurs in need of lessons. Szell was standing on the podium, getting more and more impatient. We could see he was really mad. Finally at the end of Szeryng's lecture he said, "You've told us how *you* play it. Now we're going to show you how *we* play it."
>
> So we began rehearsing. Szeryng was a fine violinist and I was listening intently when suddenly I realized he was looking straight at me while he played. He had melting brown eyes and those eyes locked on mine. I couldn't look away. He was playing so gorgeously, all the time looking at me. I had the feeling he was playing for me alone. The beauty of what he was doing was just for me. Those eyes! And that playing! I started imagining all sorts of things. It was like some movie scene where a man and woman see each other across a room and the next thing you know . . .
>
> Well, I was in a tizzy. I felt sure our personnel manager was going to come over to me at intermission and say Szeryng wanted to see me in his dressing room after the concert. I was sort of spellbound, thinking what I should wear and how I'd better wash my hair and fix my makeup.
>
> In the locker room that night before the concert, I confessed to one of the women what had happened between Szeryng and me. Her mouth just fell open. She said he'd looked at her the same way. She thought maybe he'd fallen in love with her. And then another woman joined us, saying the same thing.

Somehow he had managed to look at each of us, making us feel he'd fallen instantly in love. Talk about an operator.[23]

But something else happened: Szell gave Szeryng a hard time, criticizing his playing and insulting him. He got so mad he actually walked off the stage before the end of the rehearsal. It was quite a scene. He couldn't stand Szeryng's attitude and his lecturing. And then he did something so awful I still get the shivers thinking about it. During Szeryng's performance in Carnegie Hall a month later, Szell conducted the accompaniment slightly too fast so Szeryng had to scramble to keep up. He cued the orchestra to come in just a bit too soon to make it seem as if Szeryng was wrong and all of us were right. Szell kept doing that through the entire concerto. He was fixated on ruining that man.[24]

Naturally the next morning we rushed to get the reviews. They were even worse than we anticipated. The orchestra got raves, but Szeryng was consigned to the junk heap. I'll never forget that incident. As far as I know, that's the only time Szell ever did such a thing. Can you imagine what it takes to do something like that? Well, anyway, Szeryng didn't suffer much harm from it because he gave a lot of recitals and always got good reviews. He really was a fine violinist, but he sure didn't get off on the right foot with Szell, who was far beyond him musically. He should have known better. Some soloists have tunnel vision.[25]

That was hardly the first time Szell treated a visiting soloist badly. He had frequent altercations with other artists whose playing didn't please him: violinist Nathan Milstein, pianist Clifford Curzon, and even violinist Erica Morini and pianist Rudolf Serkin, both of whom had known him since they were prodigies together in Vienna.[26] But he had never done something in public as bizarre as the night when he deliberately ruined Szeryng's performance. His inner demons had gotten the best of him.

CHAPTER 8

The Brass Section

THE BRASS SECTION is capable of blowing the rest of the orchestra to smithereens. Knowing this, the composer Richard Strauss famously warned young conductors, "Never look at the brass. It only encourages them."[1] He knew what he was talking about; his father had been a professional French horn player. Woodwind players have to sit in front of brass players and be deafened when pieces by Wagner or Strauss call for an augmented brass section.

In contrast to violinists, who can begin playing at the age of three or four, brass players have to wait until they are several years older. They need strong enough muscles in their lips to cope with metal mouthpieces. Boys gravitate toward the glittering gold instruments they see and hear in marching bands.

Male predominance in brass sections is taken for granted by professional musicians and conductors because women are thought not up to the task of blowing a horn. This assumption is belied by women's feats in endurance sports, especially long-distance swimming. Their exploits would seem to prove that at least some female lungs are up to the requirements of a Wagner opera or a Bruckner symphony with their large brass sections blowing hair-raising sounds. Nevertheless, until recently, if a woman wanted to play a brass instrument she had to resign herself to an amateur orchestra or band. Once in a great while a female French hornist can be seen in the brass section of some professional orchestra where she is grudgingly accepted. But this never occurred in the Cleveland Orchestra during Szell's reign.

The orchestra's brass section was composed of four trumpeters, five French hornists, four trombone players, and one tuba player. If Szell decided to program a Mahler, Bruckner, Strauss, or Wagner composition, additional players had to be hired, bringing the total to twenty or more brass players. The extra fees could be expensive, and he didn't allow himself very many such occasions.

The lower brass instruments aren't merely the ponderous foundation of a symphony orchestra; they can be fleet and nimble too. A musician spoke admiringly of a virtuosic tuba performance in John Philip Sousa's *Stars and Stripes Forever* that he never forgot: "It was one summer in San Francisco. This band had a fantastic tuba player who could do Sousa's famous piccolo solo. He was unbelievable. I'd never thought the big tuba could be made to play as fast as the little piccolo. In a band the tuba is usually just required to play oompahs. But this guy was playing stuff written for a high instrument and making it sound easy."[2]

That virtuoso may have been Ronald Bishop, whom Szell hired away from the San Francisco Symphony in 1967. Bishop was a champion swimmer and had developed strong lungs and great stamina. His favorite composers were Bruckner, Prokofiev, Strauss, and Wagner. No wonder. Their music gave him a chance to show what he could do.

An absence of aggressive behavior in the orchestra's brass section was perhaps due to their not having to prove anything; their instruments did it for them. The brasses usually gave Szell little trouble once he established the kind of sound he wanted, and they produced it on their American instruments that were easier to play than European ones.

The genial trombonist Al Kofsky was well liked by his fellow musicians for his modesty and ability to get along with everybody. When personnel manager Zauder needed an assistant, Kofsky was tapped for the position.

At first I didn't want the job. Just a lot of headaches. But they kept pressing me and finally I gave in. Somebody had to help out Zauder. So I was given an office next to Zauder's that I shared with his secretary. Pretty soon I was being handed all the problems that Zauder didn't want.

People lost their tempers with me and I had to calm them down and mediate. They could get pretty hotheaded and use strong language. Sometimes arguments would get blown out of proportion and go to Szell. He would speak to each player and I was always impressed at how judicious he could be and how fair. He'd hear both sides and then decide who was wrong in the argument. He was very observant and usually knew what was going on and who was the troublemaker.

I think about Szell all the time. There was nobody else like him, and he molded the orchestra into the great thing it was. He was a very precise person, a genius really, and all of us knew it. He stuck to what he did best—the Germanic repertoire mostly. He didn't like chitchat during rehearsals and didn't have much small talk, but he had a sense of humor and liked jokes. He had a temper with some people though, people he thought weren't taking their job seriously.

Most of us listened to the Sunday afternoon WCLV broadcasts of our performances. We were constantly involved with finding better equipment for our instruments, mouthpieces especially. Each brass player has to have a mouthpiece that's right for his lips. It entails trying out a lot of them to settle on the exactly right one. They regularly need replating with silver or gold.[3]

The orchestra's brass players were lucky to have the White Instrument Company in Cleveland, where they went to buy mouthpieces and have their horns repaired or relacquered. The craftsmen at White—it later changed its name to Selmer-Conn—worked with the players to develop better instruments and parts. They used some of Kofsky's ideas for improving their trombones. He recalled that they were always glad for suggestions.

Every once in a while there's something innovative for brass instruments like the extension valve for the trombone. It's great because with a flick of that little valve you can play an octave lower without having to extend your arm way out. You can switch registers faster with it. We brass players have it easy compared to the woodwind players who have to make their own reeds and constantly adjust their gouging machines. Their instruments get played out after several years, not like ours that last for decades. I have trombones that play fine after fifty years.

We don't have as many exposed solos as the woodwind players do. Sure, we have to practice to stay in shape and keep the tubing in our instruments cleaned out, but we don't have their reed-making worries. All of us in the brass section own various different instruments that we play according to what the music calls for, what key or what kind of sound. I can play tenor, alto, and bass trombone. Trumpeters can play slide trumpet and piccolo trumpet and B flat or F or C trumpets. Except for the French horn, brass instruments are much easier to play and more stable than woodwind instruments.

Talented trumpeter Dick Smith joined the orchestra in 1956 and was made principal trumpet in 1958. Szell liked his playing, but as the months went on, Smith's personal problems affected his performance. Szell sent him to a therapist, paying the bills himself.[4] Smith, however, could no longer play as brilliantly and dependably as needed in such a prominent position. Szell loyally kept him in the orchestra as a section player and hired someone else as principal trumpet.[5]

Smith's replacement was thirty-two-year-old Bernard Adelstein, who, with many years of experience playing under Antal Dorati and Fritz Reiner, was a seasoned expert. Adelstein had asked for and received a trumpet for his eighth birthday. This started a love affair with that instrument, and he joined a professional orchestra when he was only sixteen. While he was playing principal trumpet in the Minneapolis Symphony, Szell, who was guest-conducting that orchestra, heard him and took note. A year later, in 1960, Szell telegraphed him to come and audition for the principal trumpet position in the Cleveland Orchestra.

"It was a surprisingly easy audition," Adelstein would later recall. "He didn't have the audition folder in the room and I hadn't brought any music. He just said, 'Play.' So I did some of a Haydn concerto and a few famous orchestral excerpts. And that was it. He hired me. I'd grown up in Cleveland. I knew how great the orchestra was. Now I was returning to head its trumpet section. Kind of 'local boy makes good.'"[6]

At his first rehearsal Adelstein was astonished by the orchestra's perfection; it never seemed to wane. "Each week the music always sounded breathtaking on the very first run-through. I'd thought I was hot stuff, but I found out I had a lot to learn from Szell. He was a master at balancing the sections of the orchestra so the brasses and percussion wouldn't cover the strings and woodwinds. And he insisted on rhythmic precision. That's a tricky thing for brass sections because of the length of tubing in our instruments. It takes longer to start the sound. If we blow exactly with the beat, the sound gets out front slightly behind the strings. There's a small time lag. We have to compensate for that by blowing slightly *ahead* of the beat. Szell knew that and allowed for it. And he was big on subdivisions. An eighth note followed by two sixteenth notes shouldn't sound like three even triplets. Everything had to be precisely played as it was written on the page."[7]

Like other members of the orchestra, Adelstein was to find out that Szell knew a great deal about his instrument. Szell's constant curiosity combined with a fabulous memory enabled him to know the fingerings of all the instruments, their characteristics, and their problems. "One time," Adelstein said, "he called me into his office and said, 'The E is a flat note on the trumpet isn't it.' I said, 'Yes, but I use an alternate fingering to bring it up.' He said, 'With that fingering the note gets too sharp.' And I said, 'Well, I use a trigger on the first valve to get it in tune.' Then he said, 'Well, the octave E is still out of tune.' He knew exactly what the trumpet could do and all those regular and alternate fingerings."[8]

In addition to his knowledge of the workings of brass instruments, Szell had definite opinions about their sounds. He was repelled by what he perceived as harshness from American brass instruments, preferring the mellower sounding European ones that he wanted his players to use. Adelstein remembered Szell's adamant pronouncement concerning a certain trumpet's tone quality: "Once he called me into his office and criticized my playing in Poulenc's *Gloria* that we had just performed with Robert Shaw conducting. I'd been using a Martin trumpet because it had a piercing quality that I thought Shaw wanted in that piece. Szell was disgusted with the Martin and said, 'That sound has no place in the Cleveland Orchestra.'

"He rarely complimented me," Adelstein continued.

In Vienna the orchestra played an all-Gershwin concert with Louis Lane conducting, and I had a great night. Afterwards Szell came up to me and said, "Fantastic trumpet playing." That was the height of his compliments.

Everybody got corrected all the time. We all feared for our jobs because he was so critical. The only way you knew you pleased him was if he didn't say anything. Then you knew you were okay.

One day I went into Szell's office to ask about a mistake I thought I'd found in a Walton symphony we were rehearsing that week. My part was in unison with the violins except for one passage where my part didn't match theirs. Szell faced me, and, without the music and without looking at the piano keyboard, began playing the score to explain why there wasn't a mistake. It was uncanny because the piece was something he'd never conducted before, totally different from his usual repertoire. He had studied it so well he knew it cold.[9]

Szell was a great pianist. I first realized it during one of our Northeast tours. I went to the hall early—I can't remember whether it was in Boston or New York—and saw two people on stage, one of them playing the piano and the other one watching. I thought it was Leon Fleisher playing because he'd been performing Beethoven's *Emperor Concerto* with us on tour. He was one of Szell's favorites and played with us often. We called him our house pianist. He was so great.

As Adelstein got closer he was surprised to see that Fleisher was standing, and it was actually Szell who was playing. He was demonstrating a difficult passage in the *Emperor* and explaining it to Fleisher like a professor and his student.[10]

"He was playing it beautifully too. That was really impressive because he didn't have time to practice the piano for hours every day. He was busy all the time conducting. But he had such a fine piano technique he could sit down and play something difficult without having worked on it. If he hadn't decided to become a conductor he would have been one of the world's great piano soloists."[11]

Szell's rejection of salary raises discouraged most of the underpaid musicians. But, confident he deserved it, Adelstein decided to risk asking for more money.

In those days Szell was in charge of salaries so I went to his office and requested a raise. He sat me down and gave me a fifteen-minute talk on economics to explain why I couldn't have it. It was like a lecture from a Harvard professor. He was really well educated on many other subjects than music, including medical things.

I had to have a hernia operation and when I returned to work Szell wanted to know about it. Who was my surgeon? How had my operation gone? I said I couldn't tell him much because I'd been under anesthesia. He said he'd had that operation, too, and stayed awake the whole time so he could watch. He started telling me exactly what had happened. He was so curious about everything that he'd insisted on watching his own hernia operation.[12]

Szell knew a lot about the trumpet and its mouthpieces and had a preference for the tone quality of brass instruments made in Germany and Austria. Over time, however, the brass section convinced him that American instruments are easier to play. "Balancing chords was something he was a master at," Adelstein said. "Each note in the chord had to be the same volume and quality as the ones around it. He liked a dark sound in the bottom registers. And he kept a tight rein on things. He always insisted on such precision that we couldn't play freely. There wasn't a lot of spontaneity."[13]

Szell could become fixated on someone or something out of all proportion. "One time," Adelstein recalled, "we were rehearsing the Brahms *Second Piano Concerto* with its big cello solo in the slow movement. Lynn Harrell played it and it was so absolutely gorgeous that at the end we all shuffled our feet and clapped in appreciation. We'd never heard such fabulously beautiful cello playing. But Szell said he'd have to play it again. This or that wasn't right. He kept raking Lynn over that solo. It was ridiculous. It couldn't have been more beautiful."

Szell never left anything to chance. According to Adelstein, Szell once told the orchestra they would play "Happy Birthday" for Artur Rubinstein.

"Instead of just telling us to play it in the key of C, he had Louis Lane write out a part for each musician, and then he rehearsed us in it, a simple little tune we all knew. He had tremendous pride in his orchestra and wanted even the most insignificant thing to be perfect."[14]

Adelstein remembered when brass sections from three orchestras got together to record some Gabrielli antiphonal pieces. "We didn't have a conductor. We just told the technician to start the tape rolling. We didn't tune at first, simply started playing, and things fell into place. The record came out and sounded great. It won a lot of awards. Szell listened to it and came up to me several days later asking who had conducted it. I said, 'Nobody.' That sort of threw him. I guess he couldn't quite believe a bunch of musicians could make excellent music without a conductor."

As did others of his colleagues who needed a paycheck during the summer months, Adelstein left Cleveland to play in classical music festivals such as Aspen and Casals. Szell knew where they went and why, but he didn't like it. "One time, right after the first rehearsal of the fall season, I got called into Szell's office," Adelstein recalled. "We'd been playing Debussy's La Mer with some exposed solo trumpet passages. He said, 'You were in Aspen last summer weren't you? It has spoiled your rhythm. Everyone who comes back here from Aspen has bad rhythm.' It wasn't true, of course. He just resented our playing for some European conductor he used to know."[15]

When Szell guest-conducted various orchestras in the United States, he had more on his mind than just the music; he was taking note of which players he might steal for the Cleveland Orchestra. Because the 1946 contract he signed in Cleveland had a clause giving him the power to hire anyone he wanted, he used it to carry out marauding forays. One of his conquests was the French hornist Ernani Angelucci, who had joined the Cleveland Orchestra in 1937 but seven years later defected to the Philadelphia Orchestra to make more money. Upon hearing Angelucci in Philadelphia, Szell immediately hired him to come back to Cleveland. Certain that the trustees wouldn't balk at paying the hornist the salary he asked, Szell got what he wanted—and then some.

Angelucci slyly declined to play first horn, saying he desired the lesser position of second horn.[16] Szell accepted the request, thinking he could soon push Angelucci into accepting the more responsible position of third horn. When he then asked Angelucci to be his third hornist, Angelucci said he would need a raise if he were going to do that. Szell gave it to him. But, with more responsibility, the situation was not to Angelucci's liking; he wanted to enjoy life and not have to play important solos. When his contract came up for renewal, he requested that he be demoted to fourth horn, while at the same time asking Szell for *another* raise. Somehow he outwitted Szell, got the raise and the position he wanted, and stayed in it for many years thereafter. "Enjoying life" included devising pranks to play on his fellow brass players, joining in the long-running poker games in the locker room, and demonstrating his impressive horn technique to his students. He had no desire to shine in the starring role of first horn.

All the musicians conceded that Angelucci was not only a good hornist but also a clever fellow, an expert poker player, and a scamp. Warm-up time before rehearsals gave him the opportunity to switch valves in his colleagues' instruments and enjoy the mistakes that resulted. His practical jokes were known to Szell who nevertheless tolerated Angelucci's mischievous pranks for the sake of his fine playing.[17]

The five-man French horn section was in constant flux, players going from one demanding position to another less demanding one, and new people replacing old ones who couldn't stand the pressure of Szell's demands coupled with the treachery of their instruments. But Angelucci remained. Content and ambitionless, he was a perfect fourth horn player.

Eight years after Szell took up his post in Cleveland, he hired a young French horn player, Mike Bloom, to play third horn. He then proceeded to hector him in his usual way with newcomers. After a year of this treatment, Bloom, thinking he could never please Szell, decided to accept an offer from another orchestra. He went into Szell's office to announce his resignation. Hardly had Bloom begun speaking when Szell realized that he was about to lose someone who possessed the most beautiful tone on the French horn he had ever encountered. "But haven't you heard?" Szell improvised. "I've made you my first horn." This was too much for Bloom. Here was one of the world's greatest conductors choosing him for the most prominent position in his orchestra. In that instant he became Szell's devoted disciple.

The whole orchestra agreed that Bloom's phrasing and tone quality made him one of the world's outstanding hornists. "His tone was just so full of color," reminisced cellist Diane Mather. "When he played you knew there was nobody else like him."[18]

Szell had always known the problems of the French horn. In his youth he had tried to play the instrument with negligible results; one of his friends likened Szell's sound on the French horn to that of a motorcycle. Knowing from his own experience that the French horn was the most temperamental of all orchestral instruments, Szell was able to appreciate Bloom's talent and daring and was aware that the slightest thing could cause a horn player to crack notes. He stopped criticizing Bloom, who then flourished in that important and nerve-racking position.

Sometimes the horn just won't play. Once that happened in Brahms's *Second Symphony*. The famous horn solo in the first movement didn't appear because, though Bloom blew, nothing came out. There was complete silence where the horn solo was supposed to be. Afterward Bloom couldn't explain to Szell what had happened. But his job was safe because Szell, for all his knowledge, didn't know what ailed the hellish instrument either. Nor did the other men in the horn section. Among themselves they all resignedly agreed, "That's what the damned thing does."[19]

Bloom was not cool. He was a bundle of sensitivity and idealism, and his mobile features when he played his solos revealed the effort he put into every note. He tolerated nobody's criticism but Szell's, and the two could be seen listening to a playback at a recording session, heads together over the score. They were as one in their commitment to the music.

Admired for his unusually beautiful sound, Mike tried to explain how he created it. "I wanted to make the horn sound like a cello. I mean the cello as played by Pablo Casals and Emmanuel Feuermann."[20] He did more than that. No cello could soar like Mike's French horn.

An early fixation on meaningful phrasing and beautiful tone quality happens to many musicians. They discover something they can't describe, something infinitely alluring. Their dedication to this nameless sound-and-phrasing concept sets them apart from nonmusicians whose ears aren't attuned to it. It's what one player calls "the music in the music."

The most romantic sounding of all the brass instruments, the French horn is also the most treacherous. It has problems in its high register; the twelve-foot length of its wound-up tubing and high notes closely spaced together make precision extremely difficult. Moreover, French horn players' lips—like everyone else's in the woodwind and brass sections—can give out after several hours of playing, and dental problems can affect their performance. Why do they keep at it? One hornist made this confession: "We love the French horn and music. Many of us would probably keep on with it even if we hardly ever got paid." He was careful not to voice this sentiment during contract negotiations. No use giving the management ideas.[21]

Until 1955 the orchestra's brass players had to cope with Severance Hall's sound-deadening carpets and drapes. That year Szell ordered them removed.

At the first rehearsal after the renovation was completed, everyone could hear the improvement in resonance and clarity. Szell looked out at his brass section and said, "I've just given you ten more years of life."[22] He meant that they no longer had to blow as hard to be heard, thus saving their lips and lungs for longer careers. "But just a few minutes after he'd said that," Kofsky later recalled, "he was asking us to play louder. Our lives weren't much improved after all. But at least we could hear ourselves better. And the orchestra sounded better too."

CHAPTER 9

Auditions and Mavericks

ONE OF THE STRANGEST former prodigies Szell ever hired was violinist Robert Menga, who, it later turned out, had been fired from nearly every symphony orchestra in the country. Menga's virtuosity was so apparent from the first notes he played at his various auditions that conductors immediately snapped him up, no questions asked. Szell did likewise, hiring him to play in the first violin section.[1]

It was obvious Menga could play anything. Unfortunately, he played his anythings whenever he felt like it, including while Szell was talking and during rests. At rehearsals and concerts, while his colleagues performed a symphony, he softly played snippets of violin concertos. His zany behavior was driving his stand partner crazy.

The climax came during one concert when he started tapping his bow on the music instead of playing. His partner whispered that if he kept that up he was going to get a hit over the head. Menga went on tapping and got a whack from his partner's bow. Undeterred, he tapped again and got another whack. The tapping and whacking continued through the entire piece, Menga hugely enjoying the situation. As everyone filed off stage afterward, the two were told Szell wanted to see them in his office. They went to their fate while fascinated bystanders wondered what was going to happen in there.[2]

Several weeks previously, some of the musicians who had attended Menga's recital had been bowled over by his playing, which included a flawless rendition of a difficult Mozart rondo. At the end, when he received a standing ovation, he played an encore. Announcing, "Here's a piece I used to play," he sat down at the piano and performed a difficult movement of a Prokofiev piano sonata. He was just as fabulous on the piano as on the violin.[3]

Discussing this phenomenon, some of the players conjectured that Szell, surely treasuring such a fine musician, would try to put up with his behavior and gradually civilize him. It was not to be. Szell had his number: Menga was a nut. There could be no nuts in the Cleveland Orchestra. He could go and play his concertos elsewhere.[4]

Cleveland violinist Roberta Strawn was a former prodigy of a much different stripe. She had attended Cleveland Institute of Music and then decided to audition for the Cleveland Orchestra. Practicing hours a day, she memorized the entire contents of the audition folder. On the day of the audition she took special pains with her appearance, teasing her hair into the currently fashionable beehive and donning a form-fitting cocktail dress and high heels. But finding the heels too high for comfort, she jettisoned them in favor of tennis shoes.

As Strawn walked onstage, Szell took in the coiffure, inappropriate dress, and tennis shoes, and asked assistant conductor Louis Lane, who was sitting next to him, "What social circles does she travel in?"[5] Unaware of the visual impression she was making, Strawn played her prepared solo. Then she confidently opened the audition folder to perform various difficult excerpts from Szell's repertoire. Since she knew them all from memory she hardly needed to look at the music.

But as she glanced at the first piece, *Don Juan* by Richard Strauss, she received a shock. It wasn't the *first* violin part she had practiced so assiduously, but instead was the *second* violin part. She stared at the unfamiliar music, trying to figure out what to do. There was only one thing she could think of. She played what she had memorized—the first violin part. Szell leaned forward in surprise. This strangely outfitted girl wasn't playing what was in front of her. Quickly realizing what was going on, and deciding that anyone who could play all those excerpts from memory deserved the job, he hired her.[6]

Strawn was soon asked by Bill Steck, one of the assistant concertmasters of the orchestra, to be the second violinist in a quartet he was forming with a view to giving concerts. Steck was an ambitious musician who would later become concertmaster of the National Symphony and then the Atlanta Symphony. He wanted his quartet to play compositions the way composers had intended. In his zeal for authenticity he was influenced by a phenomenon that had recently appeared on television.

An English spiritualist named Rosemary Brown claimed to have been visited for several years by dead composers who dictated new compositions to her. She played Beethoven-like and Brahms-like ditties for the television interviewer and explained that Chopin, Schubert, Liszt, and other composers appeared in her parlor telling her what to write. Liszt even pressed her fingers down on the piano keys. She knew it was Liszt because "he wore a black cassock and had long white hair just like in his pictures."[7] These visitations caught the attention of various musicians, including André Previn and Leonard Bernstein, who agreed that what she was playing was unusual for an amateur and maybe something out of the ordinary was happening.

Along with millions who watched that television program, Steck pondered the existence of famous dead composers in another dimension. Was it possible he, too, could communicate with them and receive answers about their compositions? It didn't take long before he was leading Ouija board sessions after quartet rehearsals. The four, placing their fingers on the board, asked it musical questions. Bill had the most questions because he, as leader of the group, needed to guide the others to his well-considered opinions.

One evening they were rehearsing Mozart's *Oboe Quartet* with John Mack when Steck insisted the measure before the return of the main theme in the first movement needed to slow down. Mack and the other two objected. It was too obvious. It was cheap. It was tacky. Steck disagreed. Mozart would surely have wanted a ritard even though he hadn't written it into the music. The only way to settle the argument was to communicate with Mozart via the Ouija board. All eyes were glued to the planchette as Steck asked the spirit of Mozart the question: "Should there be a ritard just before the reprise of the main theme?"

The planchette crawled to "Yes."

"Uh huh," Steck crowed. "Just as I thought." Mack, skeptical of the venture but not wanting to alienate his colleague, later commented, "Bill runs a tight little Ouija board."[8]

Once in a while a prodigy breaks away from an orchestra and makes it on the world stage. The rest continue to labor anonymously in the symphonic vineyards, frustrated and hoping to move up from second violin to first, become an assistant principal and, perhaps, concertmaster. Occasionally the progression is halted because some conductors like to have highly qualified violinists in the backs of sections to balance things. Back-of-the-section frustration can lead to misbehavior, however. Forestalling this, Szell maintained discipline by constant surveillance. His eyes, magnified by his thick-lensed glasses, seemed to see everything. Since he memorized all the music, he was able to maintain a ceaseless watch. Only a Menga type would dare to do anything overt.

But when the cat was away, the mice would play, and not nicely. Word reached Szell that guest conductors had a tough time keeping order; their concerts were never as good as his own. The great Cleveland Orchestra was famously well disciplined, but mischief could break out as soon as Szell's back was turned. The less competent maestros had a tough time with a talented bunch that could discern in just a few minutes whether the person facing them was mediocre. Returning from six weeks of guest-conducting other orchestras, Szell was in shock when he heard the sound coming at him. Clearly things had deteriorated. "What has happened to my orchestra?" he exclaimed. Whipping it back into shape took only part of one rehearsal. The unruly animals returned to their cages.[9]

Joseph Gingold, concertmaster of the Cleveland Orchestra from 1947 to 1960, tried to keep the shenanigans to a minimum by appealing to his colleagues' better natures. "Gentlemen! Gentlemen! Please!" His appeals usually worked but not always.

Russian-born Gingold and Szell admired each other and were friends. Gingold was that rarity, a person cherished by all his colleagues. He had an angelic nature coupled with unworldliness: he never learned to drive. So acerbic cellist Harry Fuchs drove him to and from rehearsals and concerts. In contrast with Fuchs, who considered most conductors to be his enemies, Gingold regarded Szell and Toscanini as the greatest conductors he had ever played under and spoke of Szell's interpretations. "Under him, every little note was a diamond. Each individual note had its own value. For me, his orchestra was the greatest in the United States and I don't say that just because I played in it. Szell was a great teacher and you can always learn from great musicians."

But after thirteen years of playing under Szell, Gingold longed for a less stressful way of life, so he consulted him about an offer he had received to head the violin department at Indiana University. Although Szell was greatly disappointed to hear his valued concertmaster was considering leaving, he put Gingold's well-being ahead of his own needs. "Listen, you don't have a university degree. You are fifty years old. You won't get another chance like this. Take it." So Gingold left the orchestra to teach, a move lamented by the entire orchestra.[10]

He was replaced by violinist Raphael Druian, Gingold's exact opposite. The newcomer quickly alienated his colleagues and didn't seem to care about the orchestra's reputation. Although his mastery of the difficult Alban Berg violin concerto established him as an artist, he and Szell didn't see eye to eye. When Druian played a Mozart violin concerto somewhat out of tune, his departure became a matter of not if, but when.

Druian had rehearsed the piece at Severance Hall with Szell at the piano. A musician happened to hear them arguing over the pitch of various notes.[11] Each note to which Szell objected, Druian justified, citing basic rules of music theory. This note was a leading tone and therefore had to be high; that note was the middle note of a minor chord and had to be low. Szell listened to these justifications and said little, but thereafter he was laying for Druian. Eventually the opportunity he was waiting for arose.

Druian's dressing room was on a level with the stage and separate from the rest of the musicians' locker room in the basement. So he was accidentally overlooked when the personnel manager told everyone down there that the next morning's recording session had been canceled. Druian came to the hall the following day, saw nobody onstage, and rushed upstairs to fume at manager Barksdale. Convinced he'd been singled out for an insult, he raged, threatened to resign, and huffed out of the office. He then decided to show his contempt for the orchestra by staying away from the next day's rehearsal. This was taken as a violation of his contract and he was informed he'd been fired.[12] Szell hadn't created the mix-up, but he took full advantage of it. The musicians weren't surprised. They knew nobody could dare instruct Szell in music theory and get away with it.

Assistant concertmaster Danny Majeske had been sitting under Szell's nose long enough to be a known quantity. Majeske was a born-again Christian and led an exemplary life. He, too, had been a prodigy, gone to Curtis, and was a natural replacement for Druian. Szell called him into his office and offered him the coveted concertmaster job.

"If God wills it, I accept," Majeske said.

"God has nothing to do with it," Szell replied. "*I* will it."[13]

The changing of concertmasters was quite different from the 1968 clash between Szell and two of his violinists that ended up in court. At the beginning of each season, Szell issued a seating chart for all the string players. Looking at the bulletin board in the musicians' locker room, first violinists Gino Raffaelli and Bert Siegel were shocked to see they had been moved into the second violin section. This demotion was humiliating. They protested and, getting no satisfaction, decided to sue.

They hired a lawyer; management hired one also; the parties went to court. The judge heard the testimony of the two angry violinists and then perused Szell's contract with the Musical Arts Association. There it was in black and white. It specified that Szell had the right to do whatever he wished, including the right to leave the employ of the Musical Arts Association if at any time his authority was questioned. So no illegality existed. Raffaelli and Siegel would have to remain in the positions Szell had assigned them—visual proof to their colleagues, if any was needed, that dissenters would not be tolerated.[14]

A year later the orchestra's violinists were fascinated by yet another seating chart. Siegel and Raffaelli had been transferred back into the first violin section. The players collectively scratched their heads. What did it mean? Why had Szell done it? The two men weren't playing any differently now than they had a year previously. There was conjecture. Perhaps this was a tacit admission that Szell was ashamed of what he'd done. Or maybe he just changed his mind. Or maybe—this theory was the most popular—he had deliberately taken the two players out of the first violin section and then put them back in to establish once more his absolute power over them.[15]

Occasionally Szell had problems with his principal cellists and he would demote them to a lesser position. Some of them resigned themselves to this indignity, but not Harry Fuchs, who was terribly hurt when he was demoted to assistant principal. Married to a department store heiress, he played a wonderful Amati cello, lived close to Szell in a fine neighborhood, and drove a Rolls-Royce to the daily rehearsals. The humiliation was more than he could bear. He found a way to retaliate. He began walking his St. Bernard in front of Szell's house, encouraging it to relieve itself on Szell's lawn.[16]

One day at Severance Hall, recording engineer Vlad Maleckar heard the two of them in conversation. Harry was doing most of the talking, citing all the things that were wrong with the orchestra and his position in it. He ended his monologue with bitter words to Szell, "You have all the power."

"Yes, but Harry," Szell replied, "you have the Rolls."[17]

Szell went through several more principal cellists until he found one who was later to achieve international fame: nineteen-year-old Lynn Harrell, son of the well-known baritone Mack Harrell. Lynn had inherited his father's musical gifts and played on a glorious old Venetian cello. His beautiful tone quality and virtuoso technique set him apart from the other cellists in the orchestra, and Szell realized he had found someone who could more than ably fill the principal cellist position. He first placed Harrell in the middle of the cello section to allow him to gain orchestral experience and then, after three seasons, offered the principal cello position to him. Harrell signed a contract making him the youngest principal player in the orchestra. A few days later, Szell regretted what he had done.

Harrell, young and feeling his oats, was often seen smiling at his colleagues during concerts, showing off his wonderful technique and exhibiting a lack of gravitas as leader of his section. Upset that Harrell didn't seem to respect the great honor and responsibility conferred upon him, Szell demanded the contract back. Harrell refused to relinquish it. Thereafter, Szell was on the lookout for anything he could criticize in Harrell's playing. No matter how gorgeously Harrell played, he couldn't please Szell. The two of them were often seen backstage before a concert, Szell rehearsing Harrell through some minor solo passage. Harrell knew his solos from memory and tried to please his abuser. It was no use. Szell was convinced that his gifted principal cellist was immature. No amount of exquisite playing could change his mind.[18]

He had better luck with another cellist he hired, Diane Mather, a slender beauty with sparkling brown eyes, who had studied with Leonard Rose at Curtis. Rose, who had played in the orchestra before Szell's time, encouraged her to audition for Szell. With only a weekend to prepare, she went to Szell's apartment in New York and rang his doorbell. Szell himself answered the door, looked down at her, and said, "Come in, my child."

"I wasn't a child. I was twenty. So I thought that was kind of funny. Because I'd recently given a recital, I had various solos prepared. He asked me to play the cello part in Brahms's *Double Concerto* and also the second line in the divided cello section of Debussy's *La Mer*. He was interested in how well I took direction and whether I could incorporate his suggestions into my performance. At the end of the audition he said to me, 'How would you like to play in my orchestra?' I hadn't seriously considered playing in an orchestra because my dream was to get a Fulbright to study in Europe and then be a soloist. So I hedged, saying I'd have to ask my parents. That was to gain time to think over his offer. I decided that I'd play in his orchestra for just a year or two to earn some money and then try for a solo career. So I telephoned the orchestra's personnel manager and was told I'd be sitting on fourth stand."[19]

Mather was the only woman in the cello section. After several years Szell promoted her to first stand, where she was given the title of assistant principal and seated next to Harrell. It was a well-deserved promotion and at the same time promised to bring a measure of decorum to the cello section. Szell may have thought that an attractive, mannerly female seated next to high-spirited Harrell might keep him somewhat tamped down.

Whatever Szell's reasons, the two young cellists were amicable musical partners. It was obvious they could play anything in the symphonic repertoire. After a performance of Richard Strauss's extremely difficult tone poem *Don Juan*, Mather said to one of her colleagues, "I played every note." Since lesser musicians usually scramble through this complicated piece, even faking particularly demanding passages, Mather could be justifiably proud. And Szell, his antenna tuned to everything going on in a performance, could be content that he had two virtuosos sitting at the head of his cello section.[20]

Mather's first rehearsal with the orchestra was a revelation. "The sound was amazing," she later recalled. "I'd never played in a professional orchestra before, and I was kept busy trying to fit in with the rest of the cello section." Szell had been kind to her at her audition, but on the podium he was all business. If he enjoyed having an attractive female cellist in close proximity, he gave no indication of it, treating all the cellists alike—except Harrell, whom he frequently berated. He couldn't forget that Harrell had defied him by refusing to forfeit his contract as principal cellist.[21]

Although Szell was known for his clear beat—which in part accounted for the precision in his performances—he once confused Mather during a particular passage. "I must have shown puzzlement regarding the beat and he saw my questioning look," said Mather. "The second time the passage appeared he flicked a definite beat and smiled significantly at me. There was no mistaking his intent: 'You wanted a clear beat and here it is.'"[22]

Was Szell, while conducting a performance, able to simultaneously observe all one hundred of his musicians and know what each was thinking? It would seem impossible, yet many players, having had an experience like Mather's, believed he could read their minds or at least their countenances. The surveillance was constant and unsettling. Those all-seeing eyes![23]

Szell made a shrewd decision when he hired Abe Skernick to head the viola section. Skernick had served in World War II and was glad to be out of the army and in a wonderful orchestra headed by a great musician. He and Szell became friendly, and Skernick was the person many musicians turned to if they needed someone to intercede for them. His laid-back presence had a calming effect on the viola section, resulting in a notable lack of friction in that quarter.[24]

Two musicians were more than grateful to be members of Szell's orchestra: violinist David Arben and trumpeter David Zauder. They had been in concentration camps in Germany, and their forearms bore tattooed numbers. The highly disciplined Cleveland Orchestra must have seemed a haven of calm after the terrible things they had suffered at the hands of the Nazis.

During Zauder's five years in concentration camps, he vowed to his dying father that he would survive, get to America, and do something worthwhile with his life. After liberation, he worked his way through various jobs, finally making it to Detroit, where he fell in love with the trumpet. Impressed by trumpeter Harry James, who had married movie star Betty Grable, he decided he too would become a professional trumpeter and marry a glamorous woman. He achieved both goals and then joined the Cleveland Orchestra.

Szell watched him for several years in the brass section of the orchestra and noticed that Zauder had begun carrying a book around. Curious, he asked what Zauder had in mind and smiled encouragement when Zauder answered he was taking a business course. That smile portended more than Zauder realized. Shortly afterward, Szell began finding fault with Zauder's playing and said he would only consider renewing his contract if he agreed to take on the assistant personnel manager's job. Thinking he had better comply, Zauder agreed, and thereafter his playing was deemed acceptable.[25] This was Szell at his most manipulative. Zauder eventually stepped into Trogdon's shoes as personnel manager, inheriting all the arguments and complaints that went with the position.

"This is your conscience calling," Zauder would say over the telephone to musicians who called in sick. He visited them in the hospital with crossword puzzles and joke books, doled out cigars from his stash when his wife gave birth to their daughter, rounded up miscreants, and raised spirits that had been trampled on by Szell.

One unhappy spirit was a new violinist, singled out for an infraction he had committed. Szell halted the music and eyed him. "You!" Szell said. "Stand up. Yes, you. Why aren't you following the bowings the rest are playing? They've been written into your part." The guilty one stood humiliated and red-faced. Afterward he went to Zauder to complain about his treatment. Zauder knew he couldn't help him. Szell's bowings were sacred. They weren't merely suggestions; they were orders, and anyone who didn't follow them wouldn't last in the orchestra. The newcomer played till the end of the season and then disappeared. Individualism within the ranks of the string sections was not tolerated.

Players complaining that Szell had mistreated them were consoled by Zauder, who would wax amiably philosophic. "Yes, you are right, but it's because of his high standards. He puts himself under a lot of pressure. Here, have a cigar. Go home. Relax. It's a job. We're all in this together."[26]

The orchestra members knew Szell gave preference to musicians who had fled war-torn Europe. Even orchestra members who feared and disliked Szell admitted he had a decent side. Then, during one notable tour, they realized he was more than decent; he actually had a noble streak. It manifested itself in 1961 when the orchestra toured the South. This was before integration, when Negroes were barred from restaurants and hotels and had to sit in segregated areas in movie theaters.

As cellist Don White attempted to enter the concert hall in Birmingham, Alabama, he was stopped by a guard who said Negroes were not allowed inside. It did no good for several orchestra members to insist that Don was a member of the orchestra's cello section. Observing the scene, orchestra manager Barksdale, himself a Southerner, understood what was going on. He interceded on White's behalf, saying that if White wasn't allowed to play, the rest of the orchestra wouldn't play either. He then went to Szell and confessed what he'd done.

Szell backed Barksdale completely. He had hired White and was satisfied with his playing. Nobody was going to tell him who he couldn't have in his orchestra. Underlying his dislike at being told what to do was likely his scorn for prejudice and his experiences of anti-Semitism that had culminated in the Nazi killing of millions, including his own parents.

The manager of the hall weighed his options. What if there was a riot? On the other hand, canceling the concert would cause considerable fuss. He relented. White would be allowed to play alongside his colleagues.

There was tension onstage as the hundred musicians filed out to take their seats, White prominent in the cello section. They warily eyed the audience, wondering whether there was going to be trouble. But Szell proceeded to the podium, lifted his baton, the music began and nobody took offense at the sight of a black man playing Beethoven. Either the audience was in shock or under the spell of beautiful music.

The players still talk about Barksdale and Szell resolutely defying Jim Crow in a place known to stage lynchings. The rest of the Southern tour was uneventful. White was always visible, nobody challenged his presence, and he stayed in the various hotels along with his colleagues. Thus the Cleveland

Orchestra integrated many concert halls and hotels in the South—at least for a couple of weeks.[27]

Several years later, Szell again showed a nobility of spirit. Cellist Mather, who had taken part in the nationwide protests against the Vietnam War, recalls what she and a few other Cleveland Orchestra musicians did after the infamous shooting of students by the National Guard at Kent State University on May 4, 1970, that resulted in the deaths of four of them.

"Some of us in the orchestra were deeply affected by this horrific event and we decided to wear black armbands at that week's concert. We were determined to do it; yet we were scared how Szell would view such a public display. We walked out on stage and took our places, waiting for Szell and worried about what might happen. When he came out, he stepped onto the podium, and then, to my amazement, instead of raising his baton to start, he turned toward the audience. And what he said I will never forget. 'Please stand and join me in a moment of simple human recognition of the tragic events of this last week.' In those seconds he grew a foot taller in my estimation."[28]

CHAPTER 10

Conductor Wannabes

OCCASIONALLY SOMEONE WATCHING a symphony conductor waving his arms and lunging about on a podium thinks, "I can do that." He gets a recording of a symphonic work and stands in front of a mirror waving a pencil in time with the music. It's exactly as he thought. He's a born conductor. He hires a hundred musicians, rehearses them, and announces a concert. The players, used to various levels of ineptitude on the podium, rally together to achieve a workmanlike performance. Applause results. The amateur maestro is lauded for having done a difficult thing without falling on his face. As long as his money holds out, he can keep up his act.[1]

Danny Kaye once conducted the Cleveland Orchestra in a benefit concert. Severance Hall was packed and Kaye was amazing. He explained afterward that he had listened to recordings of the compositions prior to appearing and knew how they were supposed to go. But he wasn't leading the orchestra. He was following it, as the musicians knew.[2]

Did their impressive playing without a real conductor prove the Cleveland Orchestra could function without one? The orchestra's trustees knew better than that. They knew full well that conductors Sokoloff and Rodzinski had molded the orchestra in its beginning and intermediate stages, and Szell had driven the undertaking to greatness. They also knew that important work took place at rehearsals when Szell hounded his troops into compliance with his orders. What the trustees probably never considered, however, was what took place *before* rehearsals.

As Szell studied a music score at home in his second-floor studio or in his office at Severance Hall, he heard the sounds that the printed notes represented. He had honed this skill in his prodigy years. In a symphony orchestra, five strands—first violins, second violins, violas, cellos, and double basses—have to combine with fifteen strands in the woodwinds, fifteen strands in the brass section, and five or six strands in the percussion section. With everybody doing something different at the same time, order must be made of it all. It's a task akin to playing three-dimensional chess.

Szell reduced some forty strands to ten or fewer that he played on the piano, pondering which strands were foreground, background, or equal in importance.[3] Each note, each phrase had to have a specific character and volume. His fabulous memory then wove those phrases into patterns that became a sonic landscape, as if the musical score were laid out like a horizontal scroll depicting mountains and valleys of sound. Within these outlines, he mentally highlighted significant moments after carefully weighing all the elements present.

Szell had to take into account the various abilities of his musicians and their instruments. A violin passage could go only as fast as his talented violinists could play it without falling apart. Cloyd Duff could hit his tympani only so hard before the skinhead of the instrument would split. Mike Bloom could play his French horn solos only up to a certain volume before he cracked notes. It was a delicate balance, and Szell knew the capabilities of his musicians, perhaps better than they did themselves. One player said of Szell's demands, "He made you play better than you could."[4]

His decisions were first communicated to his players by the marks the librarian penciled on the players' individual parts. These marks, copied from Szell's score, which he had peppered with words and signs, dictated how each musician should play. Some composers, like Mahler, larded their scores with these interpretive marks. Others, like Mozart, employed marks sparingly. It was Szell's task to add marks if they didn't exist or follow the ones already in the composer's score. Since composers' ideas aren't always appropriate for a specific orchestra or hall, it's the conductor's job to decide on gradations of speed and volume.

Szell's insight into the music often brought out ideas that the composer hadn't considered. The musicians usually agreed that Szell was right. It was almost as if, in bringing out the beauties of a piece of music, he had composed it himself. He went even further with his creative marks, inserting split-second silences—eighth rests, sixteenth rests, thirty-second rests—into his score, which the librarian had to meticulously copy into the players' parts. The famous clarity of Szell's orchestra was partly the result of his insistence on those tiny pinpricks of silence that separate a phrase from the one following it and one chord from the next. His obsession with those silences and coordinated entrances used much rehearsal time as he drilled everyone into compliance.[5]

Some of his musicians grumbled. They didn't understand why they needed to again rehearse a piece they had recently played. What more could possibly be done? But Szell didn't count on them to remember everything he had previously fixed. So he again raked them over the same passages, keeping everyone in a constant ferment. Part of the orchestra's great reputation resulted from Szell's taking nothing for granted. Perfection four weeks previously was no guarantee things would remain that way.

The rests between the slashing strokes of chords in the funeral march of Beethoven's *Eroica Symphony* became a particular trial to his musicians as they strove to give Szell what he wanted. The result can be experienced in the orchestra's 1957 recording of the piece. Szell demanded that his players abruptly cut off their chords so they lasted mere split seconds in duration. The stark chords interrupted by stark silences result in almost pictorial drama. One of the most dramatic moments in classical music comes in the middle of the *Eroica*'s march when the violins softly fade out on a high A flat followed immediately by a blasted low A flat hurled by the cello and bass sections. It was here that Szell's constant drilling of his orchestra paid off. The twenty players, as one, struck their lowest string at the precise microsecond Szell jabbed his baton at them. That note became a great stone slab crashing down. Under Szell's implacable baton the sudden low blast was chilling.

One season Szell would decide exactly which notes of Beethoven's *Eroica* or some other piece should be brought to the fore and a year later he would change his mind as a result of further study. His more recent decisions, gleaned from yet more delving into his scores, kept his players off balance and alert. He knew there was no one right way to interpret a piece, and so he continually rethought his interpretations. If not the absolutely *right* way, at least a *righter* way. His conclusions were born of utter confidence, a driving force that communicated itself to the musicians through his piercing eyes and the precise movements of his baton.[6]

Beethoven had some thoughts on the subject of interpretation. A young woman, after playing one of his piano sonatas for him, asked whether her interpretation was correct. He answered that her performance wasn't how he had originally conceived the work, but her interpretation was as valid as his own. So she should go on playing it her way.[7]

Another composer, Béla Bartók, was once visited by a musicologist who was writing his thesis on Bartók's music. He wanted to know whether his theory on a particular passage in one of Bartók's compositions was correct. Bartók studied the musicologist's conclusion and then exclaimed in surprise, "So *that's* what I did." A composer, while creating, can be so caught up in what he is doing that he doesn't realize the full import of it. Knowing that was sometimes the case, Szell considered it his duty to bring out those things that can add to the significance of a great work.[8]

Certain compositions propel a conductor and his musicians into becoming mere servants of a force greater than themselves. The composers of such music are caught up in this force that goes beyond the usual definition of inspiration. Igor Stravinsky talked about this phenomenon when he said about *The Rite of Spring*, "I was the vessel through which *Le Sacre* passed."[9]

Szell seldom put into words how he became the servant of a musical composition. He spoke of the need to "love music more than oneself." He spoke of "artistic morality." What he actually did was akin to Michelangelo's alleged explanation of how he'd carved David out of a large block of marble: "I simply removed the parts that weren't David." The great sculptor, before he even picked up mallet and chisel, had a visualization of his finished creation.[10]

Similarly, though it was an act of auralization, Szell studied a work until he "heard" the composition in its entirety. This enabled him to plot the pacing of each movement, make one phrase lead to the next, bring out the highlights and forge a sonic totality. Oboist Bob Zupnik commented on this particular ability of Szell's: "He not only made each movement of a symphony logical, he brought the four movements together, making a perfect whole. I can't recall playing under any other conductor who could do that so perfectly."[11]

Even after Szell had rehearsed his crew into compliance with all his interpretive demands, there was yet another element that had to be taken into consideration: the concert halls in which the orchestra performed. He knew that overly resonant acoustics can turn even the most carefully rehearsed piece into muddy blurs. On the contrary, a hall lacking in resonance, in which every note is starkly delineated, can ruin smooth phrases by rendering them chopped up and disconnected. Aware of these problems, he always insisted on an acoustical rehearsal in halls the orchestra encountered on tours. He had an assistant conductor or apprentice sit in an audience seat and judge the orchestra's sound as he conducted. Or else he ceded the podium to one of them while he stood in various places around the hall drawing his conclusions. Then, returning to the podium, he adjusted the various sections of the orchestra according to what he had heard.

One of his colorful pronouncements about Philharmonic Hall in New York showed his continued distaste for the place even after it had undergone an acoustical renovation. "Let me give you a little simile," he said. "Imagine a woman, lame, a hunchback, cross-eyed and with two warts. They've removed one wart."[12]

All Szell's efforts and all his musicians' strivings would have been written on the wind if their performances hadn't been recorded. So it is fortunate that the early 1950s brought about improvements in recording techniques, and that by then the Cleveland Orchestra was attracting attention as one of the world's greatest symphonic ensembles. As a result, there are examples of their work preserved for posterity: their many recordings for Columbia Records.

Szell's recordings were usually preceded by five rehearsals and three concerts at Severance Hall. When tape recorders entered the scene it became possible to splice together the various recorded sections of a composition called "takes." Szell and the musicians always gathered to listen to playbacks so they could evaluate their performances and he could decide which takes had to be repeated.

Soon afterward, he would go to Columbia Records' studios in New York to work with an audio engineer responsible for splicing the successful takes for the final pressing. It was a finicky process, time-consuming and hard on the nerves of both of them. One particular day the various engineering cubicles were occupied by Szell, Bruno Walter, Leonard Bernstein, and Leopold Stokowski, all of them heavily involved in editing their recordings.[13]

In the early days of Columbia's recordings of the Cleveland Orchestra, they used Andrew Kazdin as their recording supervisor. Kazdin's multitrack recording equipment and sixteen microphones enabled him to separate the sound of each section of the orchestra and thus control its volume and quality. Determined to incorporate his own ideas, he used his sensitive mixing board to override Szell's interpretations.[14] Listening to the resulting playback, Szell was enraged at the changes he heard. Thereafter, he insisted on being included in every recording decision, controlling each step of the process, from microphone placement to final editing of takes.

The resulting records are more than just a great conductor's legacy. They are examples of what can be achieved by putting an ideal ahead of ego. What Szell asked for and received from his musicians was a love of music as great as his own, a servitude to masterpieces. One player's remark spoke for all: "We knew he cared first for the music."[15]

CHAPTER 11

The Percussion Section

PRINCIPAL OBOIST JOHN MACK put the orchestra above everything else in his life. Summoned to Szell's office for coaching, he went willingly, honored to be tête-à-tête with the great conductor. When Szell rehearsed him in his solos backstage just before he went onstage to play, he eagerly took direction. He called Szell "Maestro," took it upon himself to quell dissension in the woodwind section, and assiduously copied all Szell's verbal corrections into his part.

Mack harbored an almost military sense of the chain of command. At the top was the conductor. Next in line was the concertmaster, followed closely by the principal oboist—himself. A little further down the line were the other principal woodwind players, followed by the principal string and brass players. Mack could admit that timpanist Cloyd Duff was important, but he thought of the rest of the players as privates. He made no secret of how he judged percussionists; they were malefactors who needed to be confined to the guardhouse. "I hate the percussion," he frequently said.[1] As far as he was concerned, if he could hear them at all they were too loud, and their instruments were noisy gadgets.

Since orchestral protocol rules that musicians never turn their heads to look back at their colleagues while they are playing, Mack never looked at the percussion section. So he never saw the effort and concentration they expended, never saw their eyes glued to the conductor as they tensely counted measures waiting for the precise moment to strike. It never occurred to him to consider what kind of expertise might be necessary to play the tambourine. In his lexicon, the entire percussion section should be removed and the music would be the better for it.

Szell didn't agree with such an opinion. If a composer indicated a cymbal crash at a certain place in the music, that crash was appropriate and absolutely had to be heard. At the same time, however, like many other conductors, he wasn't very knowledgeable about the fine points of the various drums, triangles, cymbals, and bells. Many of these instruments weren't used in the classical and romantic works he specialized in, and so he had never felt much need to study their individual characteristics. It was only when he conducted impressionist and modern pieces, with their colorful percussion passages, that he had to consider those instruments at all. Then he usually demanded only precise rhythms and split-second entrances. Perhaps his ears weren't attuned to the subtleties in tone quality between a small triangle and a medium-sized one.[2] But the percussionists themselves were well aware of the differences and knew which size of instrument should be used.

Composer Béla Bartók, who wrote *Concerto for Orchestra* in 1943, couldn't have known that, two decades later, the drum taps in the first eight measures of the second movement of his famous composition would cause a crisis in the percussion section of the Cleveland Orchestra. Nor did Szell, who chose to conduct the piece, realize it would give one of his musicians a chance to get the better of him.

Bartók gave a few directions on how the taps should be played. The drum part states that the snares are to be turned off the snare drum, thereby turning it into a plain side drum. Bartók's measures are simple. They instruct a lone drummer to play thirty-two taps in a simple asymmetric pattern within a 2/4 meter. The score specifies that the drummer should start out medium loud, accent certain taps, and get progressively softer in the last two measures. The drum taps are executed against a silent orchestra.

Did Szell have an idea how these measures should sound before the rehearsal started? Or did he wait until the drummer had tapped out the solo to arrive at an interpretive decision? None of the musicians present at the rehearsal of Bartók's composition could figure out what Szell wanted. This incident became a legend among Cleveland Orchestra musicians, its dramatic climax a source of much glee.[3]

Bob Pangborn was expert on the snare and side drum, and it was his job to play those thirty-two taps in Bartók's second movement. After he played them, Szell cut off the music, saying he didn't like what he heard. Back to the beginning.

Pangborn tapped again. Szell said that wouldn't do, but he didn't say why. He ordered it played again.

Pangborn tapped once more and then asked what he was doing wrong. Szell didn't explain and testily ordered another percussionist to take over.

Bob Matson then tapped. He also was found wanting, for no discernible reason.

The next victim in line was ordered to play the solo. He, too, was rejected for failing to please. By then the entire orchestra was on edge. Something simple was turning infernal. None of the drummers could control their nerves as the tension mounted. Clearly there was going to be hell to pay. The whole percussion section might be fired and a new bunch hired just before the Carnegie Hall concert.

Intermission was declared by the personnel manager, and timpanist Cloyd Duff was ordered into Szell's office while the traumatized percussionists huddled fearfully backstage. Inside his office, Szell fumed to Duff that everybody in the percussion section was worthless. Therefore Duff would have to play those thirty-two notes. Duff said that was ridiculous, that he was a timpanist, not a drummer, and that Szell had just ruined the best percussion section in the country. "Every one of those men is capable of playing those measures perfectly. But you've made them so nervous they can't do it."[4] Duff, secure in the knowledge that he was a fine timpanist, simply refused to do Szell's bidding. Szell insisted. Duff was adamant. But then he got an idea.

He agreed to play the taps on the condition that he wouldn't have to rehearse them, that Szell wouldn't look at him during the performance, and that nothing more would be said about it. Having exhausted his options, Szell accepted these restrictions. He resumed rehearsing the concerto while omitting the offending drum passage.

Days later at the concert the musicians waited for the notorious solo, wondering how Duff would play it. They all froze during the brief silence at the end of the first movement. Szell then lifted his baton for the beginning drum taps of the second movement. What ensued must have been one of the shocks of his life.

Cleveland Orchestra trombonist Al Kofsky talked about it fifty years later. "Duff beat the daylights out of those measures. He whacked them out double forte and Szell had to stand there taking it. He knew, and we knew, that he was getting his comeuppance for having terrorized the whole percussion section over nothing. We couldn't exhibit any awareness of the crazy way Duff was playing. But, oh boy, backstage after the concert we almost carried Duff on our shoulders. He was our hero. And you know what? True to his promise, Szell never said a word about it afterwards. He knew he had it coming. Duff saved the entire percussion section from getting fired because the way he played that solo said more clearly than words that Szell had been in the wrong. And Szell understood. He really did."

After that dust-up, Pangborn having voluntarily left to play in the Metropolitan Opera Orchestra, Szell needed a replacement. Among the hopefuls at the auditions was twenty-three-year-old percussionist Richard Weiner. Years later Weiner recalled that crucial audition.

For several months I'd been practicing eight to twelve hours a day because I knew I'd have to demonstrate my abilities on all the different percussion instruments. On the Severance Hall stage at that audition was an entire array of the standard percussion instruments, plus Louis Lane and Cloyd Duff. During the audition things went well and I realized I had a real chance to win the job. Then Szell, who had been sitting out front in an audience seat, called, "Have him play the castanets." I started playing the castanet solo in *Carmen*, but Szell interrupted me saying, "Too fast. Follow me." Suddenly my legs got shaky because it looked as if things had become really serious. But my hands stayed steady, and I stared out at him and played the solo following his beat. After the audition I was told to see manager Barksdale in his office, where I was offered a contract.

At the first rehearsal with the orchestra I thought to myself, "Holy cow! These guys are good." I was so nervous playing tambourine in *Roman Carnival Overture* that, in one spot, I entered a bar too early. Szell just smiled at me. I guess he was used to newcomers being a little rattled.

Weiner's ambition was to become principal percussionist in a major orchestra and Szell, having observed him for five years, offered him the position in 1968 when Duff stepped down from it (staying on as principal timpanist). Weiner spoke about his new responsibilities:

The principal of the percussion section has different duties than the other principals in the orchestra. While sections of the brass and winds have designated players for the first, second, and third chairs, there are no such designations in the percussion section. So the job of the principal percussionist is to assign the various percussion parts based on the abilities of each player and the requirements of the composition. For years before computers became available, I kept a card catalogue of each piece the orchestra played and what percussion instruments it needed. Then I was able to choose the right player for the part and save time in making assignments.

Our instruments must be positioned so we can move between them when necessary. This is especially true when performing contemporary works. Some conductors want the timpani in the middle of the percussion section, but that positioning makes it difficult for us to move around while playing. I prefer to have the timpani on the side.

Percussionists' jobs have become more interesting in the last several decades because contemporary compositions call for more percussion effects than in the classic symphonic repertoire. Many contemporary composers call for unorthodox actions like smashing glass in a garbage can.

Though Szell's repertoire didn't usually include exotic percussion effects, Mahler's *Sixth Symphony* requires hammer blows in its finale. They are achieved by hitting a sturdy wooden "Mahler box." The sound is supposed to be a monstrous thud, representing a deathblow. Szell asked Weiner to use a sledgehammer for the desired effect.[5]

Many years later, when the orchestra performed the Mahler *Sixth* again, Weiner recalled that he worked with the stagehands to build a six-by-six-foot wooden box. "I climbed steps to stand on top of it and hit it with a heavy block of wood fixed to the end of a wood shaft for the enormous crashes. The box was positioned in the percussion section so the entire audience could see those dramatic moments."[6]

For some time after Duff's drum bashing in the Bartók *Concerto for Orchestra*, Szell remained wary of revealing his less-than-complete knowledge of percussion instruments. Nevertheless, he wished to maintain some semblance of authority over the triangles, and so he meddled. He knew that if the beater remains a tiny fraction of a second too long on the downward stroke, the triangle's sound doesn't resonate properly. He commanded Weiner, "Lift, lift, lift." When the lifting didn't look fast enough, he walked back to the percussion instruments and tried to demonstrate proper lifting technique. Grasping the small beater, he briskly struck the triangle. The resulting sound was more plunk than plink. He tried again with no better result. Backing off, he said, "You see, the secret is in the lift."

Weiner didn't learn anything from Szell's demonstration, but one thing seemed clear. He had better raise his triangle up high and execute a dramatically rapid wrist movement. Obviously Szell heard with both ears and eyes, and things had to look right to sound right.[7]

Still meddling in things triangular, Szell informed Weiner at one rehearsal that he needed to hear all the triangles in order to pick the best-sounding one for a particular piece. Weiner and the other percussionists busied themselves hanging many triangles of different sizes, and Szell came back to the section at the rehearsal break to listen to them one at a time. After hearing all the triangles, he said he needed to listen to them from the hall. Once again Weiner struck the triangles and then looked for Szell out in the auditorium. But he was not there. Either he trusted Weiner to choose the best one or he didn't want to admit he couldn't come to a decision. The rehearsal resumed with nothing more said about triangles.[8]

CHAPTER 12

Szell's Methods, Touring Travails

SZELL ALWAYS HAD TO keep the human element in mind. There were two groups he had to deal with, the first being the board of trustees, whose wealth enabled the costly enterprise to stay afloat. He used a genial manner on the occasions when he met with them in the boardroom. At receptions after concerts he employed his Viennese charm, smiling and kissing the hands of the wives of the board members.[1] These women thrilled to his European gallantry; no one else ever kissed their hands. In that moment they became star-struck teenagers. Their husbands responded to Szell's aura also. A famous man, a genius, was shaking their hands. It was worth thousands of their dollars to be in such a presence. Musical history was being made, and they were part of it.

Charm, however, isn't usually effective with an orchestra that has to be knit into a cohesive ensemble. With this disparate bunch Szell used fear to achieve his ends: fear of losing their jobs and fear of humiliation. But fear wasn't the only weapon in his arsenal. His musical superiority was daunting. It was obvious he knew far more about the music than any of them. In addition, his constant surveillance kept him informed of their every move onstage. His piercing eyes behind his thick-lensed glasses didn't miss a thing.

Oboist Felix Kraus tried to avoid those frightening eyes by positioning his own glasses far down on his nose so the frames would block out Szell's eyes. This ploy was immediately noticed, and Kraus was told Szell wanted to speak with him in his office after the rehearsal. He entered warily and saw

Szell sitting at his desk holding a small piece of paper. The maestro got right to the point.

"Mr. Kraus, your glasses need adjusting. They are slipping too far down on your nose and I can't see your eyes. I must see your eyes. Here is the address and phone number of my optometrist. Make an appointment to get your glasses fixed."[2]

From his height on the podium Szell could look down on his string players and see what fingerings they were using. He could hear the differences in tone quality between the four violin strings and had opinions on which strings should be employed in certain passages. The concertmaster usually seconded Szell's orders with Szell watching like a hawk as all thirty-two violinists wrote the changed fingerings into their parts.

A few violinists groused about Szell's snooping into their fingering choices. They were unaware of his years playing with Polish violinist Henri Temianka. When the two had performed duo recitals, Szell closely observed Temianka's fingerings and bowings. Known for his beautiful tone and artistic interpretations, Temianka would employ an unorthodox fingering on a string if it caused the melody to sound smoother.

Szell wanted his violin sections to use Temianka's fingering principles to give the most uniform sound. If they had to play further up on the fingerboard to avoid string crossings and assiduously practice the passage to get it just right, so be it. That was *their* problem.[3]

"Looking right" extended to all his string players. Their bows should move in unison with the others in their sections. There was to be no willful free-for-all, bows going helter-skelter according to individual preference; there was to be military precision. When he marked his scores with directions on nuances, he also wrote in bowings for the string sections: up bow indicating a bow traveling left, and down bow indicating a bow traveling right. He was convinced that bow direction affected the sound and hence the interpretation. Theoretically there's a tiny increase in volume as the bow travels left. Most string players try to eliminate this fluctuation, and Szell sometimes imagined more than he heard because, for him, *looking* right was closely connected with *sounding* right.

The correlation didn't extend only to bows. John Rautenberg, one of the flute and piccolo players, was told by Szell that he wanted him to play an all-wood piccolo because the sound was superior to that of piccolos with one silver section. Rautenberg privately greeted this command with dismay.

His half-metal piccolo was much easier to play and didn't vary with temperature and humidity changes. So he did something that could have gotten him fired if Szell had discovered it. He covered the silver section with black paint and played the camouflaged result at the next rehearsal. Szell smiled and nodded at him approvingly, sure he was hearing the all-wood piccolo's supposedly superior tone quality. None of the other members of the flute section tattled. They were amused that somebody had been able to put one over on their leader.[4]

One time, while rehearsing a Weber overture with the Chicago Symphony, Szell noticed something different during the clarinet solo. At intermission he called clarinetist Jerry Stowell to his dressing room and asked why the solo, certain measures of which involved the least mellifluous range of the clarinet, had sounded so unusually good. Stowell, relieved that his playing was being complimented, explained he had used an unorthodox fingering which incorporated a side key, allowing the melody to flow without a change in tone quality. Immediately interested, Szell asked him to bring his clarinet to the dressing room and demonstrate the two ways of playing the passage.

Several years later, when Szell conducted the Cleveland Orchestra in that same overture, he instructed principal clarinetist Robert Marcellus, "When you play your solo, use the side key fingering for the B flat." The astonished player muttered to his colleague on the left, "Ye gods. Now he's studying the fingering charts."[5]

Some of Szell's prying stemmed from his conviction that he could solve most problems. One evening the personnel manager came to him before a concert, saying that cellist Harvey Wolfe couldn't play because his cello's endpin wouldn't stay in position. It was unacceptable to Szell that a mere endpin would cause the loss of a cellist. He hurried downstairs to the musicians' locker room, where Wolfe was sitting disconsolately. Getting down on his knees in front of the cello, Szell began trying to tighten the endpin's screw, which seemed to have stripped its threads. After minutes of fussing he had to give up. Wolfe was excused from playing that night, and Szell went back upstairs with the irritating knowledge that he couldn't fix everything.[6]

But that failure didn't faze him. Many months later, when he received word that Duff was having trouble with one of the calfskin heads on his timpani, he went backstage to Duff and his instrument. Several musicians watched as the two of them bent over the balky piece of leather, trying to fasten it to the sides of the timpani. Szell was sure he could figure out the problem; no piece of calfskin was going to get the best of him. None of the musicians watching his effort can now remember how it ended. What they instead remember is Szell determinedly struggling alongside Duff, the two united against a common foe.[7]

Szell's confidence in his abilities may have resulted in success with a nonmusical problem. The orchestra's annual February tour of the East Coast took them to colleges and cities prior to appearing at Carnegie Hall. They usually traveled the short distances between venues by bus, and harsh weather conditions created hazards. Bob Zupnik remembered when the orchestra's bus got stuck in a snowdrift on the Massachusetts highway between Smith College and Mount Holyoke:

> A bunch of us piled out to push the bus and we weren't making much headway. Szell, who'd been riding with us, was sure he knew what to do. He got out of the bus and went to the rear where he began conducting us, indicating who should go where to push. Then he went in front of the bus and started conducting the driver which way to steer and when to gun the motor. It was pretty funny, him making big motions with his hands and arms as if we were playing some wild piece of music. We finally shoved the bus out of the snowbank. Szell's conducting may have gotten us going again, though I'm not sure about that. Anyway, we made it through the snow and arrived at Mount Holyoke.
>
> When we went out on stage there we were dismayed at the dim lighting. We could barely see the music. Well, right after the overture, Szell turned to the audience and scolded them for the terrible lighting. And we were never invited back.[8]

Poor-quality touring conditions plagued the musicians well into the 1970s. Nevertheless, oboist Felix Kraus relished an interesting experience in a low-cost hotel room during the orchestra's stay at Miami's Voyager Inn:

> When the orchestra checked in, the lobby was bustling with a film crew and its equipment. A movie was being filmed and it turned out that my room was right next door to the action. Trying to ignore them, I began practicing my parts for that evening's concert.
>
> But within a few seconds there was a knock on my door. I opened it and was confronted with an aggrieved member of the film crew who said they couldn't work with all that noise going on next door. I said I was in the Cleveland Orchestra and had to warm up for that evening's concert. We came to an agreement. When the crew needed quiet they'd bang on the wall and I would stop playing. There was an incentive. I'd be welcome to come into their room

and watch the filming. It was a low-budget operation, had to be completed in six days, and the working title was *Deep Throat*. I was curious, so I took him up on his offer.

There wasn't much happening at first, just a couple of people adjusting bedsheets. Then a woman came in whose name was Linda something. But I had to get back to practicing, so I didn't stay. Every once in a while they'd bang on the wall and I'd stop playing.

When I got back home I told my wife about it and said, "What kind of movie gets made in six days in a cheap hotel room with only one actress? It'll never get off the ground." Turns out I was somewhat mistaken about that.[9]

One time Szell's convictions concerning rightness met up with strong opposition. Wrongness appeared in the person of pianist Glenn Gould. The rehearsal began with Gould coming on stage in an overcoat, scarf, and gloves. He was accustomed to dragging along an adjustable folding chair made for him by his father. Minutes passed as he lowered, raised, and lowered the homely piece of furniture until he found the most comfortable level. String players close to the podium, watching this fussy routine, saw Szell become increasingly impatient. Finally they heard him snap, "Perhaps if we were to slice a sixteenth of an inch off your derriere, Mr. Gould, we could begin."[10] Gould, busy taking off his gloves and scarf, didn't reply. Then, placing his chin level with the keyboard, nose nearly touching his fingers, he played and hummed his way through the concerto. Szell had heard about Gould's eccentricities, but seeing them up close was too much to bear. After the concert he swore to Louis Lane he would never conduct that nut again.

A few years later, Gould's popularity was such that Szell had to give in and have him back with the orchestra. But he refused to conduct this oddity. Somebody else would have to put up with Gould's shenanigans. At the subsequent concert Szell, listening to Gould's astonishing clarity and fine interpretation, had to admit rules could be subject to a few exceptions. Sometimes sight doesn't affect sound. Speaking to Lane after Gould's wonderful performance, he said, "Well, no doubt about it. That nut's a genius."[11]

Proving that, for Szell, sometimes even more was at stake than sight and sound was the famously surreal encounter that took place between pianist André Previn and himself. It was famous because Previn enjoyed recounting it.

Previn had arrived at Szell's Los Angeles hotel room for a rehearsal of Richard Strauss's *Burleske*, but there was no piano in evidence. He asked how he was supposed to play the piano when there wasn't one. Szell replied he could use the nearby table. Thinking this was something he must go along with, Previn sat poised to play. Szell hummed the introduction, and at the correct moment Previn began fingering the table.

"No, no. It needs to go faster," Szell exclaimed.

"You'll have to excuse me, maestro," Previn apologized. "I'm not used to the action on this table."[12]

That witticism earned him the cancellation of his contract. For Szell, there was no joking about great music. Unless the joke came from him. In such a case appreciative laughter was rendered by his dutiful crew.

Szell's own ability on the piano enabled him to assess other pianists, and he conducted many of the best of them. Some he tyrannized when their ideas didn't agree with his own. Because he and Rudolf Serkin had been close in Vienna when they were both young prodigies, Serkin affably gave in to Szell over musical matters to ensure that their venerable friendship remained intact. The always jovial Serkin, understanding Szell's musical obsessions, didn't take offense. After one rehearsal Vladimir Maleckar, the orchestra's recording engineer, overheard the two of them—their musical differences forgotten—reminiscing about their youthful days in Vienna. Szell sighed. "Ja, Rudy, we are the old ones now."[13]

CHAPTER 13

Prodigies, Masterpieces, Boulez

IN 1903, WHEN GEORGE SZELL'S proud parents had taken him to Vienna's foremost piano teacher, Theodor Leschetizky, they probably expected a warm reception. Leschetizky had founded a school of piano playing in Vienna that had earned a worldwide reputation for the soundness of its methods and the eminent artists it produced, the most famous being Ignacy Paderewski. But little George was rejected. Perhaps the aged pedagogue had developed an antipathy to child prodigies, who were known to fizzle in their teenage or young adult years. He would probably have been quite skeptical had he been told that this child whizzing up and down on the keyboard would become one of the world's greatest conductors.[1]

Yehudi Menuhin's parents took him to violin teacher Louis Persinger, who, realizing he had a magnificent talent in front of him, nurtured it. By the time Yehudi was twelve years old he was world-famous, and Arturo Toscanini, enamored of the child's beautiful playing, wanted little Yehudi to call him "Papa." Mrs. Menuhin knew that her three children were musical prodigies and that Yehudi was the finest of the three. He was home-schooled, dominated by her, and not allowed to go anywhere by himself, not even to cross the street alone. Never having experienced a normal childhood, he tried in his early twenties to become independent, achieving mixed results. At the same time, he suddenly realized he didn't know how he played so brilliantly. He had never worked on scales, arpeggios, or études. Where did his violin technique come from? He had no idea. It had all been so easy and natural. And then one day it wasn't.[2]

The crash many times occurs when a prodigy fatally wonders how he *does* it. At that moment something happens in his brain, and he becomes mortal, unable to prance on the tightrope he had been so nimbly negotiating. Put onto the concert stage too early, before he has had time to mature and fully master his art, he is inevitably overtaken by adulthood with its realizations and concerns. He tries to analyze and think logically. Alas, he has forged no mental muscles except memory. He will need years to build what he lacks. Meanwhile, audiences notice mistakes, reviewers begin to point out his fall from grace, and concert bookings dwindle.

So why didn't that happen to Cleveland Orchestra principal keyboardist Joela Jones? Perhaps the only thing separating her from hundreds of other prodigies was her mother, who had an analytical mind and was psychologically astute, carefully steering her little daughter in the right direction. Joela remembers her childhood years:

> I started playing the piano when I was six. Mother played the piano herself and noticed right away that I was good at it. But I disliked boring scales and exercises. So she picked out difficult passages in my solos and told me I could make games out of them. It was fun because it was a challenge. I conquered a lot of difficult pieces by doing what I thought was just figuring out puzzles and playing musical games. That way I improved at my own pace, learning to analyze my playing. In two years I started performing in public.[3]

Knowing her talented daughter needed a good piano teacher, Mrs. Jones took her to the best one in Florida, Ernst von Dohnanyi, a composer who had emigrated from Germany and was teaching at Florida State University. Young Joela bowled him over with a difficult Chopin ballade, and he immediately accepted her as his youngest pupil. But after a year he told her mother, "There's nothing for her here in Florida. Take her up north where the good music schools are." Following his advice, Mrs. Jones took Joela to the Eastman School of Music in Rochester, where she was given a full scholarship to study not only piano but theory and harmony as well. Mrs. Jones also persuaded the principal of the junior high school Joela attended that she should only have to attend school half a day.

> Mother made a schedule for me. I'd come home from school at noon, have lunch and practice for several hours. Then I'd go for a walk or play outside. We'd have dinner and I'd practice some more. That way I would practice four hours a day and six or eight hours a day on weekends. She'd sit beside me and whenever I made a mistake she'd call attention to it and have me decide

what to do to make the passage perfect. She couldn't play my pieces herself, but she always knew when something wasn't going right. I got into the habit of figuring things out for myself.[4]

This regimen—encouraging a child to analyze difficulties—avoided one of the kinds of teaching that cause many prodigies to fail in their teen years. The combination of fun and challenging games not only keeps a child interested but also gives it confidence in its own mental and physical abilities.

Joela was soon discovered, first by Arthur Fiedler, who featured her in his many concerts throughout the country, and then by Szell, who was looking for a pianist capable of playing a difficult contemporary concerto. Soon after Jones's success with the concerto, he asked her to play Stravinsky's *Petrushka* with the orchestra. While sitting out front listening to the *Petrushka* rehearsals, he came to a decision and a few days later again approached Jones, this time with an offer.

"He said to me, 'How would you like to play keyboard in my orchestra?' I was thrilled. Here was one of the world's greatest conductors offering me a job. It was beyond anything I'd ever dreamed of, way beyond playing solo concertos with various orchestras."[5]

In hiring Jones, Szell did something unprecedented in the Cleveland Orchestra. He created the new position of principal keyboardist especially for her, stipulating that she was to play not only piano but also organ, harpsichord, and celesta and perform solo concertos with the orchestra. She would eventually solo with the Cleveland Orchestra more than two hundred times in more than fifty concertos.

"He cared about the whole person," Jones recalled,

> not just a player's performing ability. I played piano during a recording session of Kodály's *Háry János* and saw Szell calling attention to a slightly out-of-tune horn note that was unusual for Mike Bloom. He asked Mike to listen to the playback so they could ascertain together what to do. He gave the impression that all the players and he were in an undertaking together, forging a relationship between themselves and the composer's music. Many times when I wasn't actually performing, I attended rehearsals and watched how Szell worked with his principal players. It was usually kindly, two people interested in understanding the score and its needs. But one time it was shocking, and I saw how angry Szell could get when he thought somebody wasn't taking the music seriously.
>
> It was during the first rehearsal of Richard Strauss's *Bourgeois Gentilhomme*. There's a very prominent cello solo that starts out in the high register of the

cello. Lynn Harrell was playing it and Szell got in a rage, accusing him of not having practiced it. He leapt off the podium and dashed at Lynn with his baton upraised. It looked as if he was attacking Lynn, and Lynn raised his arm to ward off the blow. Szell didn't actually hit him, but it was an awful moment. Szell was maddened that his principal cellist seemed so unconcerned with that big solo that he hadn't mastered it before the first rehearsal.[6]

Szell was involved with everything that went on at Severance Hall, including rehearsals and concerts when guest conductors were on the podium. He would sit in an audience seat far in the back of the hall listening and observing. "His eyes were always on us and we knew it," Jones said. "Nothing got by him. We had to listen to each other and watch him constantly. He behaved the way he did because he was always thinking of the music and not himself. Szell was totally honest."[7]

Szell's honesty extended to appraisals of his own conducting. He knew he had limitations. His area of expertise was the symphonic and operatic music of the great classical composers—what is known as "the meat and potatoes" of the repertoire—from Haydn to Richard Strauss and pieces by such composers as Béla Bartók and William Walton. When he ventured afield and conducted impressionist and contemporary works he was on less familiar ground.

Because Debussy's *La Mer* was so popular with the public, he conducted it several times and couldn't help but insist on some of his favorite things: clarity and rhythmic precision. His Teutonic approach to a French impressionist piece depicting water and sunlight prompted the musicians to dub the piece under his baton *Das Merd*.[8] Similarly they called Ravel's *Daphnis and Chloé*, when Szell conducted it, *Daphnis und Chloé*. Try as he might, gauziness and subtle blurring were foreign to his nature. His baton had none of the graceful airiness of the hands of such conductors as Erich Kleiber or Leopold Stokowski.[9]

Precision was the point. Precision and clarity. Szell's baton described angles and jabs in the air leaving no doubt about the beat and subdivision of the beat. This led some audience members to believe what their eyes rather than their ears told them. Szell must be a cold fish because he didn't emote on the podium or trace rainbows in the air with a flexible wrist. He didn't *look* the way Mahler's heart-on-the-sleeve music *sounded*.[10]

A lack in his conducting extended to irregular meters. The 5/4 movement in Tschaikovsky's *Sixth Symphony* always got his goat. He thought it was unnatural. And Stravinsky's *Rite of Spring* was his *bête noire*. He agonized over its constantly shifting meters and accents and threw in the towel. Somebody else would have to conduct that complicated masterpiece.[11]

The somebody was composer Pierre Boulez, internationally known as the world's best conductor of contemporary music. Boulez, being French, also had an affinity with his nation's impressionist composers. In 1969 Szell designated him the Cleveland Orchestra's principal guest conductor. Under his expert direction, *Das Merd* turned back into *La Mer*, and *The Rite of Spring* reveled in convincing barbaric asymmetry.

Stravinsky's masterpiece isn't only a test of a conductor's ability to lead an orchestra through rhythmic hazards and dissonances. It's also a test of the orchestra's timpanist. Just minutes into the primitive setting, the music co-alesces into a menacing beat that portends the savagery to come—a young virgin dancing herself to death while tribal elders look on. The rhythms for this scene are pounded out by a timpanist surrounded by five differently pitched timpani. Placement of the timpani thuds is so crucial to the piece that just one mistaken thud can throw off the conductor and the entire orchestra.

Luckily for the timpanist in that 1913 premier performance, an invention for timpani tuning had been made two years previously. To replace tuning handles on the rim of the instrument, pedals were invented, enabling the player to use his feet to tune his instruments. This innovation allowed pitches to be changed quickly, and Stravinsky availed himself of the new invention to write intricate lines for the timpani. Decades later, tuning became even easier when someone invented a pressure gauge that could be fastened to the side of the timpani. The player can depress the pedal and watch the gauge to get a perfectly-in-tune note. It works with levers and cogs fastened to the pedal.

One timpanist commented on the *Rite*'s hazards. "In every audition I've had to play *The Rite of Spring*. All timpanists have to. You take that for granted. I can't imagine how the timpanist played it at its 1913 premiere. There were no recordings to go by and nothing else like it in the repertoire. He didn't have years to work on it as we do now. Even after a century it's still considered the most difficult thing in the standard repertoire. So, of course, all conductors want you to play it at your audition. You'll never make it into a professional orchestra if you can't ace that thing."[12]

When the Cleveland Orchestra performed the piece in 1969, the audience saw principal timpanist Cloyd Duff on a riser above the rest of the orchestra, surrounded by five timpani. Eyes glued to conductor Boulez's beat, lips count-ing those beats and arms pistoning over his drums, Duff pounded out the thuds depicting frenzy and death. The piece is a nerve-racking test of a timpanist's ability to count while playing complicated rhythms. Duff and Boulez were dependent on each other to keep the piece from going off the rails.

All the musicians admired Boulez's efficient conducting; difficult modern pieces were his specialty. But his ability to lead the orchestra through the sonic thickets of *The Rite* would have been of little avail if Duff had made a single mistake in counting. During this tour de force Duff turned into a machine of steely resolve. Listening out in the audience, Szell must have realized that Duff was his superior when it came to complicated rhythms and meters.

In view of Boulez's bold pronouncement "The symphony is dead" and his intellectual compositions that left Cleveland audiences confused, it could be considered strange that Szell would want to share the podium with him. So it's a measure of Szell's broadmindedness that he realized music was moving on, new styles of composition were capturing the public's interest, and contemporary compositions had a right to be heard.

Boulez's ease with the most mathematically complicated music won the respect of the Cleveland Orchestra's musicians. With his appearance at Severance Hall, program notes became spiced with explanations of combinatorial set theory, aleatoric sequences, atonalism, and serialism. He didn't have to look far in his quest for anarchic music because that was now the norm. He was less successful when he had to conduct Bach, Haydn, or Mozart, because he had as little sympathy with those composers as Szell had with serialist Anton Webern and I-Ching aficionado John Cage.

With Boulez conducting, Cleveland audiences heard the latest and newest. Although many judged those pieces "interesting," older patrons grumbled.[13] Where was the beauty they were accustomed to? It returned only when Szell was on the podium. Then, once again, melody and harmony reigned. They had to admit, however, that Boulez represented progress. And who wanted Cleveland branded as a backwater? Cleveland was just as cosmopolitan as New York because it had Boulez. And Szell had chosen him.

CHAPTER 14

Concert Experiences

CHILD PRODIGIES SUPPOSEDLY exist in three main categories: chess, mathematics, and music. But there are many bright and ambitious children who don't fit into the recognized groups. Bobby Conrad in Kankakee, Illinois, was one of those children. In 1938 five-year-old Bobby made a pretend microphone out of a cardboard toilet paper tube and informed his mother he was going to be a radio announcer. Mother Conrad said in that case he had better start learning to pronounce all the words in the dictionary. Bobby was lucky to receive such counsel. A different parent might have dismissed his statement as mere prattling.

Taking her advice to heart, Bobby began reading dictionary words into his "microphone" and writing his own scripts, heavily influenced by what he was hearing over the airwaves. Bobby grew up to become Robert Conrad, cofounder of WCLV-FM, Cleveland's classical music radio station.[1]

From the 1920s to the 1950s, radio reigned supreme in the United States. Five thousand radios were sold in 1920; four years later, sales of radios jumped to an astounding two and a half million. By 1929, people were tuned in to 606 radio stations operating throughout the country. As millions of youngsters raptly listened to *Captain Midnight* and other serialized programs aimed at them, they were inadvertently exposed to classical music.

"That's because many of those programs used symphony music as their themes and to set a mood," Conrad reminisced decades later as he sat in the downtown Cleveland office of radio station WCLV.

Everyone knows *The Lone Ranger* music was Rossini's *William Tell Overture*. But they probably don't know that the name of another piece on *The Lone Ranger* was Liszt's *Les Préludes* along with Wagner's *Rienzi Overture*. All of us who listened to those serials when we were kids identified with the music being played. *The Green Hornet* used Rimsky-Korsakov's *Flight of the Bumblebee* as its theme melody. *Sergeant Preston of the Yukon* used the overture to a little-known opera, *Donna Diana*. And Sibelius's *Valse Triste* was the theme song for *I Love a Mystery*. Most of the programs used classical music, and it became part of our lives.[2]

From serial programs and hours spent in front of the family radio, young Robert went on to a part-time job at a local radio station where, at age seventeen, he became known as Sagebrush Bob.

While I was in high school I had the good luck to take private speech and drama lessons from a fabulous teacher, Beryl Danforth. She gave me exercises to improve the quality of my voice—I had a loud voice as an early teen—and sharpen my diction. There were vowel drills to work on pitch and quality. To adjust pitch and resonance I would read, in various voices, Shakespearean excerpts like "Oh, that this too, too solid flesh would melt." I give Beryl credit for making my voice into what it turned out to be.[3]

Although he didn't know it at the time, his teacher's insistence on honoring commas, stressing certain words and syllables to make sense of phrases, clarity of diction, and adjustment of volume paralleled Szell's concerns with rests, accents, tone quality, and phrasing.

While enrolled at Northwestern University, Conrad worked from six to twelve p.m. every night at Evanston's FM station, using what he had learned from Danforth. "I was determined to become a full-time professional announcer." His work paid off; he had a breakthrough. "I entered a contest for 'The Most Beautiful Voice in America' and came in second. But since the first-prize winner was a woman, I could claim the distinction of possessing the most beautiful *male* voice in America."

After a stint in the army during which he was posted to Hawaii, Conrad returned to the states and teamed up with an advertising executive to purchase an FM station in Cleveland. "When we became its owners in 1962, we changed its call letters to WCLV, relocated it, and had a tower built. Eventually we acquired a library of twenty thousand records, all given to us by recording companies who viewed our broadcasts as free advertising for their products."[4] WCLV was one of the reasons that many northeastern Ohio listeners became classical music fans.

In the aftermath of World War II, the U.S. emerged as a prosperous nation, its citizens swelling the ranks of the middle class. Suddenly hundreds of thousands of Americans had the wherewithal to take vacations, buy their own homes, and purchase tickets to concerts. But regular symphony attendance is expensive. Even with their new affluence, many classical music lovers in Cleveland could afford to go to Severance Hall only once or twice a season. In the hall's impressive lobby they momentarily brushed shoulders with elegant socialites going to their boxes on the mezzanine. Opening their program books, these single-ticket holders would read about the music they were going to hear and then, proceeding to the last pages, could peruse the list of wealthy Clevelanders who supported the orchestra with their generous donations.

It was through the community's largesse that the Cleveland Orchestra, Severance Hall, and George Szell existed among them. It was well known that ticket sales didn't support the orchestra. Instead, the cost was borne by the box holders in their jewels, furs, and formal evening wear.

WCLV provided a way for Clevelanders to hear classical music that didn't entail dipping into their savings to pay for tickets, nice apparel, and a babysitter. They could simply turn on the radio and tune in to Conrad's WCLV station. In their homes and cars they could hear Beethoven symphonies, Schubert songs, Rossini overtures, and whatever else had been selected by Conrad and his staff. Listening to these pieces became habit-forming, and some people wanted more. Just as baseball fans listening to sportscasts yearned to go to Ebbets Field and see the great Babe Ruth, classical music lovers in Cleveland wanted to go to Severance Hall and see the great Szell. Then, sitting there, they were hooked. Severance Hall's beautiful interior coupled with beautiful sounds caused the everyday world to drop away. In minutes they were transported to a distant realm of color and emotion conjured by a hundred black-clad musicians and one man on a podium.

For additional entertainment they could purchase a pair of opera glasses and get a close-up view of principal hornist Mike Bloom, whose mobile features showed the effort he was putting into each note, see timpanist Cloyd Duff visibly counting measures as he waited to strike, and watch members of the woodwind section lean forward in unison, eyes shifting from their music to Szell's baton, as they attacked their notes. Such moments counter the idea that watching a symphony orchestra is boring. In fact, such things seen through magnifying lenses reveal the harrowing tension of performing symphony music before an audience.

The tension was once commented on by Szell in a taped interview with Conrad:

> I would suggest that perhaps a musical performance which happens only once and is unique in the philosophical sense and unrepeatable, where the performer and the community of listeners find themselves in the same space, in the same spot, in one moment and live through one performance with all its hazards and all the grace of the moment it may have—I would like to hope that this experience in the real sense of the word will still seem very covetable to the audiences, that the excitement of the moment it just happens, and when it could go wrong and doesn't go wrong, that this will still be, in a way, superior to the cut and dried repeatable-put-together-faultless-but-always-the-same record.[5]

These words, coming from a man famous for rehearsing and overrehearsing, could be considered misleading in view of his efforts to anticipate every problem. But there was no way of avoiding the unforeseen. His players' nerves, screwed almost to the breaking point, might indeed unravel. An audience member could see the strain if he used his binoculars at crucial moments.

Szell's words may reveal an additional reason for his preference for live performances: an addiction to the thrill that comes with risk-taking. Whether racing his car on the Autobahn, or conducting a difficult piece played by skilled musicians, there was the constant knowledge that the unexpected might happen. That, as the music sped along, something or someone could cause it to go off the rails. He, and only he, at the steering wheel could avert disaster. He must be completely in command, watchful, wary and yet calm enough that his musicians would feel they could trust his every gesture and facial expression. Each performance was a test of himself. It was exhilarating knowledge.

Always on the lookout for ways of capturing audiences for his orchestra, Szell recognized radio's importance and wanted his finger in that pie too. People were becoming more and more interested in classical music through hearing it on the air every day. Surely their interest could be harnessed. They might use some of their new prosperity to buy tickets to Cleveland Orchestra concerts.

During one interview with Conrad, Szell spoke of the earliest days of recording, when the technology was in its infancy and the equipment resembled

RCA Victor's logo of a dog listening to its master's voice coming through a gramophone. "They used a funnel-like horn to capture the sound, and in order to get the orchestra close enough to it they packed us into a tiny room with the players on three tiers. You couldn't hear the bass section at all. So we had to substitute a tuba. It sounded awful, but that was the best to be had."[6]

In view of the deplorable sound of those early recordings, it's surprising the public bought any records at all. But something was better than nothing, and inventors like Thomas Edison kept tinkering and improving their products. Bakelite records gave way to celluloid and were then superseded by vinyl 78s, 45s, and finally LPs. At last a complete symphony could be heard without interruption. The LP years and the introduction of woofers, tweeters, high-resolution Dolby sound, better turntables, and diamond needles made manifest the full glory of a hundred-piece symphony orchestra. And Szell could exult that his orchestra's greatness had been captured for all the world to hear.

Conrad recalled WCLV's first experience with the Cleveland Orchestra. "In 1965 Szell wanted WCLV to broadcast Cleveland Orchestra performances so he had the orchestra's manager Beverly Barksdale contact the station. Until then we'd been using recordings of other orchestras and performers. We began working with Barksdale, and an agreement was worked out. After the expense of broadcasting their performances, the money left over would go into the Cleveland Orchestra musicians' pension fund. Szell very much wanted that arrangement.[7]

> Before format radio—all rock or all country and western or all classical—the general media felt it was their duty to get classical music to the public. Important radio people like William Paley and David Sarnoff thought there should be a variety of music, both popular and classical. It's surprising to think of now, but in 1990 there were ninety commercial classical music stations in the United States. By 1996, those stations were selling for more than their owners ever dreamed they were worth.
>
> Of course, things changed radically when television became so popular. But just because there are symphony orchestras going bankrupt in the country doesn't mean there isn't an audience for classical music. It's there all right. People become patrons of orchestras after exposure to classical music on the radio. A survey by the National Endowment for the Arts showed that about fifteen percent of the general population listens to classical music on the radio at least once a week. So the classical music situation in the U.S. is in better condition than some people think.[8]

In 1970, knowing symphony orchestras are always financially strapped, Conrad initiated a three-day marathon in which listeners could call in and request a certain Cleveland Orchestra performance to be played if they donated a small sum. This caught the attention of his listeners to such an extent that calls were made to the station requesting something to be played in honor of their spouses, relatives, girlfriends, cats, dogs, and various worthy causes. From Friday through Sunday evening, calls came in and the donations piled up. "We raised ten thousand dollars in the first twenty-four hours," Conrad recalled. "By signoff time on Sunday evening we had raised $33,000." The marathon weekends became an annual event.[9]

"In the first two years, we broadcast from our own studio. But then we took the broadcasts to shopping malls like Severance Center." Local businesses donated merchandise for auctioning, and a few bold types even auctioned off dates with themselves. "We held those marathons for twenty-seven years, raising a total of four million dollars for the orchestra," Conrad recalled.[10] The marathons were not only financially successful, but also responsible for bringing the orchestra to the attention of the general public.

There were other ways to bring money into the orchestra's coffers: benefit concerts featuring some celebrity. In 1960 when it was proposed to have Jack Benny host a benefit concert for the orchestra, Szell agreed but said he wouldn't be able to take a speaking part in any comedy routines because spontaneity wasn't his strong point. Made aware of Szell's inability to ad lib in a comedy routine, Benny arranged to have a member of the orchestra join him in a joke.

At the moment in the concert when Benny was supposed to play his violin, he professed himself unable to adjust his music stand and asked for a different one to be brought onstage. An overalls-clad stagehand emerged from the wings, bearing the requested stand. Benny fussed over it, trying to raise it to the proper height and then asked the stagehand to hold his violin and bow while he made some adjustments. The stagehand took Benny's violin, tucked it under his chin and expertly tossed off the opening measures of a violin concerto. The fellow wasn't a stagehand at all; he was Sidney Weiss, one of the orchestra's best violinists. Benny did his famous slow burn during this virtuoso exhibition, and then, acting miffed, ordered the interloper off the stage. The audience loved it. That benefit concert brought in many thousands of dollars.[11]

One benefit concert featured a stunt that didn't involve a stagehand but rather the entire orchestra. Popular entertainer Bobby McFerrin occupied the podium and went through his repertoire of voices, mimicking the witches in *The Wizard of Oz* and carrying on in frenetic fashion. After that, he turned to the orchestra and led them in the *William Tell Overture*. The famous opening fanfare was played by the trumpet section. But then, instead of *playing* the rest of the well-known tune, all the musicians put down their instruments and *sang* their parts, da-da-da-ing, humming and bleating in falsetto. The audience went wild. They had never heard such a performance. It was the high point of the evening and conclusively proved that their Cleveland Orchestra could do anything, even upstage Bobby McFerrin.[12]

WCLV's broadcasts of the Cleveland Orchestra brought Conrad into some of its inner workings. One Sunday afternoon he found himself in Szell's living room at the maestro's request.

> We received a phone call at WCLV from Szell. He said he wanted to discuss the broadcasts. He wasn't happy with the sound he was getting. Because nobody else was making the same complaint, I thought it might have something to do with his speakers. So I went to his house.
>
> When I entered his living room—after removing my shoes because outdoor shoes weren't allowed on their light carpet—I couldn't see any speakers. I asked where they were. Szell said they were behind the sofa. Mrs. Szell, while rearranging the furniture, had ordered them put back there because she considered them unsightly.
>
> Szell didn't seem to be aware that radio waves have trouble going through upholstery if it's smack up against a speaker. I said I'd have to put the speakers out where there wasn't any interference. So I started moving the sofa. Mrs. Szell was there and she said, "George, help him." So he pitched in too.
>
> As soon as we got the speakers out from behind that sofa, things greatly improved. But he didn't have an antenna on his stereo. I explained that, without an antenna, reception wouldn't be optimum. I had brought along a twin-lead T-bar antenna, and I asked him to raise it up high and walk around the room to find out where the best spot for receiving was. He did as I requested and found the location where reception was most clear. It was funny watching him pace around the room, arms over his head, holding up that T-bar.[13]

Although Szell had definite and well-informed opinions about acoustics, his knowledge of radio waves was nonexistent. In this he was like most people who turn on their radios with never a thought about how they work. Strangely, although he had insisted some years before that all sound-deadening velvet hangings and carpets at Severance Hall had to be removed, it seemed not to have occurred to him that thick upholstery against the front of his speakers could impede radio waves.

Helene couldn't have been pleased to have her carefully arranged living room sullied with boxy components, cables, and an antenna. Her oriental screens and beautifully upholstered furniture were desecrated by the necessities of her husband's profession. But she had to retreat. Décor was secondary to music.

In the late 1950s, before WCLV broadcasts of the Cleveland Orchestra had begun, audio technician Herb Heller made a series of tape recordings of the orchestra's rehearsals for Szell. Because doing so was expressly forbidden by the players—for once backed up by the union—Szell had to do his spying secretly, aided by Heller. Microphones hanging over the stage were supposed to be used only for taping the performances to be broadcast. But Szell, determined to listen to playbacks of rehearsals, had Heller place hidden microphones to be surreptitiously turned on while the orchestra rehearsed.

Later he and Heller met in an empty room in which Heller had positioned high-quality speakers, and there Szell listened to the illicit tapes. He could clearly hear each nuance, and these tape recordings gave him the information he needed to prod his players into ever better performances. Then the jig was up one morning at a rehearsal, when he accidentally spilled the beans. "Gentlemen, I have been listening to the rehearsal tapes and there are some things I want to fix." No sooner had the words left his mouth than there was a ruckus. He'd been spying on them after all! The angry players brought the Szell-Heller listening sessions to an end.[14]

From 1965 on, people could tune their radios to WCLV's Sunday afternoon broadcasts of Cleveland Orchestra concerts. Szell and his players heard those broadcasts too. So it was hardly necessary for Szell to point out any inadequacies at the following Tuesday morning rehearsal. The musicians already knew when their playing had been less than stellar. But they also heard when they had all played superbly. Coming off the stage after concerts with Szell on the podium, the musicians frequently had the conviction that no other orchestra was ever going to play those pieces better than they just had.[15] Such knowledge kept them full of respect for their taskmaster, who continually demanded their best.

CHAPTER 15

Szell's Haydn and Schumann Interpretations

IN 1946, HIS FIRST YEAR of conducting the Cleveland Orchestra, Szell listened to the players he had inherited and fired sixteen of them.[1] Their faults? Some of them didn't play in tune. Others produced sounds that weren't pleasing to the ear. Still others didn't play their notes at the exact split second he flicked his baton. The trick of quality linked to simultaneity was difficult enough to put various musicians out of their jobs.

The musicians hired to take their places soon realized what kind of man stood in front of them. Szell was a person with a brain like no other they had ever encountered. Not only had he memorized hundreds of thousands of notes, he knew the significance of those notes and exactly who should be playing them at any given moment. Determined to bring forth meaningful sounds, he marked up his scores with penciled instructions and then was pitiless in enforcing them. "I need that rest," he called to one of his sections.[2] They knew why he'd said it and made haste to briskly hop off their note. Mushiness was a major crime. Indulgent lingering on pretty tones wasn't tolerated.

Clarity of sound and rhythmic precision led some European critics to say the Cleveland Orchestra played "too perfectly." It was overrehearsed; there was no allowance for individuality; there were whiffs of Teutonic regimentation. Such comments amused Szell, who knew that getting one hundred musicians to play perfectly together was a rare feat. As for the criticism about regimentation, he had a thought about that too: "I want this to sound spontaneous, but as a result of meticulous preparation," he said.[3] The musicians laughed, knowing he was making fun of a few carping critics.

In Austria the orchestra received rave reviews mixed with a few cavils when they played Strauss waltzes. More warmth was needed. Some schmaltz—wayward rhythms, slight blurrings between notes, casual intonation, a breezily unbuttoned air—that was the spirit of a Viennese waltz. Szell would have none of it. Schmaltz was merely sloppiness. His witty interpretations of Haydn symphonies were rebuttal enough. He conveyed warmth and humor not by sloppiness but by carefully separated upbeats from downbeats, subtle differences in tempo and clever highlighting of heretofore concealed melodies, all of it catching his listeners off guard and bringing out Haydn's droll originality.

Among Haydn's 104 symphonies, his *Symphony No. 88* was one of Szell's favorites. Its felicities include an unusual trio in the middle of the minuet movement. Here Haydn wrote a bagpipe effect totally different from the rest of the piece, causing listeners to wonder, "Where did *that* come from?" Szell's way of conducting Haydn's works wasn't simply surprising and charming; his Haydn recordings with the Cleveland Orchestra between 1949 and 1969 fully manifested Haydn's genius.[4]

Between 1958 and 1960, Szell recorded the four Robert Schumann symphonies. As a result of that album he was hailed as a great Schumann interpreter. He defended Schumann's symphonies to detractors who criticized their orchestration. Maintaining that careful attention to balances and details would show these compositions to be masterpieces, he said they simply needed help in certain places for their greatness to be revealed.

His words, however, don't explain what he *really* did to Schumann's scores. His alterations of many passages by such things as adding notes to buttress important phrases and removing string sections' reinforcements of woodwind solos can best be comprehended by looking at his penciled-in changes. These changes achieved lightness and precision, enabling Schumann's beautiful melodies to emerge more clearly. Proof of Szell's clever reorchestrations can be heard in his recordings of those four works.

Oboist Bob Zupnik commented, "Szell heard things in the music that aren't usually noticed, and he brought out those things with such clarity it was as if you'd never really heard those pieces before."[5]

But Szell wasn't just bringing out what Schumann had written. Violinist Jerry Rosen, who joined the orchestra in 1959 as one of its apprentice conductors, shed more light on Szell's way with the Schumann symphonies:

> He altered the orchestration on just about every single page in those four scores. You can look at them and see all the markings that he wrote in.

I quit the orchestra in 1962 because I went to college to major in math and philosophy. But I came back two years later in 1964 to listen to a concert at Severance Hall. Szell was conducting Schumann's *Symphony No. 4*.[6] As they played the transition from the scherzo to the finale I had an epiphany. I got chills. That's when I realized that music is more than a profession. It's a calling. And that's when I was called . . . maybe not chosen, but certainly called. I have rarely been so deeply moved by anything in my entire life. I knew then I had to get back into his orchestra.[7]

Szell rehired him, this time for the first violin section. The combination of Szell and Schumann was, for a musician of Rosen's talent, irresistible.

The orchestra's present music librarian Robert O'Brien corroborated Rosen's statement on Szell's changes to Schumann's scores:

> Nearly every page of those four scores has Szell's reorchestrations, especially *Symphony No. 3*, the Rhenish. He changed some horn writing, and completely rewrote the brass choir section of its fourth movement, revoicing it.
>
> In Schumann's *Symphony No. 1*, Szell totally altered the timpani line from the original. He used colored pencils when he marked his scores. Red was for places that had to be stopped and fixed in rehearsals, blue was to call attention to something, and green meant that his changes had to be copied into the parts. He was always trying to achieve dynamic balance. He frequently copied his alterations into the various parts himself rather than leaving them to the librarian.
>
> Conductors and musicologists have come to the Szell library to study Szell's scores and have given up trying to copy out his changes, particularly in the Schumann symphonies.[8] It would take countless hours. That's why nobody else has been able to record those symphonies to sound as great as Szell's recording of the two-disc album he began in 1958 and finished in 1960.[9]

Sometime in the middle to late nineteen-fifties, Szell, at the peak of his intellectual and musical powers, undertook the Schumann symphonies project that would occupy him for several years. Well in advance of his recording of them, he began their reorchestration. Free of the time constraints of rehearsals, he could spend the months necessary to fix their inadequacies. He must have derived great satisfaction from improving those scores and knowing that he was one of the few musicians in the world who could do what he was doing.

A revelation in Schumann's *Symphony No. 2* comes in the third movement, the beautiful adagio espressivo. There Schumann wrote one of the most exquisite set of notes ever penned, a yearning melody that offers up its heart with all the poignancy of love and loss. This solo was oboist Marc Lifschey's meat. Listening to him play it, one can understand why Szell so highly prized his artistry.

The orchestra recorded Schumann's *Symphony No. 4* and then his *Symphony No. 3.*[10] Its beginning breaks forth joyously, Mike Bloom soaring in his horn solos. The fourth movement foreshadows Schumann's end, when he would go insane, attempt suicide, and finally die. In a little more than five and a half minutes, the brass choir forges the image of solemn processions through a vast cathedral. This magnificent movement, architectural in concept, uses the various entrances of the theme like levels in space.

Finally, on October 21, 1960, the two-year recording project came to an end. The results have never been equaled.

CHAPTER 16

Attire, Duty, Respect, Decorum

THERE ARE RIGHT WAYS and wrong ways, and Szell had strong convictions on which were which. He controlled everything that went on at Severance Hall and didn't hesitate to lay down rules. Quality and appropriateness were his criteria, imported from the Vienna of his youth, where music reigned supreme and one's wardrobe and demeanor denoted social class. He applied his mental yardstick to many things in addition to music: audience behavior, grooming, clothing, colors of concert halls, punctuality, and marriage.

Besides quelling unruly musicians, he tried to steer his audiences to a code of conduct brought from Europe. He considered U.S. audiences to be tainted by sports arenas, where noisy, unruly behavior was part of the general ambiance. And he knew that most U.S. radio audiences listened to broadcasts of music while talking, eating, and driving. Clevelanders were no different. Most of them, even classical music lovers, failed to come up to Szell's standards of proper concert behavior. He was convinced that their casual deportment detracted from the music, ruined everyone's concentration, and had to be stamped out. What he required of his audiences was attentive silence during performances and then appreciative, though brief, applause at the end of each piece.[1]

This stern approach extended to his presence on stage. He would walk to the podium, barely acknowledge the applauding audience with a cursory bow and step up to the business at hand. At the end of a piece he would bow and briskly leave the stage. Only prolonged applause could entice him to come out and bow more than twice. His bows were rarely accompanied by a smile. After various principal players performed their solos, his recognition of their artistry was a perfunctory motion ordering them to briefly stand for recognition at the end of a piece. Not for Szell the milking of applause by motioning one player after another to stand until the entire orchestra was on its feet as the audience continued clapping. Instead, each soloist was expected to rise, stand modestly without bowing and then sit down.

That Spartan routine caused orchestra members to resign themselves to little glory on the Severance Hall stage. As a result, they were surprised and gratified when they experienced standing ovations from audiences at Carnegie Hall. They frequently contrasted unresponsive Cleveland audiences with the wildly enthusiastic people who attended their concerts in New York. Most were unaware that Szell's austere stage demeanor set the tone in Cleveland, and the lack of prolonged applause—standing ovations, whistles, and stamping feet—was in part due to his forbidding appearance.

Lawyer William Buss, who as a teenager attended concerts with his parents at Severance Hall during the 1950s, recalled instances of Szell's dealing with audience disruption:

Once he did something really shocking. In the middle of acknowledging the audience's applause, he noticed someone snapping his picture. He stopped bowing, glared at the photographer and barked, "Give me your camera." The surprised fellow left his seat, walked to the front of the stage amid dead silence from the startled audience and held up the offending camera. Szell leaned down, snatched it from his hands, opened it up and yanked out the film. Then he returned the camera. The poor embarrassed guy slunk back to his seat. None of us had ever witnessed anything like that. Word got around and, as far as I can remember, nobody else ever tried to take an unauthorized photo of Szell.

Buss recalled other Szell moments:

One of the funniest times was when the concert included a contemporary piece. It wasn't very attractive and we were all impatient for it to end. I guess Szell sensed the piece wasn't being well received because there was a certain amount of rustling and inattention. At the conclusion, there was hardly any applause. Then, instead of bowing, Szell looked out at us all and said, "This is a very short piece. So we will play it again." The second playing took place in an atmosphere of rigid silence. The audience probably thought if it didn't behave itself it would be given a third hearing.[2]

I think the message was that we were supposed to give a new composition our polite attention even if we didn't like it. I always wondered whether Szell himself liked that kind of music or if he programmed it every once in a while because he thought it was good for us. Like cod liver oil.

Buss's conjecture was near the truth. Szell wasn't keen on most contemporary music, which he called "temporary music." He usually left the more dissonant compositions to his assistant conductor or some modern-music expert like Pierre Boulez.[3]

On one occasion Szell was so incensed by the audience's behavior he did something drastic. The orchestra's management, in an attempt to boost ticket sales, had announced a concert of light classics to be held in downtown Cleveland's cavernous Public Hall. For this event audience members would be seated at small tables where drinks would be served, thus fostering an atmosphere of casual entertainment. When Szell was informed of the plan he perhaps ignored its potential for disruption, thinking only of how he and the orchestra would perform some well-crafted Strauss waltzes.

Predictably, the waltzes had to compete with the din of chatter, clinking glasses, people walking about, and chairs scraping on the floor. It was obvious to the orchestra members that their performance was being relegated to mere background music. Szell's grim face mirrored their thoughts.

At the end of the first piece on the program, he ordered the orchestra to leave the stage and not return. He strode off without acknowledging the scattered applause and then, backstage, gathered all the players around himself. Standing at the edge of the group were Vladimir Maleckar, the orchestra's recording engineer, and Irving Kolodin, the well-known music critic. These two heard Szell address his humiliated musicians. "Ladies and gentlemen, I apologize for the behavior of the audience and I promise you this will never happen again."[4] What he must have said afterward to manager Barksdale isn't known. But that was the first and last time he and his musicians performed in such a setting.

Male hair was a subject about which Szell had definite ideas. His Viennese years influenced his thinking. In pre–World War II European cities, most fashionable men were beardless and kept their hair neatly slicked back.[5] He adhered to that style himself and preferred to see the same on those around him. Hair on the face could be a small mustache, but beards were strictly forbidden. Hair on the arms had to be covered by long-sleeved shirts and on the legs covered by calf-length socks. Hirsute chests were to stay safely out of sight beneath buttoned-up dress shirts. Absolutely no male ponytails. These rules were enforced by the personnel manager, who was answerable to Szell. Very little was left to chance.

The women of the orchestra could arrange their tresses as they saw fit, though they couldn't wear sparkling jewelry; glitter took people's minds off the music. Cleavage was similarly verboten, tolerated only on famous sopranos. Szell had to bite his tongue during rehearsals with prima donnas who would come onstage in full-length mink coats that they then tossed off to reveal many inches of skin.[6]

There would probably have been a scene had he been on the podium in 1967 when the English cellist Jacqueline du Pré rehearsed with the orchestra wearing an extreme miniskirt. At the evening performance du Pré—her long blond hair floating in the air—appeared wearing a slinky red-satin dress with a plunging neckline. As she walked out on stage, a low moan of ecstasy arose from the males in the audience. Afterward, some people couldn't remember what concerto she had played, proving Szell's conviction that cleavage distracts from the music.[7]

When on tour, orchestra members had to be neatly dressed at all times. Casual garb shouldn't be seen in hotel lobbies, restaurants, trains, airplanes, or buses. They weren't ordinary people; they were members of the great Cleveland Orchestra and had to look that way. The moment they left their hotel rooms they were in the public eye. Wives of orchestra members, aware of sartorial strictures, were expected to provide freshly laundered and pressed white dress shirts, bowties and vests, shined shoes and frequently cleaned suits of tails. Playing under Szell created a lot of nervous sweat.

Twenty-one-year-old Jerry Rosen, one of the former prodigies in the violin section, was occasionally scolded by Szell for his unkempt appearance. Rosen was not only a fine violinist and pianist, but also a composer and one of the orchestra's apprentice conductors. Practice on his instruments and studying scores left little time for grooming. This was bound to get him in trouble with Szell. Rosen remembers what happened to him when the orchestra played in Eugene, Oregon.

> I had asked Szell to look over the score of one of my compositions and he said to meet him for dinner and score studying at the hotel's restaurant. When I arrived in the lobby and approached him, he immediately noticed a black mark on my collar. He said, 'What's that on your collar?' I replied that it must be a stain from my violin's chin rest. I'd just come from practicing.

He said "I won't eat dinner with anybody with a stain on their collar." I tried to reason with him, but it was no use. He said, "I'll look at your score but I certainly won't eat dinner with you." By then we had walked out of the lobby and were outdoors on the sidewalk. Right there in public he grabbed me by the collar and with both hands lifted me off the ground and shook me like a misbehaving puppy. I'm only five foot three inches tall and he was six foot one. It was a real manhandling. Then he walked off by himself and I was left standing there.

Perhaps Szell, later reflecting on his treatment of Rosen, felt somewhat ashamed. Or perhaps his curiosity about Rosen's score got the better of him. Whatever the motivation, several weeks later he told Rosen he wanted to see his composition. Rosen recalled, "He looked it over and made some cogent corrections and suggestions that were really helpful."

But another Szell favor elicited less gratitude from Rosen. "One time at an airport he approached me with a book, Dale Carnegie's *How to Win Friends and Influence People*. Handing it to me, he said, 'You have to become more genteel and Gentile.'"[8]

Szell was capable of occupying himself with such subjects as the proper colors of concert halls. Their interiors should be either red or gold, as they were in Europe. When the Cleveland Orchestra played in New York's Philharmonic Hall, he voiced his exasperation not only with the acoustics but also with the color of its walls. "Who can make music in a blue hall?" He never conducted there again.[9]

Record jackets elicited some of his most scathing criticism. Columbia Records, perhaps thinking that Szell's forbidding face on covers might put off potential buyers, decided to snag them with eye-catching art. Instead of the usual photographs of Szell and his soloists, the jackets began featuring abstract paintings, pictures of lovers, and colorful patterns supposedly related to the passion in the music, a noticeable departure from the somber jackets Szell favored.

In speaking of these changes during an interview with radio announcer Bob Conrad, Szell expressed his wrath. "I was so horrified by the outrageous, atrocious, vulgar, ignorant and downright ugly jackets that were put out by the industry generally—and for my records in particular—that I simply stipulated that the jackets have to go through the process of my approval because I cannot see the efforts of conscientious artists who have a modicum of good taste be spoiled by wrapping them in something a self-respecting supermarket would be ashamed of."[10]

His disgust with sexy record jackets must have thrown a monkey wrench into the art department at Columbia Records. One can only imagine the colorful invective he spoke over the telephone to a cringing executive at Columbia. He was certain of many things. One of them was that a nude has nothing to do with a Beethoven symphony.

Background music likewise elicited his ire, and he made that clear in his recorded interview with Conrad:[11]

I really think that the misuse, the abuse, of mechanically reproduced music, that is, the possibility of making it furnish a background noise to everyday activities, a noise to which nobody is really listening, is degrading to music. Music should be listened to with full intellectual and emotional concentration and participation just the way you listen to a speech, to a talk, to a poem. You listen inwardly if you read a book. The communication, the meaning, the sense, the significance of what is transmitted by words is of very great importance. It *should* be of very great importance for the listener, and so should the communication of what is transmitted by tones.

Sometimes the listener is a captive audience. For instance, I have a dentist who has music in his office. It's absolute torture. I would much rather endure the pain of a drill in my tooth than this constant—you call it wallpaper—noise, wallpaper music or whatever it's called. Now fortunately what comes over that system is not very important music so one doesn't have the feeling of desecration or really misuse. But this ceaseless going on of pseudo-musical noise as background is something that for me is very hard to endure.[12]

Knowing his disgust with Muzak, Helene telephoned a nearby grocery store to douse the music whenever her touchy husband announced he was going there.

As much as he disliked Muzak, inattentive audiences, bad acoustics of concert halls, mediocre musicians, inappropriate behavior, and revealing clothing, he reserved his direst opprobrium for bad music. When someone suggested he play an overture by the Bohemian composer Johann Wenzel Kalliwoda, who had fallen into obscurity, Szell rejected it with insults, using a word beyond even a four-letter one. He declared the piece was "putrid."[13]

Charming, tactful Helene tried to anticipate her demanding husband's every need. Her solicitude was noticed by Clara Rankin, the wife of a member of the board of trustees. She recalled one of her visits with Helene. "I was at their home one morning conferring with Helene about some social affair, and we talked in the breakfast room. Laid out on the table were two place settings in readiness for George's return for lunch. She felt it was her duty to have his meals on time and to make his life as easy as possible."

Helene's ideas on appropriate behavior and appearance were commented on by Rankin, who observed her at concerts and receptions. "She was friendly and outgoing and wore things that were in quiet good taste. I think she bought her clothes in Paris."[14]

Some of Szell's clothing choices were vetoed by Helene. She didn't share his admiration for a three-piece glen plaid ensemble he enjoyed wearing, believing that plaids and stripes called too much attention to their wearer. During rehearsals he should be informal in a black turtleneck sweater, a subdued sweater-vest over a dress shirt, or a long-sleeved polo shirt. And, no matter what the occasion, there should be no patterns.

Local tailor Peter Uhlir, still in business after fifty years, reminisced about his famous customer. "I was honored that Mr. Szell wanted me to make him a set of tails. We spoke Hungarian together. He wanted enough room in the shoulders and sleeves of the jacket so he could move his arms freely. I've made suits for Mr. Szell, always in solid colors. Mrs. Szell insisted on that. She picked out the fabric for a sport jacket I made for him because he didn't have an eye for color. She was very nice, very nice looking. You could see they were used to fine quality."[15]

Packing for tours was something Szell never left to Helene. He insisted on selecting which clothing items would go in his suitcases and which ones in his capacious wardrobe trunk. He neatly laid them out on his bed, folded and stacked, and placed them in the waiting suitcases and trunk.[16] His careful selection was guided by which items he would wear on which day in which city. Only he could handle this task properly, and he enjoyed coordinating. Helene never intervened in this absorbing ritual. It probably came under one of the maxims he subscribed to: "If you want something done right, you have to do it yourself."[17]

Their home exhibited Helene's refined taste in décor. The living room's white walls, white woodwork, and pale carpet set off the oriental screens and the subdued, elegant furniture she had selected.[18] She monitored the carpet with an eagle eye, and no one, including Szell, was allowed to walk on it in street shoes. This rule had a famous antecedent. Years before, composer Richard Strauss was compelled by his domineering wife Pauline to thoroughly wipe his shoes before entering the Strauss parlor. Both Szell and Strauss had to bow before their wives' carpet rules to keep peace in their families.[19] For Szell, it was a small price to pay. He knew Helene was totally dedicated to him.

Being only human, however, Helene occasionally quit her role as smiling helpmate. When she thought his antics had gone too far, she dished out some chastising. One such episode took place at an after-concert party in the home of a member of the board of trustees. Szell, unasked, had sat down at the piano and begun performing one of his famous party tricks, his own version of Strauss's *Till Eulenspiegel*. The high point always came when he dragged his cufflinks over the piano keys to imitate the clacking sound of a ratchet.[20] Helene had witnessed this act one time too many. Thinking the bombast wasn't appropriate when people wanted to talk, she strode over to the piano and slammed the keyboard lid down on Szell's hands. "Always showing off," she exclaimed disgustedly.

Another instance of her chagrin was when her husband displayed social obliviousness at an after-concert reception in Lucerne's Palace Hotel when the orchestra was touring Europe. A table bearing mouth-watering Swiss pastries was surrounded by a line of patrons and musicians, and Szell had elbowed his way to the front, intent on filling his plate. "George!" Helene remonstrated. Startled at the sound of his wife's disapproving voice, he dropped his plate, which shattered on the floor.[21] Bystanders witnessing this proof of slight cracks in the Szells' façade found interesting things to look at on the ceiling.

Usually Helene was resigned to following behind her famous husband and having doors swing back in her face as he strode along, his mind on far weightier matters than chivalry. But sometimes, tired of catering to him and standing loyally in the background, her behavior might be less than perfect. During a visit to their home, Louis Lane overheard her rejoinder when her difficult husband angrily voiced some frustrations. "Oh, George, go down to the hall and take it out on the musicians."[22]

A concern for punctuality cost Szell a considerable sum every Christmas, when he gave each of the orchestra members an expensive pocket date book. Bound in saffian leather, these small books with tissue-thin gilt-edged pages were from Smythson's in London. Intended to be dutifully inscribed with dates and times of orchestra rehearsals and concerts using the tiny pencil nestled in the hollow spine of the book, they were intimidating reminders.[23]

Orchestra members tried to keep any troubles in their marriages concealed because they knew Szell was intolerant of infidelity and divorce. In his view, emotional upheavals prevented concentration on the music.[24]

Most Cleveland Orchestra musicians knew little about Szell's first marriage or his private life. They would have been surprised to hear that he had a close friendship with a Jesuit priest. Father John Dulin, who generally eschewed the traditional priest's collar, frequently sat in the Szell box at orchestra concerts.[25] Few of the players knew that Dulin was a priest as well as a clinical psychologist. And most thought that Jewish Szell had converted to Catholicism solely for political reasons when Hitler's thugs were on the rampage, not realizing he had been a Catholic since the age of three.[26]

But keyboardist Joela Jones knew about Father Dulin's connection with Szell, as did Robert Sweeney, a retired professor of philosophy at John Carroll University. Sweeney recalled his own friendship with the priest:

> Father Dulin was formidably intelligent but wore his learning lightly, had a great sense of humor and was jolly with a ready laugh. He had bought a house, which was pretty unusual because home ownership isn't something common to Jesuits. He explained to me that he needed a private home rather than space in some office building because the VIPs who came to him for therapy didn't want to be seen. His superiors in Chicago cut him as much slack as he needed to carry on his work.

When one of his valued musicians exhibited some mental problems, Szell sent him to Dulin and paid for the sessions himself. The player told only his closest friends what was going on. Szell's solicitude for his player was in line with his abiding sense of duty.[27] He prided himself on his constant watchfulness and care. Calling himself "Papa Szell who is always right," he thought of his musicians as his children, to be disciplined and guided, believing that everything he did was for the general good.

CHAPTER 17

A New Chorus Conductor

SOON AFTER SZELL WAS HIRED to conduct the Cleveland Orchestra, he realized the orchestra's chorus needed fixing. He didn't care to conduct Mozart's great *Requiem* with the chorus he had inherited, but he wisely understood that his usual methods wouldn't work with volunteers. It wasn't possible to galvanize them through fear; they would simply quit. The situation called for someone with experience conducting choruses and possessing the ability to inspire amateurs so they'd be willing to put up with many hours of rehearsals and no pay.

There was little need to rack his brain searching for the nation's best choral director. Everyone knew who that was: Robert Shaw, leader of the famous Robert Shaw Chorale. Audiences flocked to his performances and raptly listened to his radio broadcasts. He seemed to be a Svengali or Pied Piper, leading his singers through the most intricate musical mazes and coaxing them into dramatic effects. Szell had to have him.

In 1955 Shaw agreed to become the conductor of the Cleveland Orchestra Chorus.[1] The incentives, among other things, included free rein to choose his singers, a paid accompanist, and unlimited time in Severance Hall's chorus rehearsal room to work his magic.

Taking up his post, Shaw announced to the chorus members—newcomers and veterans alike—that they would have to audition. His announcement was their first inkling that a revolution was brewing. Venerable sopranos, altos, tenors, and basses were upset at the thought of having to audition and demonstrate their sight-reading abilities. He was implacable in these auditions, and one by one various choristers fell by the wayside. Some of them managed to pass their solo auditions, performing their prepared number and sight-reading some easy pieces. But even if they passed the first audition, they had to submit to yet another one, for Shaw then held what was dubbed by one chorus member "The Saturday Night Massacre."[2]

Each singer was required to come to Severance Hall on the following Saturday evening for the second audition. Several hundred gathered and were alarmed to be confronted with a treacherous hurdle: sight-reading various passages in Bach's intricate Mass in B Minor. A musically adept soprano who succeeded in passing the final test recalled that night. "It was blood-letting. He had three cardinal rules: no obtrusive vibrato, good intonation, and good sight-reading. That final audition was designed to put on the heat and weed out the nervous nellies."

Alone, then combined in duets, trios, and quartets, the hopefuls struggled their way through Bach's difficult passages. At the end of the evening, a few prominent Cleveland singers who had been rejected went home in a huff. The lucky ones who had made the cut sighed with relief mixed with apprehension. There would probably be a lot more of what they had just gone through.

Soprano Chris Miles, who had successfully negotiated Shaw's hurdles, remembers her years in his chorus:

> I wasn't really a singer. I had been a piano major at Baldwin Wallace University Conservatory of Music and I'd had courses in solfege and Dalcroze so I could sight-sing. But I didn't possess a huge voice or a rounded tone. Well, apparently that didn't matter to him. He seemed to be most interested in a quick assimilation of the printed notes and a willingness to do things his way. It was a complete singing education and the most memorable thing that ever happened to me.
>
> And that Bach B minor Mass. It must have been one of his favorite pieces because he not only used it to get rid of the mediocre singers at the second audition, he also prepared us for the Severance Hall performance of it. That concert was the high point of my life. I had an out-of-body experience. It happened during the Sanctus movement. I was inside a sound that was so gorgeous, so wonderful, climbing higher and higher as the music modulated, that I was borne upward, looking down, observing Shaw and the chorus. And at the same time I was singing, feeling tears and my whole body was shaking. I can't hear that Sanctus movement to this day without remembering that fantastic moment. It was like I was part of the cosmos. The piece erects a cathedral of

sound and the cathedral goes on and on, and you are in the sound and being propelled. Afterwards I was completely undone.

But it wasn't only the music affecting me. It was the music combined with the way Shaw had prepared us. After our first rehearsal Shaw sent each one of us a sermon about it. Well, I call it a sermon but it was really a wonderful explanation and analysis of what the piece was about, not religious, but inspiring. And in another few days we all got another page or two about it. And then we'd go to a rehearsal, and following that there'd be something else in the mail from him. By the time we got to the performance we were all so galvanized we'd have followed him and that piece right off a cliff if he had told us to jump.

Oh, those rehearsals! We'd come in the evening, tired from work, hardly any time to eat supper, and he'd have us do these physical things for eight or ten minutes to relax us. I think it was his own method he'd invented to relax people and make them bond with each other. We'd each turn to the person next to us and massage his shoulders and back. Then we'd turn to the person on the other side and do the same thing. All that massaging and light tappings on our backs relaxed us, and gradually the day's cares just dropped away. We'd open up and sing. Sing like we didn't know we could.

Singing is totally physical. It resonates in your head. When you're in the midst of enormous sound it gets so emotional it's actually scary because you feel as if you aren't in control. You lose your sense of identity while singing a great work under a great conductor. All of us had a conviction of rightness, of having found *the answer*. It was wonderful and disorienting at the same time. I'm pretty sure every other choir member felt the same as I did—that it was something fantastic we were doing, and we were all in it together, going toward a common goal. It was just Shaw and the music and us.[3]

Unlike Szell, Robert Shaw hadn't been nurtured by wealthy parents and a great teacher in a musically sophisticated city. Instead, born in Red Bluff, California, in 1916, Shaw had endured a childhood marked by poverty. His father, a minister with a wife and five children to feed, received no salary beyond what the collection box yielded each Sunday. All five Shaw children were singers, gathering around their mother Nelle, who had a rich, commanding voice, equally adept with hymns and the latest popular songs. They could sing in four-part harmony—father Shaw on the bass line—and as they moved from parish to parish the family formed the nucleus of his various church choirs.

Hours of family singing gave Robert an unerring sense of correct pitch and an ear for which harmonies went with which melodies. His mother's singing was a model of how a voice could create mood and color in a song. He wasn't shy about telling his friends how they should sing, conducting them in sing-alongs and bossing them into shape. And he absorbed something that was to stand him in good stead. His father's sermons were models of persuasiveness about the need to find Jesus, walk in His way, forsake sin and come into the fold. Robert, steeped in these injunctions and their style, became adept at the art of persuading singers to follow him.

The messages of hymns—their biblical phrases wedded to uplifting melodies—indelibly marked the young musician, as had his father's sermons. He decided to follow in his father's footsteps; he would study for the ministry at Pomona College, where he had been offered a scholarship, and devote his life to serving God.[4]

Pomona was founded in 1888 by Congregationalists. Its curriculum in later years became progressively less religious, and by 1934 it emphasized modern poetry, as well as Darwinism and other modern theories. These changes of direction soon began eroding Shaw's religious convictions. Caught up in glee club activities, he took little notice of the iconoclastic atmosphere's effect on his vow to dedicate himself to God.[5] Pomona offered the usual music courses of liberal arts colleges of the time, but Shaw availed himself of few of them, preferring to spend most of his waking hours conducting singers.

Within two years his ability to lead choruses was recognized by the college's administration, and they offered him five hundred dollars to conduct the prize-winning Pomona Men's Glee Club while its regular conductor was on a leave of absence.[6] Spurred by this recognition of his talent, Shaw began looking into Pomona's music library, discovering musical worlds he had never imagined. He was soon caught up in sixteenth-century madrigals, medieval Gregorian chant, and works by Schubert and Mozart and other classical composers.

Pomona's reputation for singing attracted the attention of bandleader and producer Fred Waring, who needed a musical environment for the shooting of a movie. He, his Pennsylvanians, and a movie crew moved onto the Pomona campus in 1934 to film *Varsity Show*.[7] Waring noticed young Shaw, who was leading one of the glee club's performances included in the film, and realized he had found something. He offered Shaw a job but Shaw turned him down. Under the impression he was committed to his father's profession, Shaw said he was studying for the ministry; conducting was only a sideline. In truth, he wasn't doing much studying. The "sideline" filled his days and nights.

When the filming of *Varsity Show* ended, Waring went back to New York and once more offered Shaw a job. By then Shaw realized his heart was with music. So Waring prevailed after all, sending Shaw a check for one hundred fifty dollars to travel to New York. Frugal Shaw chose to go by bus, the cheapest way, keeping the leftover sixty-seven dollars to live on when he arrived in the city.

He started working with Waring, picking up experience with microphones and acoustics and learning choral arrangements that featured more vocal lines than the customary four he'd been used to. In Waring's scores, interesting harmonies resulted from up to eight separate lines. Robert assimilated these complicated arrangements, his acute musical ear enabling him to rehearse choristers in songs that went over the airwaves.[8]

During these successes Shaw, by then permanently settled in New York, came to the attention of a music professor, who advised him to study at the Mannes School of Music. At that conservatory he would get the musical education he needed. Shaw's time at Mannes was brief. While there he took four lessons from a well-known European conductor on the staff, George Szell, who took little notice of a student whose unprepossessing demeanor, lack of piano technique, and ignorance of orchestral scores would have marked him as a nobody unworthy of any attention.[9]

Szell had a low opinion of conductors who weren't fine pianists.[10] Virtuosity at the keyboard was the only accepted way to demonstrate one's ability to sight-read orchestral scores and prove one's musicianship. In addition, he considered U.S.-trained conductors to be severely handicapped by their lack of experience in European opera houses. In Szell's eyes, Shaw, with his years at a small liberal arts college in California, was a musical cipher. Never having seen Shaw lead a chorus, he was unaware of his great talent and ambition. It was more than a decade before Szell had occasion to reverse his opinion.

After a brief stint in the navy, Shaw won a Guggenheim Fellowship for a year of concentrated musical study. And Fred Waring was left far behind when Shaw's Collegiate Chorale was hired to join forces with Toscanini's NBC Orchestra for Beethoven's Ninth Symphony and other choral-orchestral works broadcast by NBC. The high point of this collaboration came when Toscanini kissed Shaw on both cheeks after the young man had led a rehearsal of the Ninth's choral movement. Referring to their collaboration, Toscanini said, "In Robert Shaw I have at last found the maestro I have been looking for."[11]

Toscanini's pronouncement about Shaw sparked Szell's interest. He had been on the lookout for someone to whip the Cleveland Orchestra Chorus into shape. Observing that Shaw shared his obsession with creating great musical performances, he resolved to hire away Toscanini's favorite. In 1955 he succeeded. Shaw came to Cleveland.[12]

To capture his Cleveland choristers' interest and loyalty, Shaw began communicating with them via letters meant to galvanize and inform them prior to rehearsals. These letters enabled him to spend rehearsal time profitably with little talking. One longtime chorister, baritone Gerald Hughes, recalled Shaw's rehearsals:

> He was completely in the grip of the music and wanted to convey everything to us. He had a temper too. When he became upset about people coming to rehearsals unprepared, he would grab a pencil and snap it in two. There were times when he would have been justified in reprimanding someone for lack of attention or a blatant mistake. But he never attacked anyone personally. I remember one woman who wasn't paying attention and was throwing people off. Instead of insulting her he blamed himself, saying, "It's my fault for choosing you."[13]

Long before he was hired by Szell, Shaw had perfected his methods of teaching amateurs how to sing in his choruses. It's noteworthy that his ideas so closely mirrored Szell's. They both said the same thing about musical performance. "First, second, and third, it's rhythm, rhythm, rhythm."[14] Without rhythmic accuracy it's impossible to get one hundred orchestral musicians or two hundred singers to achieve clarity. Shaw's attention to detail was comparable to Szell's, and they both insisted on strict discipline in rehearsals. But the similarity ended there, because Shaw used a disarming "Aw shucks, I'm just a country boy" persona to bond with his choristers,[15] whereas Szell was a cultivated intellectual whose prodigious musical knowledge enabled him to dominate everyone.

Shaw's letters to his singers usually started with the salutation "Dear People." What followed would be a fascinating mix of the King James Bible, Cranmer's *Book of Common Prayer*, Robert Frost, Walt Whitman, Dylan Thomas, Rudyard Kipling, Moby Dick, the United States Constitution, jazz jargon, Shakespeare, Lincoln's speeches, and bits of comic strips. They had the desired effect. Here was their conductor communicating with them in colorfully unforgettable words.

One memorable Shaw letter was typed in the shape of a dagger.[16] It must have taken him quite a while to form the words into a pictorial threat. Its recipients were fascinated that their conductor was expressing himself graphically, and although it conveyed his disappointment in the previous night's rehearsal, it was received with amusement. Here was their Robert enjoying himself while letting off steam. Szell would never have sent such a letter; he never wrote to his orchestra players at all. But Shaw had no qualms about the familiar way he addressed his chorus. At rehearsals he exhorted, educated, threatened, and cajoled, using slangy phrases and even a few profanities guaranteed to get the group's attention and inspire them with the glory of the music.[17]

Great urgency was a regular part of each rehearsal. Shaw worked himself into a lather of sweat that flew in all directions. This sent his choristers a message: if their leader was giving his all, they should too. There were lighter moments. Shaw's sense of humor was usually quick to break through in moments of tension. And his loss of temper when he thought people weren't trying hard enough often was followed by a joke. One year his Christmas present to each chorus member was a tape recording of himself reading A. A. Milne's *The House at Pooh Corner*. Such a humorous gift was far from Szell's annual pocket datebook to his players.[18]

In unfortunate contrast to the adulation Shaw enjoyed from his chorus members was the daunting reception he received from the Cleveland Orchestra players. Ever alert to any inadequacy on the podium, they sensed immediately that Shaw had rarely conducted an orchestra, knew little about orchestral instruments, and certainly knew little or nothing about the standard orchestral works. Within a few minutes of Shaw's first rehearsal with them, he saw what he had gotten into. Long repressed by Szell, some of the musicians dared to cut loose and show their worst sides, asking questions intended to bring out Shaw's ignorance of instrumental technique and indulging in other disruptive juvenility. His excessive sweating was noted with glee, and his inability to control them resulted in rehearsals totally at odds with the orchestra's public image as a well-disciplined group.[19]

Hoping to win their friendship, he abased himself by taking Christmas gifts to various members of the orchestra. Among those he tried to placate in this way was oboist Marc Lifschey, who usually made Shaw's life miserable whenever he appeared on the podium. Showing little sympathy for what Shaw had to suffer from him and his colleagues, Lifschey told about his once-a-year visitor. "Every Christmas Eve Uncle Bob in his Santa hat rings my doorbell with a present. All the principal woodwind guys get something. Probably we aren't the only ones he brings gifts to. It's pathetic."[20]

Shaw's gifts were an obvious plea for better treatment by the orchestra members. To no avail. Every rehearsal with the orchestra was an unnerving trial. Like bratty schoolboys, they were out to get him. Even as he became more skilled as an orchestral conductor, some players managed to constantly remind him he was no Szell. Before one rehearsal, keyboardist Joela Jones noticed his tension as he waited to face the incorrigibles. "While we were talking backstage, he was beating his baton against his leg. He was so wound up and nervous because he had to go out there and be insulted again."[21]

There was, however, one musician who deeply respected Shaw and voiced his admiration: Szell himself. After Szell conducted one Saturday night concert with a Shaw-prepared chorus he said, "It is astonishing, like some sort of magic. Simply by the quality of the beat one can make an instant change in tone, tempo, balance or color. This chorus is more responsive than an orchestra."[22]

Shaw's methods with his chorus were similar to Szell's with an orchestra. He had refined a technique of achieving clarity through rests—split seconds of silence—that separated words and phrases. Joela Jones recalled some of the ways Shaw trained his chorus:

> As far as I know, Shaw was the first choral conductor to come up with a special way of getting his singers to enunciate words. For example, with final consonants the sound had to be cut off at an exact moment, which made a precise ending. Two hundred people doing that perfectly together was a revelation. It clarified the words. There were exercises he led them through to achieve that. He had exercises for vowels too. The first rehearsal of a piece wouldn't be singing the work as it was written but, instead, breaking up words into syllables. These cutoffs at the ends of notes and words were really like inserting tiny rests.
>
> Another of his ideas concerned the visual aspect of music. Reasoning that the mere sight of printed flats in their music sheets was causing many in the chorus to sing flat, he had me transpose the piano accompaniment up a half step higher. After they had learned the piece in the higher key, he had them go back down to the original key. With the higher sound in their ears, they would resist the tendency to go flat.[23]

For years Szell had routinely inserted rests into the orchestra members' parts. Similarly, Shaw insisted that his singers mark up their music with reminders about cutoffs. That was one of his ideas for achieving clarity, and he had thought of it long before he ever came to Cleveland. This attention to detail was one of the things that made his rehearsals fascinating.[24]

Jones recalled Shaw's singing:

> He didn't have a good-sounding voice himself. It wasn't a trained voice. It didn't sound as if he'd ever had voice lessons. When he demonstrated what

he wanted, he usually sang quite loudly without a nice tone quality. But he got his ideas across, and he knew what singers had to do with their mouths and throats to achieve results. He wanted them to project by opening their mouths really wide, using their "double hinge." That's what he called the muscle at the back of the jaw. I'd thought of trying to do that myself to understand what it felt like, but I didn't because I was afraid of dislocating my jaw. Anyway they knew what he was talking about, and they could do it. He was as great with his chorus as Szell was with his orchestra. In those Shaw-Szell years, performances of the great masses and requiems were really thrilling.[25]

Shaw's humanitarian principles especially appealed to baritone Gerald Hughes, who joined the Cleveland Orchestra Chorus in 1956 and stayed for fifty years. He had come to singing by way of church choirs and education at Goshen College in Indiana. "When I joined Shaw's Cleveland Orchestra Chorus I found out Shaw always wanted as many diverse groups in his choir as possible because he thought different races and ethnicities enriched the sound. He was against prejudice and intolerance. That's the kind of person he was."[26]

In December 1967 the chorus and orchestra presented, for the first time in Cleveland, Handel's rarely heard opera *Semele* with Shaw on the podium. It starred famous soprano Beverly Sills in the title role and lasted more than two hours. Nobody in Cleveland anticipated that this unknown work dredged out of obscurity by musicologists would be anything much. It wasn't until opening night that Clevelanders realized what the role of Semele entailed. It was full of trills, roulades, and leaps into the stratosphere, all of which Sills tossed off with aplomb. One high point of the evening came when she sang "Myself I shall adore if I persist in gazing" while looking into an imaginary mirror. She traded phrases with the concertmaster, the two of them soaring like larks around each other, Sills producing trills that were iridescent shimmers.

The audience was startled. This was Handel? The Handel of *The Messiah*? That bewigged baroque composer had written music for passionate seduction scenes that included words about breasts? Heretofore *Semele* had only been known as the work that contained the serenely lovely aria "Where E'er You Walk." It was clear that, in *Semele*, Handel had written something salacious— so steamy that it had been withdrawn from a London stage after only three performances in 1744. Now here it was in Cleveland in 1967 being sung by a curvaceous redhead who was obviously savoring her words. There was little doubt about what was going on in the story; the printed text in the program provided the juicy details.

Shaw had a tremendous success that night, and the orchestra members had to admit it. Never mind that he wasn't a great orchestra conductor. He was a great musician.[27]

In 1960 Shaw programmed *The St. Matthew Passion,* written by his favorite composer, Johann Sebastian Bach. This gigantic composition, lasting more than three hours while telling the story of the crucifixion as narrated in the Bible by St. Matthew, is one of the most moving of all religious works. Bach himself in 1740, a full ten years after he had composed it, realizing he had created something unusual, carefully copied the words and notes on special paper, using a ruler, compass, and two colors of ink.[28]

Shaw spent weeks making a translation of the German words into English so everyone in the audience could understand what was being sung. Given to making large statements about the works he conducted, he proclaimed in one letter to his chorus that "it is entirely possible that out of the whole history of the Western World Bach is the single greatest creative genius. Michelangelo might touch him in sculpture (though I'd have other preferences here). Who would it be in literature? R.S."[29]

The orchestra and chorus gave two performances of the *St. Matthew Passion* at Severance Hall, recording it soon after. One orchestra member who listened to the impressive recording was fascinated by Bach's mating of music and words to tell the story of the crucifixion. After thunder and lightning from the darkened heavens, there's an electrifying moment when the chorus proclaims, "Truly this was the Son of God." In wonder at the masterpiece, the bemused player, a confirmed atheist, said to his wife, "This almost makes you believe the story."[30] Together, Bach, Shaw, the soloists, orchestra, and chorus had rendered those ancient biblical events real.

CHAPTER 18

The Musicians' Insurrection

DESPITE SZELL'S TYRANNY, there had never been an insurrection within the ranks of the Cleveland Orchestra. They understood that Szell knew the music better than any of them, that he was a dedicated leader, that he was rarely wrong and that he demanded a degree of perfection benefiting them all. If he corrected a musician, it was for the musician's own good. But once in a while he got wound up berating a player, and it produced no good whatsoever. Everyone remembered the notorious drum fiasco in Bartók's *Concerto for Orchestra* when Szell came close to firing the entire percussion section because he made them all so nervous that they played badly. Several years later he created an even more dramatic incident.

The orchestra's four bassoonists were all fine players, but one of them noticeably stood out. Second bassoonist Vaclav Laksar was in a perpetual stew owing to his hair-trigger temper and propensity for accidents. As a result, he was frequently embroiled in lawsuits and constantly wary. His colleagues, knowing this, gave him a wide berth, and Szell probably knew of his mishaps. This situation was the origin of a major upset between the musicians, Szell, and the orchestra's management.

One morning during a tense rehearsal, Szell worked himself into a truculent mood that was making everybody miserable. When he heard something out of tune in the bassoons, he stopped the music and pried into the cause. There were three men sitting calmly in the bassoon section and a fourth one with an apprehensive expression on his face. Laksar. Yes. That must be where the trouble lay.

Szell started with a sarcastic remark and then tore into Laksar with progressively abusive language. The other orchestra members shifted nervously in their seats. Who was going to be next? At last Laksar was rescued by the personnel manager, who announced intermission. Szell stalked off stage, and the moment he was out of sight, concerned players tried to soothe their miserable colleague. But they knew, and Laksar knew, he was probably going to be fired.[1]

Downstairs in the locker room all hands gathered to sympathize with Laksar. The whole thing was deplorable. It could have been any one of them. Something had to be done. They decided they would return upstairs but, instead of taking their places on stage, they would sit out front in the audience seats. And they would not return to the stage until Szell apologized for his horrible abuse of Laksar and his abusive language in general. The personnel manager was delegated to relay their ultimatum to Szell.

Many minutes passed while Szell considered his options. This had never before happened—his whole orchestra arrayed against him. They seemed not to realize he had only their good at heart and were taking no account of his fatherly concern.

More minutes passed. The eating of crow takes time. At last, common sense prevailed. Szell left his office, walked to the front of the stage, stood not on the podium but beside it, and addressed his mutinous crew.

None of them can now remember his exact words. There was a waffling explanation delivered in slightly placating tones. A vague air of contrition mixed with genial phrases indicated he understood their concern and hoped they could all now return to their places and get on with it. The musicians looked doubtfully at one another, trying to decide whether what they were hearing was what they'd demanded. Possibly. Hard to tell. He was saying something though. Perhaps it was best to interpret it as an apology. So they filed back onstage.[2]

Thereafter, Laksar received no more abuse. And the orchestra members had gotten a taste of victory. If they stood together maybe they could prevail in a far more important struggle: a battle over their working conditions.

For years the players had endured tours involving long bus rides, cheap hotels—during their New York appearances they were frequently quartered at the rundown Wellington, where they shared the elevator with resident prostitutes—and paltry per diem.[3] In addition, they coped with summers of unemployment and a local musicians' union that turned a blind eye to all of it. These were the prevailing conditions from the beginning of the Cleveland Orchestra. Only a few principal players made a living wage. The others had to teach and work part-time at various nonmusical jobs during the hours they weren't playing in the orchestra. And they had to maintain expertise on their instruments through daily practice.

Finally, in April 1963, those players who didn't occupy first chair positions—and therefore received minimum scale—selected a committee charged with improving their lot. Told by management this subversive committee could not hold meetings inside Severance Hall, it met instead in the vestibule of the hall's side entrance. There, huddled in overcoats against the April cold, they agreed on a course of action.[4] It involved calling a players' strike if the orchestra management didn't meet their demands.

Their resolution wasn't popular with some of the musicians. What if management simply let them strike indefinitely? How long could they hold out before succumbing? Who really needs classical music anyway? It's a luxury commodity paid for by the rich.

Ignoring the timid among them, the players' committee went ahead and presented a list of its demands to management. It included higher salaries, better working conditions, the right to ratify their own master contract, protection against firing without just cause, and a voice in the hiring of new players.

The orchestra's board of trustees contended that the Cleveland Musicians' Union held the key to contract negotiations. Local 4 had always negotiated with the Cleveland Orchestra management; union officers, not the orchestra players, ratified the master contract. The trustees admitted orchestra salaries were low but argued that the cost of living in Cleveland was correspondingly low. Money shouldn't be the object of an arts enterprise anyhow. Classical music is nonprofit; it's not a business. Besides, there was no more money to be had. And where was the gratitude for providing the musicians with a beautiful hall in which to play? Where was the gratitude for providing them with one of the world's greatest conductors?

In the middle of this hornet's nest was Szell. Some of the very conditions that had led him to choose Cleveland as the city where he could accomplish his goal of creating a world-class orchestra were paradoxically now working against him: A board of trustees that had given him unlimited authority to hire and fire. Patrons whose great wealth enabled them to underwrite a costly cultural jewel. A musicians' union that didn't protect its Cleveland Orchestra members. And a body of players so fearful for their jobs they were afraid to speak out.

Now, however, the musicians realized that they, too, had power. They had demonstrated their ability to stand as a body and protest Szell's harassment of them and the orchestra's second bassoonist. As a world-famous orchestra, they knew that they deserved better pay and that they could change their poor working conditions if they presented a united front.[5]

It was a pivotal moment in the orchestra's history—and a dangerous one. The board of trustees and Szell knew things could not go on as before.

Adella Prentiss Hughes, 1869–1949, founder of the Cleveland Orchestra in 1918. Photo courtesy of the Cleveland Orchestra Archives.

An impeccably clad George Szell in the 1950s. He was always neatly and appropriately dressed in custom-made suits and jackets. Photo by Editta Sherman, courtesy of the Cleveland Orchestra Archives.

Austrian artist Victor Tischler's oil portrait of glamorous twenty-four-year-old Helene Schultz, who, years later, became Szell's second wife. Photo courtesy of John Teltsch.

The Cleveland Orchestra's home, Severance Hall, which opened in 1932. It is considered one of the nation's finest concert halls. Photo by Peter Hastings, courtesy of the Cleveland Orchestra Archives.

Szell's fourteen-room brick home in Shaker Heights, Ohio. Szell's studio, with its upright piano, was on the second floor, third window from the right. His grand piano occupied the bay window area of the first-floor living room. Photo courtesy of present owners, Mr. and Mrs. James Diener.

Szell posed outside Severance Hall with his new Buick. He loved powerful cars and routinely drove over the speed limit. Photo courtesy of the Cleveland Orchestra Archives.

Helene Szell, Cleveland mayor Anthony Celebrezze Sr., and George Szell at a presentation ceremony. The photo shows Helene's Parisian gown and aristocratic bearing. Photo courtesy of the Cleveland Orchestra Archives.

Joseph Gingold, the Cleveland Orchestra's beloved concertmaster from 1947 to 1960. He left the orchestra to become became head of the violin department at the University of Indiana. Photo by Robert Carman, courtesy of the Cleveland Orchestra Archives.

Principals of the woodwind section in 1963. *Clockwise from top left:* Robert Marcellus, clarinet, photographer unknown; Maurice Sharp, flute, photo by Rebman; George Goslee, bassoon, photo by Peter Hastings; Marc Lifschey, oboe, photo by Robert Carman. Photos courtesy of the Cleveland Orchestra Archives.

Principals of the Cleveland Orchestra's brass section in the Szell era. *Clockwise from top left:* Ronald Bishop, tuba, photo by Herbert Ascherman Jr.; Robert Boyd, trombone, photo by Geoffrey Landesman; Bernard Adelstein, trumpet, photo by Herbert Ascherman Jr.; Myron Bloom, French horn, photo by Geoffrey Landesman. Photos courtesy of the Cleveland Orchestra Archives.

Szell manifesting his joy in music while rehearsing the Cleveland Orchestra in Leningrad during the orchestra's eleven-week USSR-European tour in 1965. Photo by Oleg Makarov, courtesy of the Cleveland Orchestra Archives.

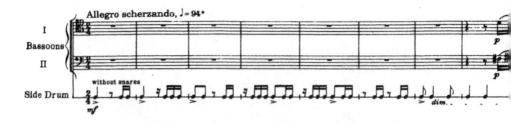

Top: The beginning of the second movement of Bartók's
Concerto for Orchestra. Bottom: Cloyd Duff, principal timpanist
with the Cleveland Orchestra from 1942 to 1981. He once defied
Szell, belligerently banging out the above measures, thus saving
the jobs of several percussionists. Photo by Julian Apsel Studio,
courtesy of the Cleveland Orchestra Archives.

Principal harpist Alice Chalifoux played in the Cleveland Orchestra from 1931 to 1974. In the absence of women's dressing rooms, she made do with her harp case. Photo by Geoffrey Landesman, courtesy of the Cleveland Orchestra Archives.

Pianist Joela Jones rehearsing with Szell and the Cleveland Orchestra in 1967. In 1968 Szell created the position of principal keyboardist of the orchestra especially for her. Photo by Peter Hastings, courtesy of the Cleveland Orchestra Archives.

Famous choral conductor Robert Shaw (*far right*) rehearsing the Cleveland Orchestra Chorus. Photo by Peter Hastings, courtesy of the Cleveland Orchestra Archives.

Shaw's threatening dagger letter to his chorus members in 1965. From the collection of baritone Gerald Hughes. Reproduced with the permission of Thomas Lawson Shaw.

Atlanta, Georgia
January 14, 1965
vvvvvvvvvvvvvvv
We might as well
get right down to
the nitty-gritty
of it. Last Mon-
day night's re-
hearsal was a de-
bacle, completely
unworthy of the
Cleveland Orchestra Chorus.
The first reading of the Britten War Requiem was superior in every way. The first rehearsal of the season —
even with the attendant disruptions of new member regis-
tration, music allotment and exchange of greetings— was
better motivated, better mannered and more constructive.
This chorus is not a social club.
Such satisfactions as we gain because of musical excellence are
achieved through self discipline
and undivided responsibility.
The fact that we enjoy our col-
laborator's company is a splen-
did bonus, but even this would
disappear did we not address
ourselves firstly, secondly,
and throughout to the music.
/// Rehearsals of a chorus
of this calibre should not
ever be primarily a place
for note-learning. The
problems of ensemble are
complex enough. Most of
the note-learning should
be done at home. Monday
night should be an oc-
casion for pooling our
skills and knowledge,
not our ignorances.
/// Look at our re-
hearsal schedule.
Obviously we will
have to concentrate
on the Beethoven
Ninth Symphony. It
should be sung
from memory in
Cleveland and
New York. ///
Consider how
little time
there is fol-
lowing that to
conclude prep-
arations on
the Britten
War Requiem
— far too
little to
allow the
lack of at-
tention
by which
l a s t
Monday
night's
rehear-
sal was
betray
ed. //
//So
them
t t
R

Robert Conrad, announcer; cofounder of radio station WCLV, Cleveland's classical music station; and member of the board of trustees of the Cleveland Orchestra. Photo by Roger Mastroianni, courtesy of Robert Conrad.

Architect Peter van Dijk, who designed the Cleveland Orchestra's Blossom Pavilion, built in 1968. He worked for Eero Saarinen before coming to Cleveland. Photo courtesy of Westlake/Reed/Leskosky/ van Dijk.

Top: Structural engineer Richard Gensert, who worked with architect Peter van Dijk on the Blossom Pavilion design. Photo courtesy of Carrol Gensert. *Bottom:* Structural engineer Miklos Peller, who designed the Blossom Pavilion superstructure. Photo courtesy of Miklos Peller.

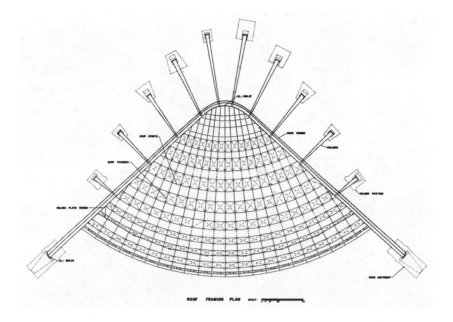

Top: Structural engineer Miklos Peller's scale drawing for the web of trusses holding up the Blossom Pavilion roof. Drawing courtesy of Miklos Peller. *Bottom:* Aerial view of construction of Blossom Pavilion showing the arch-beam held up by ten columns. Photo courtesy of Westlake/Reed/Leskosky/van Dijk.

Architect Peter van Dijk's 1966 presentation of his model for Blossom Pavilion. In the Cleveland Orchestra boardroom, standing left to right: acoustician Christopher Jaffe, assistant conductor Louis Lane, conductor George Szell, architect Peter van Dijk. Photo by Peter Hastings, courtesy of the Cleveland Orchestra Archives.

The three men primarily responsible for the creation of Blossom Music Center. Left to right: architect Peter van Dijk, conductor George Szell, president of the Cleveland Orchestra board of trustees Frank Joseph. Photos courtesy of Westlake /Reed/Leskosky/van Dijk.

The most dramatic moment in the construction of Blossom Pavilion: the enormous keystone being lowered into position between the sides of the giant arch-beam. The gigantic sections met within three-eighths of an inch and were jacked together by workmen standing dangerously close to the edges. Photo by Imperial Studios, courtesy of Miklos Peller.

Blossom Pavilion, seen from above, its vast roof sheltering more than forty-five hundred people. Its originality and bold simplicity of design have earned it a place among the world's great structures. Photo courtesy of the Cleveland Orchestra Archives.

An ailing Szell acknowledging audience applause after the orchestra's final concert in Tokyo in May 1970. On the extreme right is principal violist Abraham Skernik, Szell's closest friend among the players. Photo by Peter Hastings, courtesy of the Cleveland Orchestra Archives.

CHAPTER 19

Picketing and Resolution

SZELL HAD ALWAYS BEEN AWARE that the musicians' salaries were too low and that working conditions needed to be improved. The short season meant that most players needed to take on summer jobs. Some of his efforts on the players' behalf, however, met with a lack of enthusiasm from the board of trustees. They had already given hundreds of thousands of dollars to keep the orchestra running and had solicited large donations from their friends. There was a limit to how much money they could raise. Among themselves they agreed that the musicians' demands were unrealistic. If they thought their working conditions were unacceptable, they could simply leave. Other, more sensible, musicians would be glad to take their places. Nobody was irreplaceable except for the maestro himself.

When his orchestra began hemorrhaging players in the early sixties, Szell had initially let matters run their course. Just one or two at first—violinists and cellists going to greener pastures.[1] Nothing to be alarmed about. But he couldn't bear knowing some of his handpicked principals were planning to leave, the ones he had connived for, stolen from other orchestras, and cajoled into coming to Cleveland by telling them they were joining the world's greatest orchestra.[2] They were the ones he had hectored, molded, and encouraged. If all those key players left, they would be taking pieces of his magnificent creation with them. He was nearly seventy. Never again would he have the time and energy to rebuild the orchestra. The losses would be a permanent setback.

So he played the card he had kept up his sleeve for twenty years. He reminded the board about the crucial clause in his contract that gave him the right to terminate it at any time. This warning focused the attention of the board as nothing else had. It was one thing to lose a few musicians. It was quite another to lose their very own genius, the man who had given them what was being proclaimed as one of the greatest orchestras in the world. They knew it was time to address something their maestro had long been advocating: year-round employment for the musicians.

In a 1966 letter to manager Barksdale and meant to be relayed to the trustees, Szell stated his wishes for a summer venue for the Cleveland Orchestra. Cleverly not mentioning his struggling musicians, he instead appealed to the trustees' pride. His request called for something impressive and aesthetic, something no other orchestra owned, something that would be unique. While acknowledging the uninspiring Cleveland landscape, he proposed how it could be transcended. Specifying the large amounts of money that would have to be spent, he emphasized two of his obsessions: rightness and quality. At the same time he anticipated the probable concerns of the trustees by stressing that they should think in large terms because half-measures would simply result in an imitation of what other orchestras had.[3]

His letter initiated a project that would take two years, cost more than eight million dollars, and involve people and things Szell had never concerned himself with. When he wrote the words that set in motion a costly chain of events, he had no idea his proposal would bring someone new into his life, someone as visionary as himself: an architect he had never heard of.

The news that a summer season was being planned and that the plan included an enormous multimillion-dollar building was received with mixed feelings in the musicians' locker room. It was wonderful that they would have steady summer employment, but what about their meager wages? If there were millions for a building why weren't there millions for themselves?

Some of the players were enthusiastic about the plan for a summer home, however, and four of them decided to help publicize it. Taking their instruments, music stands, and folding chairs out to the chosen site, they were photographed playing a string quartet in its vast meadow. The October 9, 1966, issue of the *Akron Beacon Journal* ran the picture. It informed the public that something interesting was in the works, something completely new.

As the days went on, section players in the orchestra veered between elation at the idea of a summer season and irritation with their hardscrabble lives. Their small salary raises never kept pace with the raises enjoyed by

the other Big Five orchestras. They were The World-Famous Clevel
chestra, not a collection of provincial third-raters. Where was the n
reflection of that?[4]

This outlook wasn't shared by many of the principal players, whose salaries
were higher than the section players and whose respect for Szell kept them
fairly content.[5] In contrast, violinists, violists, cellists, and bassists who had to
play in unison with the others in their sections never experienced the glory of
solos and recognition from their famous leader. Szell rarely addressed scale
players by their first names, never chatted with them in his office, hardly spoke
to them at all unless to criticize them for some misdemeanor or to settle an
argument. Dissatisfaction with their inferior status and low wages caused
angry venting in the locker room. The most persuasive talkers among them
corralled the others into a vote that revealed the majority to be in favor of
walking out. It was the first time the musicians had ever dared such a thing,
and many were scared they'd be doing themselves out of a job. Nevertheless,
on September 11, 1966, all stayed home, including the principal players, who
had been persuaded to support their underpaid colleagues. The entire orchestra, garbed in their concert attire, then began picketing Severance Hall.[6]

Exacerbating the situation was the stance of the board of trustees, which
consisted of wealthy businessmen and lawyers. Adroit with finances, their
eyes on the bottom line, they were united in their efforts to keep expenses
down. After all, a summer season would automatically raise the players' yearly
incomes. The musicians should focus on that. Ignoring, or unaware of, the
many hours of individual practice required for players to maintain their expertise and the hours that the woodwind players spent making reeds and
fixing their costly equipment, the trustees contended that a Cleveland Orchestra job consisting of only twenty hours of work a week—five rehearsals
and three concerts at Severance Hall—was a part-time position. Therefore
their salaries were more than adequate.

The musicians were incensed to hear their jobs were considered only part-
time. They knew better. The callused fingers of the string players and the
tired lips of the wind and brass players attested to their constant practice.
Nobody in the orchestra considered it a part-time job, not with Szell on the
podium noticing the slightest lapse in their playing. They hired a lawyer who
argued that the Cleveland Orchestra, as one of the Big Five, should receive
pay comparable to the other four in that exalted group. Management's lawyer responded by pointing out that the cost of living in Cleveland was much
lower than in New York, Philadelphia, Boston, and Chicago.[7]

The two bodies faced each other across a serious divide. Underlying the rift was a basic fact dating back centuries to the time of powerful rulers and their court musicians. Composers like Mozart and Haydn were lowly servants of royalty, and though they might eventually be hailed as geniuses, they shared some of the same working conditions as the humble players who executed their compositions.[8] With a few exceptions, most rulers looked upon music as simply a pleasant pastime, on the same order as games. This mindset was slightly altered when Beethoven appeared on the scene. But the view of musicians as mere entertainers persists. Few people comprehend the depth of feeling many musicians have for their art and the time they spend perfecting it. One Cleveland Orchestra violinist spoke of her dedication to music and her daily hours of practice. "It's my life's blood."[9] Echoing this passion but in different words, a woodwind player said, "Music is my religion."[10]

Such heartfelt convictions, held by many of the orchestra's musicians, were totally at odds with some trustees' view of the orchestra as mainly a high-status cultural amenity that enhanced Cleveland's reputation and attracted business. With the exception of board member Dorothy Humel, who had been a child prodigy pianist and knew the countless hours of practice and dedication necessary to excel in music, none of the members of the board of trustees had attained expertise on a musical instrument. Therefore they had little understanding of the deep feelings engendered by the players' lifelong devotion to their instruments and the musical masterpieces they performed.

Knowing he would have to break the stalemate, Szell intervened. He demanded that the management accede to some of the musicians' demands. What was he without his fine players? What were the trustees without an orchestra? What would they do with the fine building they were planning if there wasn't an orchestra to play in it?

With Szell's right-to-leave clause spurring them to action, the board did an about-face. Suddenly the negotiations became fruitful, and within a few days management granted a hike in wages. Minimum weekly salaries would go from $190 for the first season to $255 by the third season of the new contract with a guaranteed fifty-two-week season starting in 1968.[11]

The strike over, everyone returned to Severance Hall, and there was rejoicing that a new era had begun. In their relief, the musicians allowed some problems in their working conditions to be put on the back burner. Cleveland newspapers announced that concerts would immediately resume, that the Cleveland Orchestra members had accepted a new contract and that Szell would remain in Cleveland. There had been legitimate fears that he might leave because he regularly guest-conducted other major orchestras in the United States and Europe.

Down in the locker room, though, the atmosphere was slightly subdued. Although the musicians had achieved a victory, they certainly hadn't done it by themselves. Papa Szell had once more stepped in and asserted his authority. Years later, some of the musicians admitted he had saved them and spoke of their gratitude to the man who was their leader. As one musician put it, "He really was our father."[12]

CHAPTER 20

A Suitable Summer Site

HAVING ORDERED UP A summer home for the orchestra and settled a serious labor crisis, Szell left on his annual three-month European vacation.
Uncharacteristically, he said he wouldn't participate in the upcoming architectural project. It would all be left in the capable hands of associate conductor Louis Lane, manager Barksdale, and the trustees. Szell's stance was
prompted by his need to keep his summers free to relax in Europe, study the
scores of works he would conduct the following season, play golf, visit old
friends with Helene, and take sightseeing trips.

Szell loved to drive. Zooming at top speed on the Autobahn brought back
the exhilaration of his earlier years. He was a menace behind the wheel, and
Helene must have had nerves of steel to ride with him. Szell's vacations enabled him to return to Cleveland rested and renewed. And, too, the vacations
helped him stay healthy and able to shoulder the burdens of his position in
Cleveland.[1]

As the Szells motored about on their annual three-month European so-
journ, the orchestra's board of trustees took the first steps in response to Szell's
letter requesting a summer home for the orchestra. They formed committees
for planning, investigating possible sites, fund-raising, and the selection of
an architect.

The latter task was aided by architect Alexander Robinson, who was on
the orchestra's board of trustees. He with three others had formed the architectural firm of Garfield, Harris, Robinson and Schafer. (Partner Abram Gar-

field was the son of President James Garfield.) Moving among his influential friends, Abram Garfield had been invaluable in attracting commissions. It was his firm—now known as Schafer, Flynn and van Dijk—that was awarded the plum Cleveland Orchestra commission in 1966.[2] One of the firm's partners, thirty-seven-year-old Dutch émigré Peter van Dijk, was designated the architect of a project destined to become the talk of Cleveland.

The son of an engineer employed by Royal Dutch Shell Oil in a Dutch colony in Maracaibo, van Dijk spent his boyhood years being educated in Venezuela and Holland. He recalled the events that brought him to the United States.

> In early summer of 1939 my brother and I were at a boarding school in Holland. On September first the Germans invaded Poland, and England and France declared war on Germany. Despite assurances Holland would remain neutral, my parents decided we should leave. So we departed from Rotterdam on a ship displaying an enormous Dutch flag. The crew kept it brightly lit by searchlights at night so it would be obvious to aircraft and submarines that our ship was from a neutral country. But then on May tenth, 1940, Germany invaded Holland.[3]

His Dutch education enabled the teenager to skip several grades when he came to the United States, and van Dijk entered Cornell when he was sixteen to study electrical engineering. After two years, however, finding he was more interested in architecture, he interned with a local architect, sharpening pencils, running errands, and copying drawings of buildings. Then, having heard that the University of Oregon had a good architectural school, he enrolled there. The next four years would have been similar to those experienced by every budding architect but for one thing: he encountered Buckminster Fuller.[4]

> When I was a senior, Fuller came to the University of Oregon—it was 1953, the same year I became a U.S. citizen—for several weeks residency. His first lecture really excited all of us architecture students. He assigned us the project of constructing a geodesic dome, specifying that we use only materials we could acquire free within the United States. It was to be a lesson in organization. He wanted us to think big. The other students elected me as their leader, and we went at the task with great zeal, cutting the structural members from scrap plywood and using donated Mylar as a skin. Our geodesic dome measured thirty-six feet in diameter.
> Fuller's three-hour lectures every day were the source of our enthusiasm, and building this dome according to his principles heightened the experience

of his daily presence. He never ran out of ideas for lectures. He really gave off sparks. It was wonderful. Much of what he said had to do with understanding a problem and then searching for solutions.[5]

After graduating with a bachelor's degree, van Dijk was drafted into the army and spent two years without any exposure to architecture. Then the GI bill enabled him to attend graduate school at the Massachusetts Institute of Technology (MIT) in Cambridge. One of his professors there was the architect Louis Kahn. He and dean Pietro Belluschi were major influences on young van Dijk. His year in Cambridge brought him in contact with many noted architects and talented people, along with the diverse student bodies at MIT and nearby Harvard. It was an eye-opening experience, providing him with an encounter that was to set him solidly on his life's course.

Eero Saarinen visited MIT's architectural school one evening looking for assistants—like most other young architects we worked long hours—and Belluschi introduced me to him. He sat down next to my desk to talk. Then he surprised me by requesting that I draw him a horse in the few minutes he was away getting a drink of water. I had little knowledge of a horse's anatomy and wasn't sure how a horse's legs bent so I decided to comply with his request by sketching the horse from behind. That way I could just draw the tail and flanks with the mane and ears sticking up.

When Saarinen returned and saw the sketch—essentially a horse's ass—he was amused and impressed at how I'd carried out his request. So he hired me. I found out later that he chose most of his assistants the same way. He would talk to them and then ask them to draw something like a horse or a woman, giving them just a few minutes while he was supposedly away getting a drink of water. He wanted to see how well a person could do something spontaneous at his request.

This hiring was a decisive step in van Dijk's career because Saarinen was one of the world's leading architects, maintaining a studio in Michigan consisting of forty talented young architects, many of whom were technically experienced. Saarinen had advanced the science of building through the use of new materials and methods of construction and had many important commissions. It was considered a great honor to work for him. Van Dijk stayed with Saarinen for four years, making models involved in the design of famous buildings: Dulles Airport, the U.S. embassies in London and Oslo, the TWA terminal at Idlewild Airport (renamed John F. Kennedy Airport in 1963), the CBS building at 53rd Street in New York City, and the John Deere headquarters in Moline, Illinois.

In 1959, while working for Saarinen, van Dijk successfully applied for a Fulbright scholarship, which enabled him to travel around Europe for over a year, experiencing great buildings and being inspired by vernacular architecture, especially the Italian stone hill towns. He had married in the meantime, and with his wife and infant son he drove from place to place in their Opel station wagon, frequently camping to save money.

> It was wonderful to travel, free of duties and able to do as I wished. I covered about 25,000 miles on those travels, even going as far as Istanbul to see Hagia Sophia. I had physical reactions to many of the famous buildings and to outdoor spaces: St. Peter's, the Piazza San Marco in Venice, Siena, and famous Greek and Roman amphitheaters. Those amphitheaters are concentric circles of stone seating carved out of the hillsides. Being fairly steep, they form a kind of enclosure. Several Greek ones are magnificent sites. Syracuse in particular looks out to the sea. And the great amphitheater at Epidaurus seats fifteen thousand. All of them are tremendously large. They made a big impression on me.

Back in the United States, van Dijk returned to work for Saarinen. Around that time—the early sixties—three architectural firms were commissioned to design the one-million-square-foot Anthony Celebrezze Federal Building in downtown Cleveland. It was suggested to them that they get a person who worked for a well-known architect to be in charge of the project. Because his work with Saarinen was admired by each of the firms, van Dijk was hired. "I came to Cleveland, and when the federal building job turned out successfully, I was approached by all three of the architectural firms to join them. I decided to stay and become a partner in the firm of Schafer, Flynn and Associates."

What van Dijk needed to know—suitable conditions for a symphony orchestra's summer home—was not at first apparent to him. Then, at the behest of the search committee, he went with acoustician Chris Jaffe and manager Beverly Barksdale on a reconnaissance mission to various outdoor music festivals, including Tanglewood, the western Massachusetts summer home of the Boston Symphony—and Ravinia, the northern Illinois summer home of the Chicago Symphony. They were to discover that none of them was ideal for the orchestras or their audiences.

Van Dijk recalled some of their findings. "Tanglewood was a beautiful site, a popular place with its audiences, but it had been built on a shoestring. It had a dirt floor and the shed's low, flat roof made for mediocre acoustics. It rested on level terrain so the sightlines were bad, and interior columns blocked views of the stage."[6]

Hollywood Bowl and Denver's Red Rocks had a covered area for the musicians, but the audience was seated with no protection from the elements. Few of the sites had been planned as a satisfying art and nature experience. Of the various European summer music festivals, none provided ideal conditions either. Performances took place in buildings without air conditioning or in outdoor areas with makeshift stages and no roofs over the audience. Musicians, conductors, and audiences coped as best they could. Such makeshift structures were hardly likely to please Szell. His letter to the trustees had made that clear.

Before van Dijk came aboard, the project had a set of requirements specified by the orchestra's trustees and Szell. The structure should allow covered seating for five thousand people; it should have excellent acoustics; it should have unobstructed sightlines inside the pavilion and from the lawn; it should be within easy driving distance from Cleveland; it should be visually satisfying. And, of special importance for a symphony orchestra, there should be no noise from traffic or airplanes.

As van Dijk, Jaffe, and Barksdale traveled around to the various summer concert venues in the United States, observing the features of those facilities, they realized they would have to come up with their own solutions because none of the sites they visited were without serious flaws.

Jaffe was in his element because acoustics was his profession, but van Dijk had never before dealt with sound. He had to ask Jaffe where in a hall the acoustics were best. "That's easy," Jaffe answered. "The back of the second balcony. There's a megaphone effect; the loudest and clearest sound is up there. So maybe we should build the world's biggest balcony." Although he meant it as a joke, the two kicked around the idea, and it took hold as they—with Barksdale as fascinated onlooker—traded sketches while relaxing at the day's end.[7]

"I wish I still had some of those martini-stained napkins with our sketches," van Dijk reflects now. "They were the beginning of the design. I learned a lot from Chris Jaffe about what kinds of shapes and materials are needed for optimum sound, and we grew to like each other, becoming good friends."[8]

Meanwhile, the site committee, headed by local architect William Gould, hunted the outskirts of Cleveland trying to find a suitable spot. Gould recalled,

It took us over a year investigating places in seven counties and we were in despair that none of the places we saw were possibilities. We even took Szell up in a helicopter to look down on one of them. Unfortunately that day was very windy and the plane was shaking from side to side so we had to come down.

Just as I was about to give up, I got a phone call from a former student of mine at Kent State. He said he'd become a developer and had an option on a parcel of land close to Akron that we should visit. I went out to see it and immediately realized it was exactly what we had been seeking.

So everybody went out to see it, and then lots of people got involved. Someone on the Case faculty went to the site to test the noise level at night with sound meters; others checked out road and highway possibilities. The orchestra's summer home was originally planned to be smaller, but president of the board of trustees Frank Joseph was wise enough to know they needed a lot of land. He advised expanding the plan from the original five hundred acres to eight hundred acres. Joseph did a magnificent job directing the project.[9]

Van Dijk visited their choice and was gratified to see that the site's bowl-shaped configuration was similar to those of famous amphitheaters he'd seen in Greece and Italy. "It was a perfect site for an outdoor concert hall," van Dijk remembers thinking. "I knew they had found the spot."[10]

Contrary to what some other architects at the time were doing, van Dijk had no signature style. Nor did his mentor Eero Saarinen. Both of them practiced architecture as problem solving. Because van Dijk was young, he didn't have a body of work that was his calling card. But he had in mind the famous Greek and Roman amphitheaters he had visited years before. A megaphone effect is demonstrable at many of them, including Epidaurus, where a marble dropped onstage can be clearly heard fifty-five tiers of seats away. None of those places, however, had roofs.

In problem-solving mode, van Dijk pondered the megaphone effect with Jaffe. If the audience was sitting in "the world's biggest balcony" made possible by a steeply inclined floor, the sound would be directed toward them by a large fan-shaped wood shell over the stage.

As van Dijk got to work, the project took on great magnitude. The building would measure 475 feet from side to side—longer than a football field. The roof covering both the stage and the audience would measure more than an acre. Van Dijk already knew there must not be interior columns impeding sightlines. That meant an enormous clear span would have to be supported—somehow—without them. The strictures against interior columns that intrude upon sightlines gave van Dijk pause. Without such support, what would hold up the vast roof? While considering various ways of providing a clear span over such volume, a few things came together in his mind. What emerged was a unique idea: a single tilted arch holding up the entire roof.[11]

It's safe to say that nowhere in the world at the time did there exist a tilted arch supporting an enormous roof.[12] Furthermore, van Dijk decided this arch wouldn't be *inside* the building. It would be on the *outside*, its ends embedded in massive chunks of concrete buried in the ground, its mighty weight supported by ten exterior columns acting like flying buttresses.

This daring concept needed to become reality via structural engineering, and here van Dijk was lucky. He already knew a fine structural engineer, Richard Gensert, from the days when they both had offices in the same downtown building. Gensert was enthusiastic about working on an innovative project. Not only was he intrigued by van Dijk's concept, he also was a great fan of the Cleveland Orchestra and was a regular audience member for concerts in Severance Hall.[13]

The two men began what proved to be a happy and fruitful collaboration. Together with van Dijk's associate Ron Straka, acoustician Chris Jaffe, and Gensert's assistant Miklos Peller, the team refined the models. Their sixth and final effort convinced nearly everyone on the orchestra's board of trustees that it embodied every attribute they and Szell had specified. The concept was impressive but, just to be sure, they wanted an older, more experienced architect to pass final judgment. They invited dean of the school of architecture at MIT, Pietro Belluschi, to come to Severance Hall. He studied the model and exclaimed, "It's wonderful."[14] His enthusiastic endorsement banished any doubts. In van Dijk they had a winner. It was time to show the scale model to Szell.

The model captured Szell's interest when it was unveiled in the boardroom of Severance Hall. Recalling his initial meeting with one of the world's greatest conductors, van Dijk remembered his nervousness while awaiting the maestro's appearance.

> I didn't have much experience with presentations and especially not with someone famous. I knew who he was, having attended a few Cleveland Orchestra concerts in Severance Hall, though not very many because I had a young family to support and architects don't make much money in their early years. Szell's austere stage presence made me a bit apprehensive. But he came into the room, greeted me in Dutch, and shook my hand. It was gratifying that he had gone to the trouble of learning some Dutch to put me at ease.[15]

Also present at that decisive unveiling were acoustician Jaffe, associate conductor Lane, and several members of the orchestra's board of trustees. All were fascinated by the model before them.

During his first few minutes of inspecting the model, Szell came to the realization that he was confronting an unusual design. It resembled nothing he had ever seen. Obviously the man standing beside him was no ordinary architect. It was possible young van Dijk had conceived something destined to become an unrivaled and unique structure.[16]

Szell's experiences with concert halls throughout the United States, Europe, and South America and his stints guest-conducting at various summer music festivals allowed him to assess van Dijk's creation. He succumbed to the striking originality of its design, which incorporated acoustical solutions, unobstructed sightlines, and seamless integration into the landscape. Van Dijk's concept seemed timeless, far from a cliché. Caught up in the lure of the miniature structure before him, Szell changed his mind about keeping his distance from the project. His curiosity got the best of him. He wanted to participate in every decision.

Around this time the Ford Foundation decided to help struggling musicians in U.S. symphony orchestras while enabling audiences to experience classical music in a casual setting. It announced it would give two million dollars each to twenty of the nation's best orchestras, the money to be spent on summer orchestra festivals. The Cleveland Orchestra was one of the lucky recipients. The timeliness of the grant was perfect. It was as if Szell had ordained it. There was a caveat: the Ford money had to be matched by an equal sum from each orchestra.[17]

Energized by this gift out of the blue, the orchestra's trustees gave a fundraising dinner at the exclusive Hunt Club in Hunting Valley. The invited guests listened while van Dijk addressed them and showed his model for the proposed building. Then Chris Jaffe acquainted them with various acoustical facts.[18] After these presentations, board president Frank Joseph delivered a speech appealing to everyone's civic pride. The room hummed with enthusiasm. Immediately stepping up to the plate were euphoric members of the wealthy Blossom family, who pledged to match the Ford Foundation grant. In return, the summer home of the Cleveland Orchestra would be named Blossom in their honor.[19]

All that was catnip to another zealot, member of the board Dorothy Humel, who realized the project was rising to unprecedented heights. The summer home for the orchestra promised to be a building the likes of which the world had never seen. Szell had decreed it; a brilliant architect had designed it; the board had signed off on it.

Dorothy Humel was one of the orchestra's most ardent supporters. In her late teens her beauty and musical talent had so impressed her teacher, concert pianist Jose Iturbi, that he asked her to marry him.[20] He had gone to Hollywood to star in a movie and Dorothy visited him and surveyed the scene. It wasn't to her liking; she had other ambitions. She turned him down and returned to her home in Shaker Heights determined to play a major role in her city's cultural life.

For Humel, culture meant music, and music meant the Cleveland Orchestra. She had soloed several times with the orchestra in her prodigy years, and the thrill of being allied with it had never left her.[21] The wealth at her disposal as treasurer of her family's construction business and her commitment to the orchestra had propelled her ascent to membership on its board of trustees.

After the fund-raising dinner, Dorothy couldn't wait to get home and start looking through her list of donors. With van Dijk's model aglow in her mind's eye, she went into high gear the very next day. Telephones began ringing in the mansions of Shaker Heights. It was Dorothy on the line, inviting her friends to dinners and other functions, all with the purpose of getting them to add considerably to the money they had already given.

CHAPTER 21

Blossom's Creators

IT WAS VAN DIJK'S GREAT LUCK that Gensert had on his staff Miklos Peller, a brilliant young Hungarian structural engineer who had been one of the student insurgents protesting the 1956 Soviet occupation of Hungary. Peller, knowing his actions would result in a prison term or worse,[1] had made a daring escape through the landmine-infested border between Hungary and Austria. After enduring a stormy ten-day Atlantic crossing to New York—arriving amid New Year's Eve fireworks—he met and came to stay with his uncle who lived in Cleveland's Hungarian neighborhood.[2]

In Cleveland sixteen-year-old Peller resumed his education. Although he hadn't finished his third year in gymnasium, the Hungarian equivalent of high school, he was so advanced in science and mathematics that he was accepted into Case School of Applied Design. Several of the courses there were taught by structural engineer Richard Gensert, who soon realized that his new student was extraordinary and would be a great addition to his firm. He hired him, and Peller proved his worth, producing analysis and design, meticulous scale drawings of details, and clever elevations.

One day Gensert, busy with many commissions, returned from a meeting with van Dijk. Saying to Peller, "I've got a job for you," he assigned to his young assistant the drawings and calculations for Blossom.[3] Peller felt confident he could handle such a project. There were time constraints, however, that made for a grueling schedule that he and the other assistants faced.

"The Musical Arts Association wanted the building to be completed for a gala opening on July 19, 1968. Turner Construction Company was the contractor, and there were a lot of subcontractors. We were all concerned with meeting the deadline. I remember the hardships and strain because of that rigid time frame."

Much of the project involved doing things that had never been done before. Peller's challenges came from van Dijk's spectacular vision: an enormous fan-shaped structure measuring 475 feet from left to right, with a roof suspended from a gigantic tilted arch. The arch would be supported by huge exterior columns, the structure's sides open enough that the audience would be outdoors yet protected from the weather.

Peller listed some of the structure's unusual elements:

> The Blossom building was based on acoustics. The clear span, as van Dijk specified, was column-free in its interior. It was probably the first large building that utilized steel pipes as major structural members instead of the usual I-beams. And it was the largest music hall of its kind in the United States.
>
> I thought of the pavilion as a gigantic musical instrument with the musicians and audience seated inside. Because I played the piano and organ, the musical aspect of the project really appealed to me.[4]

In speaking of what he had done, Peller described some elements he had designed:

> The hinges I specified at the bases of the ten columns supporting the giant arch are something you find on a lot of bridges, enabling them to flex with temperature changes. The arch needed stability. I solved that by designing it in a trapezoid shape. It tapers to the axis while at the same time leaning slightly inward so rainwater falling on its surface runs off to the gutter. That keeps rusty water from staining the sides of the building.[5]

The trapezoidal arch was so massive and long that it had to be made in forty-foot sections. A foundry in Tennessee forged the sections, which were brought to the Blossom site on flatbed trucks. The lower sections were large enough for two men to stand upright, side-by-side, inside them.[6]

While recounting the steps necessary to turn van Dijk's concept into reality, Peller shed light on Blossom's beginning:

> Before any construction could take place, geo-technical engineer David Lewin had to take soil samples to discover whether the ground would support such a gigantic structure. Drills boring down eighty feet came up with mixtures of

clay and glacial till. This meant that pilings would have to be driven deep into the ground to support the ten-by-twenty-foot concrete abutments on which the ends of the arch would rest. After that was done, Turner Construction began excavating for the foundations.

The superstructure determines the size and type of foundations. So the pavilion's outlines had to be decided first. I had help with various geometric calculations. An engineer-detailer named John Hollifield took my drawings and dissected them into individual segments. He was much older than I—probably sixty at that time—and very skilled. We discussed things three or four times a day. He was indispensable because he could take my drawings and turn them into placement drawings correct to within an eighth of an inch. His role was crucial because Turner Construction relied on his calculations for ordering the steel that would go to the fabricators.

By then I was working fifty hours a week—more, actually, because I was constantly thinking about the project. I'd wake up in the middle of the night thinking about it. I was deeply involved with it because it was so innovative, and my reputation rested on the accuracy of my calculations. The pressure on all of us at Gensert's firm was enormous because we had to plan backwards from the date of Blossom's opening. There was a crucial sequence of steps all involving time. Hundreds of people had to be coordinated: subcontractors, construction workers, structural engineers, electrical engineers and mechanical engineers.[7]

The massive roof van Dijk conceived had to be supported. Gensert proposed suspending it from the giant arch. He had long appreciated nature's fine engineers—spiders who spin intricate webs suspended from stable objects.[8] It was this suspended-web idea that Gensert entrusted to Peller to render into detailed drawings. Peller designed a three-dimensional web of trusses consisting of twenty-one long steel tubes fanning out from the apex of the arch to its front rim. Hundreds of hollow steel triangles were welded to them, a tricky process. Their ends had to be cut in a precise curve and that curve wasn't easy to figure out. A specially angled cutting machine had to be used.

Not only was the web strong, its many trusses also served as sound diffusers, their rounded shapes allowing vibrations to smoothly glide between them. The result was a lightweight yet sturdy support for the tongue-and-groove wood decking laid on top. Acoustician Jaffe insisted on wood because it created softer echoes. Jaffe's knowledge of sound waves greatly impressed Peller, who said, "Jaffe relied on his ears, not sound-measuring devices, to come up with solutions. And because of him the acoustics at Blossom are even superior to those at Severance Hall."[9]

The plans for Blossom included a huge basement under the stage that would contain dressing rooms, a music library, a rehearsal space, a loading dock, a mechanical and electrical room, a broadcasting room, lockers, showering facilities, and a lounge area with a cafeteria. In addition, offices and the conductor's room were hidden in back; a walkway connected them to the pavilion. All of that necessitated extensive concrete foundations designed by engineer Don Leinweber.[10]

Turner Construction's first task was excavating for the foundations. The next step was pouring concrete into the wooden forms to create the many basement rooms. Szell wanted to be in on that. "He called me and said he'd pick me up and we'd drive out to Blossom together," van Dijk remembered. "He arrived at my place in a chauffeured limousine, and we talked during the drive there and back. He was particularly interested in the pouring of the concrete."[11]

The musicians wouldn't have been surprised had they been told their conductor was as fascinated to watch a concrete mixer as any kid. Szell was curious about everything. He had spent a lifetime prodding and grilling musicians and anybody else who might know something he didn't. The facts he elicited—coupled with a fabulous memory—had given him a storehouse of information he could instantly retrieve. That storehouse was daunting to others and gave him the confidence necessary to dominate them. And his curiosity always enabled him to learn more, although it once earned him a public reprimand.

On one of the orchestra's tours, while the musicians waited in a railroad station for their train to leave, a few of them noticed Szell climbing the metal-runged ladder of the unoccupied engine cab for a look inside. The engineer, coming out of the station, saw what was happening.

"Hey, you! Get down from there!" he shouted.

"I'm the conductor of the Cleveland Orchestra," Szell replied.

"And I'm the conductor of this train. And I'm telling you to get down." Szell sheepishly descended, his curiosity unsatisfied, his dignity ruffled.

Another time he tried to flout rules and pull rank also ended unsuccessfully. On tour, while he and some orchestra members were riding in a bus, Szell stood up to converse with a player. The driver didn't like that.

"Sit down back there."

"I'm the conductor of the Cleveland Orchestra," Szell explained.

"I don't care if you're Lawrence Welk. Sit down."[12]

Szell could count on greater deference in Cleveland, however, where his name was almost a household word. On one occasion he was on his way to

Severance Hall, driving as usual above the speed limit. A siren sounded and he was pulled over. Szell rolled down his window. "I'm George Szell," he announced. The officer halted, taken aback that he'd caught too big a fish, and Szell sped away.[13]

Blossom under construction was unlike those other situations. Szell's presence on the site wasn't merely tolerated but actively appreciated. Here was a world-famous conductor interested in the building process. It was gratifying if a bit odd.[14]

Nothing in Szell's experience had prepared him for what he saw. Details of the construction were new and fascinating. He called van Dijk, saying he'd pick him up so they could watch cranes and scaffolding erected and workmen climbing the arch to weld its sections together. With the arrival of winter, work continued in the mud and snow. Szell was out there anyway in his galoshes. So were president of the board Frank Joseph, Dorothy Humel, Peter Reed, and other members of the board, all in hard hats and bundled against the cold.[15]

Humel was still soliciting funds for the expensive project. Wealthy music lover Sam Jaffe recalled their telephone conversation one wintry day. "Dorothy was trying to get a lot of her friends to go and see what was happening. It was all so thrilling and we would appreciate it so much more if we saw it as it was being built. I said, 'Dorothy, I didn't need to see the pyramids being built in order to appreciate them now, and I don't need to go out in the mud to see that thing going up either. I'll see it when it's finished.'"[16] Jaffe knew what Humel was trying to do: get people involved who would then donate money for her pet project. He intended to contribute when he felt like it and not when he'd have to endure the cold and wet to do so. Undaunted, Humel simply called the next person on her list.

"Szell and I went together out to the Blossom construction site several times," van Dijk remembered. "I think he just wanted to get out of his office." Van Dijk's conjecture may have been true on some level, but the architect wasn't aware of Szell's inborn curiosity about everything. Never before had the maestro been involved in an undertaking involving 1,250 tons of steel, 12,000 cubic yards of concrete, cranes, scaffolding, bulldozers, flat-bed trucks, five box cars of shingles, and enormous piles of metal tubes. His dream for a summer home for his orchestra hadn't included details of its construction. Now, seeing it all spread out before him, he was captivated.[17]

He had always listened respectfully to anyone who was an expert in some field other than his own. So he paid close attention to van Dijk, who took on the role of teacher, explaining what they were seeing and the special properties of the materials. The use of Cor-Ten steel for the giant arch and its supporting columns was something Szell wanted to know about.

"It's a 1950s invention," van Dijk explained, "a copper-steel alloy that allows only the surface of the steel to rust. Then a crust forms keeping it from rusting further. Eero Saarinen was one of the first to use it, and it caught on fast because it eliminates the need to continually paint. It saves lots of time and money."[18]

Van Dijk's explanations opened up to Szell an entire body of knowledge. No doubt fascinated with what was happening and wanting a voice in the project, he began thinking up improvements and writing memorandums to Barksdale starting in 1967.

Knowing that his musicians' physical well-being directly affected their performances, and, as usual, trying to anticipate anything that might go wrong, he specified items that he knew they needed, such as comfortable chairs in their lounge area and adequate lighting between the Blossom pavilion and its buildings in back. The most expensive amenity he specified was, however, the most important: air conditioning on the stage. Cleveland's summers are hot and humid and the musicians and their instruments would be adversely affected without it.[19]

That latter item on his agenda had to wait a year for lack of funds. He didn't give up on it until he had it. The overly efficient unit, its vents located at the front of the stage, then caused the players nearby to wear sweaters at rehearsals and performances while those in the back continued to get overheated.

Early in his planning, van Dijk and a surveyor had laid out the pavilion's outline with two sets of colored tapes on the ground—one of yellow and one of red. After that, they went up in a helicopter to choose which footprint better enabled the structure to nestle into the topography of the site. The musicians' comfort also had been on van Dijk's mind as he considered the pavilion's position in relation to the setting sun. Its glare would be a serious problem for the players facing it. He addressed the glare problem by ordering trees planted at the top of the lawn in the sun's direct path. As they grew they would little by little completely diffuse the glare.[20]

Once the concrete foundations were in place, the ends of the enormous arch had to be precisely positioned in the ground. Its components arrived, and the first two trapezoidal sections of each of its sides were welded together and their ends embedded in concrete. This phase was crucial because their angle was calculated to allow the top ends of the sides to precisely meet the keystone section in the middle. Then the other sections were welded together by workers high in the air.[21]

Peller had to come up with a way of safely attaching the ten columns holding up the arch. He also had to figure out how to handle the enormous roof van Dijk had designed. This involved consulting tables of materials and their properties and calculating stresses. It should be remembered that all this took place in the era before computers were generally available. Gensert's team of structural engineers had to calculate things the traditional way, using slide rules, while at the same time coming up with innovative solutions.

Van Dijk particularly extolled Peller's designs for the large hinges at the base of the columns supporting the arch. "I would have liked to leave those hinges visible. They're pretty interesting. But they got covered with soil and grass."[22]

Giant cranes lifted the free ends of the columns to the exact points where they would meet the arch. The columns were then kept at that angle by scaffolding. Once all the columns were attached to the arch, whose sections had been welded together previously, there came one of the most dramatic steps.[23]

A crane lifted the massive keystone section up ninety feet to unite the two sides of the arch. A three-eighths-inch gap was forcibly jacked together by workmen standing perilously close to the edges. Peller and Hollifield's intricate calculations proved to be absolutely correct.

Watching as the crane slowly lowered the keystone into place, van Dijk and Gensert rejoiced that the gigantic components joined exactly as planned. This event had another witness. Szell in his galoshes was out there too.

As van Dijk had specified, the short columns supporting the roof's front rim were positioned behind the audience inside. Painted dark brown, they blended imperceptibly into the background and matched the Cor-Ten columns holding up the arch.

Construction began on the sound-projecting components of the stage once the superstructure was in place. Van Dijk described them, saying, "The orchestra shell consisted of a tall, three-sided undulating wall and a large stage canopy projecting out into the audience area. All of it was designed to reflect and disperse sound to the audience and the musicians."[24]

To test the suspension rods holding up the stage canopy, Peller daringly climbed onto the trusses.

I'd always been good at mountain climbing and wasn't afraid of heights. One of my precautions was to avoid looking down. When I was a teenager in Hungary I used to do daredevil things like hanging by one arm out of third-story windows. So I wasn't afraid to go up among the trusses and walk along the five-inch-wide pipes. I whistled to stay calm. As I inched along, I tested each suspension rod by shaking it to determine whether it was taut so there would be an even distribution of weight. What I was doing wasn't actually all that dangerous. The drop onto the canopy was just eight or ten feet. If I had fallen I would only have broken a few bones and gotten some bruises.[25]

He recalled the tall segments of the undulating stage walls: "They were mounted on casters and suspended from cables so Jaffe could tune them by adjusting their positions. After he was finished, the casters were removed and the wall segments remained permanently fixed in place."

Blossom pavilion was completed within a year. To the great relief and delight of everybody working on it, the projected date of the inaugural concert—July 19, 1968—would be kept.

CHAPTER 22

The Blossom Triumph

BLOSSOM'S OPENING CONCERT in 1968 rivaled opening night at Severance Hall in 1931. There were far more people in the audience, many of whom had perhaps never heard a professional symphony orchestra other than on the radio. In addition to the four thousand sitting inside the pavilion, more than a thousand others sat on the grassy slope surrounding it. Families came with their picnic suppers and blankets, attracted by the inexpensive tickets, casual dress, and the freedom to lie on the vast lawn under the night sky.

Little of the advance publicity about Blossom had prepared crowds for their first sight of the pavilion. As they walked from the parking lot, they saw only the top of the great roof. It was no accident that a knoll hid most of the pavilion as they approached it. Architect van Dijk had purposely designed it that way. Crediting another architect, Frank Lloyd Wright, as "a master of sequences" van Dijk said, "Like Wright, I wanted drama in the first sight of the pavilion."[1]

As people crested the small hill, they paused in disbelief, stunned by what met their eyes. After staring for a few wondering moments, they hurried down toward it, drawn by its mysterious presence. The wife of one orchestra musician voiced her astonishment upon encountering the unusual structure. "For a second or two I thought I was looking at something from outer space, hovering like it had either just landed or was going to take off. It was so futuristic."[2] Many thought it resembled a gigantic clamshell. An enthusiastic teenager summed up the general feeling, saying, "Whoever designed this is really cool."[3]

The audience that night was thrilled by what it saw and heard. As late afternoon turned to dusk, the stage lights came on, illuminating the waves of russet cedar paneling behind and above the stage, which spread a warm glow. The musicians appeared, took their places, and the usual tuning notes wafted across the lawn. Szell then came onstage and bowed to the applauding audience, and the concert began.

None but a handful of people were aware of the sophisticated sound system that allowed the audience sitting out on the lawn to hear the music exactly as those inside the pavilion heard it. Few paid any attention to the intricate circuit board at the back of the pavilion and the technician operating it. Years later, recording engineer Vladimir Maleckar recounted that technician's role in the creation of Blossom's sound system:

> One day sometime around the beginning of Blossom plans, I got a phone call from a Mr. Flickinger, who said his son Daniel was an electronics genius and needed a job. I thought that was a pretty strong statement, but I said I'd give his son a chance. He should come to my recording studio for an interview. I hired him to do some work, and it became apparent the father was right. His son really was an electronics genius.

Flickinger quickly proved that he knew everything there was to know about audio electronics. Adept with intricate equipment, he had built complete sound systems for various companies in the United States in addition to inventing numerous components, including innovative equalizers for circuit boards.

Around that time the Cleveland Orchestra management was contemplating hiring someone to create the sound system for Blossom. They had received a proposal from a European acoustician who estimated the cost of the job at $300,000. Thinking his price excessive, Maleckar obtained a copy of the estimate and gave it to Flickinger. After a few hours with pencil and calculator, Flickinger said, "I think I could bring in this whole project for about $125,000."[4]

Knowing this lower estimate would be welcome news to the planning committee, Maleckar introduced Flickinger to orchestra manager Barksdale, who in turn shared the estimate with the trustees. There was general delight that the job could be done for less than half the original estimate. They hired Flickinger, who immediately set to work ordering components and designing a complicated circuit board that could adjust fine gradations of sound and timing.[5]

No one on the various committees understood what kind of man was building the Blossom sound system. Flickinger wasn't merely a talented technician. He was a gifted inventor who would go on to create sound systems for such recording artists as Stevie Wonder, Sly Stone, Tina Turner, and Johnny Cash.[6]

Flickinger's sound consoles were regarded by many in the recording business as brilliant, much better than anything else on the market. The well-known guitarist-audio engineer Steve Albini endorsed Flickinger's inventions with unreserved praise. "I'll go to my deathbed claiming Flickinger consoles are the best sound-mixing desks ever made."[7]

Although Szell hated amplification, he conceded it was necessary for the Blossom audience sitting far out on the lawn. One of his hopes was for a sound system so good that nobody would notice it.

Sound travels at the approximate speed of 1150 feet per second. People on the grass outside the pavilion were 240 feet from the center of the stage, and so they would hear the orchestra a quarter of a second later than those inside. Therefore the sound emitted from the outside speakers had to be delayed in order to avoid a noticeable echo. Flickinger accomplished that by using a tape recorder with a movable playback head adjusted to coordinate the sound.

Maleckar had what he called a personal mantra: "If you can hear the speakers we have failed."[8] Flickinger addressed his concern perfectly. And van Dijk designed recesses in the roof's eaves to unobtrusively house the outside speakers, which were covered in speaker cloth the same color as the surrounding wood.

After much testing and adjustment, the sound system was up and running, ready for the afternoon rehearsal of the opening night concert. Several music critics from major newspapers, including Harold Schonberg of the *New York Times*, were to be given a tour of Blossom and its surroundings while the orchestra rehearsed. In his newspaper columns, Schonberg frequently inveighed against amplification, saying it was artificial-sounding, usually too loud, and unnecessary in many theaters. Knowing Schonberg's negative opinions of such technology, manager Barksdale asked Maleckar to give the critic a private tour of the premises to prove to him that the Blossom sound system wasn't obtrusive.[9]

Maleckar recalled what he did:

That afternoon I walked Schonberg about while the orchestra was rehearsing, and we wound up on the lawn outside the pavilion. He was impressed there was no amplification and said, "This sounds great." I answered that the sound was reinforced. I'd previously arranged a signal with the technician stationed at the mixing board. I raised my hand, turned my thumb down and the orchestra receded into the distance. After a few seconds I turned my thumb up and the sound came back. Schonberg was dumfounded that he had been listening to reinforced—actually amplified—sound and didn't know it. Then I said to him, "Walk down with me toward the orchestra and tell me when the reinforced sound meets up with the real sound." We walked right under the speakers and Schonberg didn't notice a thing. He couldn't tell where the line of demarcation, if any, was.[10]

The music that night was all Beethoven: *Consecration of the House* and the Ninth Symphony. Between these two works there were some ceremonial speeches, and then the chorus filed onstage to bring the triumphant occasion to an end with "Ode to Joy." After the concert, well-wishers and music critics from various newspapers gathered around Szell eager to hear what he had to say about the event and especially praising the wonderful acoustics that enabled the large audience out on the lawn to hear as clearly as those inside the pavilion.

"Schonberg knew the truth," Maleckar recalled, "and he began to protest.

He asked Szell whether or not the sound outside the pavilion was amplified. Szell caught sight of me standing at the edge of the crowd and evaded the question by saying, "Ah, here is Mr. Maleckar. He would know about that." I went into a lengthy explanation using technical terms mixed with double-talk. Szell seemed greatly amused by my speech. But when Schonberg protested that he knew there'd been amplification, Robert Marsh, a music critic from Chicago, interrupted, saying, "Harold, I didn't hear anything. Come off it."

Though Schonberg knew he was right, he wrote a review of the concert that dwelt primarily on the visual impact of van Dijk's stupendous creation, only briefly mentioning the sound system "governed by an operator at the rear of the hall."[11] It didn't occur to him to wonder who had designed something that had fooled him so completely. Nor did he know that the unnamed operator and designer were one and the same person—Daniel Flickinger.

To provide for all types of performances, Flickinger had not only placed speakers beaming the sound to the audience out on the lawn but also installed speakers inside the pavilion to be turned on only for pops groups and smaller ensembles. The ones inside weren't necessary for Cleveland Orchestra concerts because the acoustics within the pavilion had been admirably dealt with by Jaffe and van Dijk.

Blossom's second week built on the excitement generated by the first. Word was out about the fantastic building in its sylvan setting. Audience numbers swelled, and many experienced, for the first time in their lives, what magic can take place when the music is wonderful, the musicians playing it are expert, and a beautiful building in a sylvan setting lifts it all to transcendent heights.

The featured soloist was European soprano Elizabeth Schwarzkopf. She rarely sang in the United States, and insiders conjectured she came as a special favor to Szell, because their friendship dated back many years. That evening, having first performed two Mozart arias, Schwarzkopf reappeared to sing Richard Strauss's *Four Last Songs*. Arms outstretched to the audience, she glided to the center of the stage, her chiffon cloak floating behind her. As she sang, the audience was caught up in the spell of the music, the surroundings, and the night.[12]

It would be fanciful to imagine that van Dijk had planned this extraordinary moment years earlier when he had visited the great cathedrals, plazas, and amphitheaters in Europe. He had no idea then that he would settle in Cleveland and win the opportunity to design a place for one of the world's great orchestras to perform. But a seed had been planted in his mind at the time. As he thrilled to what architects of the past had designed, he became aware that vast spaces enabled many people to come together in a communal experience.[13] Whether it was cheering on gladiators in the Coliseum, watching actors in a Greek amphitheater, or glimpsing the Pope while standing in the great plaza in front of St. Peter's, the effect was the same. People were stirred by being part of an enormous crowd that was hearing, seeing, and feeling the same thing.

Now, as van Dijk observed the Blossom scene, he knew that he had created something akin to those historic places. He knew also that he had created something never done before.[14] Remembering those satisfying moments, he said,

I wanted to bring together all possible elements of an art and nature experience for many people at one time. Blossom is that. The design of the building enables people to see nature around them because the sides of the pavilion are high enough off the ground that the lawn and trees are visible. And the roof eave is high enough that people sitting at the back of the lawn can see the entire stage. Inside the pavilion there are no posts obstructing the view either. The cedar paneling behind the musicians sends the music outward and at the same time creates a feeling of warmth and enclosure. A spaciously high ceiling enables the sounds to rise and blend. And the rural setting, far from city lights and noise, enhances the experience.[15]

There were a few glitches as there always are in new buildings. A minor problem involved the two ends of the giant arch extending into the ground. Their impressive rise made them alluring to adventurous children who were soon clambering on them. To forestall their climbing the dangerous ninety-foot height, spikes were welded onto the arch ends, effectively deterring young mountaineers.[16]

The next problem wasn't as easily solved: a disruptive boom that happened during each evening concert. Much time and money was expended looking for the source of the noise. It took more than two years of searching. Peller recalled the booms and the steps taken to get rid of them:

> During the design process I had calculated that thermal expansion of the sloping columns supporting the arch would cause its apex to rise by nearly one inch as solar radiation heated up the column surfaces on a sunny summer day. When sunset approached, however, the columns would cool off and contract, letting the arch settle back down. Winter's cold temperatures would cause the columns to contract a similar amount.
>
> To accommodate those fluctuations, I had designed slide-bearing connections for the top ends of the scores of sidewall trusses. That necessitated many low-friction pads and steel guide bars. But as the contractor and steel fabricator reviewed the cost and schedule constraints, they said that the construction budget wouldn't allow for my solution. They'd have to go with a simpler one of their own design: aligned and seated steel plates that allowed sliding. These plates required temporary erection bolts that would be removed once the plates were attached.

Peller was dubious about this proposal. "I suspected that the slide plates supposed to allow movement caused by thermal expansion and contraction at the top of the side wall trusses wouldn't function as planned."[17] He was right. As the sun went down each evening, there was an enormous boom.

Nothing could be done until after the summer season. Strain sensors were then attached to the bases of the sidewall trusses and electronically scanned every ten minutes. They precisely revealed when and where temperature fluctuations were causing metal parts to scrape against each other.

Workers lifted by bucket cranes to inspect the problem areas noticed that the bolt holes for the temporary erection bolts in the slide plates had been flame-cut, leaving burrs along the edges. The burrs were hindering smooth sliding, and so workers filed them off. But the boom continued. Cranes and workers were again deployed. They discovered that some of the plates had not been seated properly during installation, causing the corner of one plate to gouge the other mating plate. Grease was applied to those joints to minimize friction. To little avail. The large boom merely changed into softer small booms that occurred throughout the evening.

There's no record of what Szell said about these noisy interruptions. His vocabulary when angered could be colorful, and Helene and Barksdale must have heard some impressive maledictions. The two local papers seized on the boom problem, and soon all of Cleveland knew that Mother Nature was using the great structure to add unwanted percussion to musical masterpieces.[18]

Tales of the boom caught the attention of the Cleveland manufacturing firm Warner and Swasey, one of whose specialties was the manufacture of such sensitive instruments as observatory telescopes. The firm came to the rescue, generously offering to donate design, materials, and labor for creating smoothly aligning plates. Peller sketched out a catwalk, which was temporarily erected on the arch, enabling welders to safely install sliding plates along the segments of the arch where the joints were located. That completely solved the problem. The booms disappeared.[19]

Peller's talent and achievements were so obvious that Gensert invited him to become a partner in his firm, thus acknowledging his young assistant's brilliance and the important role he played in the creation of Blossom.

Many years later, Peller's words about Blossom are unequivocal. "Blossom pavilion is one of the world's major structures. Not only is it great in itself, it is located in a pristine environment and complements that environment rather than clashing with it. Peter van Dijk is a great architect and Blossom is one of his finest creations. The only reason Blossom is not internationally famous is the lack of publicity about it."[20]

CHAPTER 23

The Death of the Maestro

THE ORCHESTRA'S MANY TRIUMPHS—the completion of Blossom being the latest—could surely content Szell with his achievements. At age seventy-two he could look back on having built and maintained a world-class symphony orchestra in a city not noted for its sophistication. The proof was in the national and international rave reviews for the orchestra's live performances and recordings. But as he faced the upcoming 1969–70 concert season, he confided his disenchantment to Louis Lane.[1]

Fleeing war-torn Europe, Szell had come to the United States expecting to find freedom from anti-Semitism; instead, he experienced some of the same prejudices that had poisoned those countries. Even so, he had believed in the United States and democracy. But along with millions of others, he was shocked and discouraged by the assassination of President Kennedy. Madness knew no national boundaries. And there was other upsetting news.

The orchestra's 1965 tour of Russia had opened his eyes to what was going on in Vietnam. The musicians in the orchestra who had learned Russian for the tour translated what the Russian newspapers were saying about U.S. actions in Vietnam. The conviction began growing on him that things were not as they were represented to be in this country.[2]

Discouraging, too, was the way his orchestra had, in 1966, struck for higher wages and improved working conditions. Even as plans for Blossom summer employment were going forward, the impatient musicians had given vent to their frustrations by picketing Severance Hall. Their demands were fairly modest in comparison with salaries in the other major orchestras. But Szell, knowing how hard the board of trustees was working for a summer home for the players, was incensed at what he considered gross ingratitude.

It was difficult for him to accept his players' dissatisfaction. Though their attitude had changed considerably when they found fatter paychecks and weeks of summer employment at Blossom, Szell still couldn't forget the strike and its embarrassing newspaper photos of his musicians in concert attire, marching around Severance Hall with placards. He confided to Lane that even though the orchestra played superbly and followed his every command, he felt apart from them.[3] The orchestra's many successes couldn't dispel his gloom.

There was another reason for his depression. He realized his hearing was deteriorating. This lamentable fact had come to his attention the morning after the triumphant opening concert at Blossom. He had gone to a jewelry store at a shopping mall and was hailed by Vlad Maleckar coming from a nearby store. As they stood talking in the parking lot, Szell explained he was there to get his Bulova Accutron watch repaired. Maleckar remembers their encounter:

> I said I had the same watch and that it had a tuning fork inside which vibrated at three hundred sixty cycles a second. One could hear it humming if one listened closely. I held my watch up to Szell's ear, and he listened to it for a few moments. I was quite surprised when he said he couldn't hear anything. I suddenly realized the reason he'd been complaining to me about the Blossom microphones, saying their pickup on the violin section was poor. Szell's hearing had deteriorated. He had reduced awareness of high frequencies. It happens to many older people. For him, violins playing in a high register at medium volume sounded too soft.[4]

If Maleckar was taken aback by this revelation, one can only imagine how Szell himself must have felt. Here was chilling proof that one of his greatest gifts, his hearing, was gradually declining. It was like a return to his hearing problem years before when he had undergone an operation on both his ears. This time, though, no operation could restore what he was inexorably losing.

In an uncharacteristically depressed mood, Szell packed his trunk for the May 1970 tour of Japan. He felt ill and out of sorts, but contracts had been signed, and ticket sales showed wild enthusiasm for the orchestra's concerts. Even before the orchestra appeared, Japanese audiences were primed for adulation. A fad for classical Western music, especially the music of Beethoven, had swept the country, and most Japanese considered it a duty to attend performances of Beethoven's Ninth Symphony. The "Ode to Joy" choral movement at the end was supposed to be the greatest moment in classical music. Japan's concert halls were always packed for this cultural event.

As the days went by, the orchestra receiving ovations and raves from the press, Szell felt increasingly ill. Before one concert, he called in his principal players and cautioned them he might falter while conducting. They should watch each other and carry on anyhow if his beat wasn't steady. Barksdale watched from the wings as Szell bowed to the fervent crowd and then tottered off the stage, nearly falling into his arms. The orchestra knew its indomitable maestro was ill and forcing himself to carry on.[5]

Helene bore the brunt of Szell's misery; pain caused him to become irascible. Faced with his ill-tempered behavior, she threatened to leave the tour and stay with her sister Marianne in England. Walking out of their suite in the hotel where the orchestra was staying, she met oboist Felix Kraus, whom she knew spoke and read Japanese. Saying she needed an escort for sightseeing who could translate Japanese signs, she explained, "George is as usual studying his scores and has no time for sightseeing." Pressed into service, Kraus felt honored to hold a paper parasol over her head as the two visited shrines in the area. Helene, who loved oriental art, was happy to spend several hours listening to Kraus translating temple inscriptions and looking at peaceful gardens.[6]

When Helene returned to their suite, Szell had calmed down. The two proceeded to the concert hall, where he waited in a dressing room to go onstage and she met with dignitaries, who escorted her to a box.[7]

During the concert, orchestra members saw Szell's beat become unsteady and then quit altogether as he leaned on the railing around the podium. The principal players, forewarned that there might be moments when they couldn't depend on him, rallied together, cuing their sections using what Szell had for years taught them. As one entity, intently watching and listening to each other, the players brought the concert to a triumphant close. The audience, suspecting nothing, gave a standing ovation to the feebly bowing maestro who had just been rescued by his loyal crew. As the clapping continued, two little Japanese girls in kimonos approached Szell with flowers. He took their hands and acknowledged the enthusiastic audience with a smile. Standing valiantly as wave after wave of applause rocked the hall, he finally walked offstage and into the arms of Barksdale, who understood what was happening.[8]

Szell recovered enough to fulfill his duties at their last concert in Anchorage. Then, exhausted and in pain, while standing on the stairs to board the airplane for Cleveland, he did something he would never have done under normal circumstances. He reached up and gently touched cellist Diane Mather's hair as she stood with her back to him. Only violinist Elmer Setzer witnessed the tiny gesture. He was to realize later what it foretold.[9]

The orchestra arrived at the Cleveland airport to an enthusiastic welcome from fans. Szell wasn't part of the excitement. He was whisked off by ambulance to University Hospital. In the following days he underwent a series of tests revealing what he secretly feared: his cancer had returned. The rest of the news was equally bad. His heart was weak, and he wouldn't be able to withstand an operation. Nor would he be able to conduct that summer's Blossom season.[10]

The musicians began the 1970 summer season no doubt thinking that Szell would be returning to conduct them in the fall. Pierre Boulez was expertly leading them in the summer series, Lane was in charge, and all seemed well. Szell would return. He was being cared for by experts. He would reappear in two months—his usual critical self—to conduct the fall–winter season at Severance Hall.

Even Lane, Szell's close confidante, was unaware of the seriousness of Szell's illness. He had visited him a few days after Szell had checked into the hospital and saw him resting in bed, silently conducting a score he held in his lap. Surely the maestro was experiencing only a temporary setback. Lane had come to Szell's room with a score of Mozart's *Don Giovanni* he was studying in preparation for conducting it. He knew Szell would have definite thoughts on its interpretation, and a discussion about it might take Szell's mind off his illness. He guessed correctly, and the two were soon deep into its pages.[11]

For the previous two years Lane had taken on administrative duties that Szell had declared himself no longer interested in. Lane had been with Szell since 1947. He had been privy to much of Szell's musical thought, been a guest in his home on numerous occasions, over the years becoming Szell's right hand. He was once overheard saying, when someone conjectured about Szell's salary, "They could never afford to pay him what he's worth."[12] This admiring assessment of Szell's abilities was reflected in Lane's willingness to take on whatever duty Szell assigned. In their years together Szell increasingly confided in him.

Lane had never abused that privilege, considering Szell his teacher and mentor. There was a close bond between the two, and Lane, who could have left and become a conductor of another orchestra, had never hankered after fame or autonomy. He knew Szell was head and shoulders above most other conductors and knew, too, that his boss had put his life at the service of music of the great composers. Lane's loyalty was grounded in that. They both loved the same thing.

As they talked about the Mozart score, it seemed that Szell's preoccupation with musical matters far outweighed his concern with his physical condition.[13] So it came as a shock to Lane, several days later, when he heard that Szell had suffered a heart attack and had been transferred to an intensive care unit. He wasn't expected to live much longer, even though Helene talked about taking him to Switzerland to regain his health and the doctors held out the chance of a possible remission. In denial about Szell's condition, Lane couldn't entertain the thought that his revered maestro would succumb to death. Szell had a hardy constitution; he was rarely sick; he took good care of himself. For Lane it was inconceivable his mentor wouldn't overcome this setback with his usual determination.[14]

But Szell had known for some time he had cancer. When it was diagnosed several years previously, he had endured an operation that slowed its progress but failed to eradicate it. With his customary energy and will he had refused to give in to despair, instead going about his duties. Nevertheless, he felt more tired than usual. The reduction in his energy resulted in bouts of depression. He confided to Lane that he was no longer as emotionally involved with the orchestra.[15]

It was later that violinist Elmer Setzer realized the significance of the gesture when Szell touched Diane Mather's hair as the orchestra members waited in line to board an airplane. That gentle touch was Szell's goodbye to a musician whom he liked and who represented some of the beauty he would be leaving behind. As he boarded the airplane, Szell knew it would be his last airplane trip, his last journey with the musicians he had led for so long.

At the end Father Dulin, Szell's longtime friend and confessor, administered the last rites. Knowing Szell's real religion had been great music, he nevertheless intoned the traditional phrases. And then Helene was alone with her sorrow.

That night Lane was at Blossom, where Boulez was conducting the orchestra. As Lane stood backstage, he was told he had a telephone call from the hospital. The dread news broke upon him. While the orchestra was playing, its great leader had departed.[16]

Applause swelled and then faded, the crowd dispersed into the night, and the musicians went downstairs to pack up their instruments. There they saw a devastated Lane.

"I'd never seen such a contorted face," Joela Jones said later. "Louis looked as if he were dying himself. As we listened to the terrible news that Szell had died just an hour before, we all thought the same thing. What was going to become of us? How was it possible Szell was gone? He wasn't that old—just seventy-three. We had thought he'd be our conductor for many more years. There was an awful silence. Nobody knew what to say. We just sort of drifted out to the parking lot. We were all in shock."[17]

A memorial service took place days later in Severance Hall. As the devastated orchestra members filed onstage, they saw the flower-covered podium. Conductorless, they played Bach's poignant "Air on the G String" and then looked out at the grieving audience. There was hardly a need for eulogies pronouncing it the end of an era. Everyone knew that only too well.[18]

As for a definitive statement about Szell, it was spoken decades later by faithful oboist Robert Zupnik. "He was one of the geniuses of the twentieth century."[19]

More must be said. Szell's recordings are his monument, and he wrote his own epitaph in his 1967 foreword to Robert Marsh's book, *The Cleveland Orchestra*. Here is the final paragraph:

"It is my conviction that to accomplish greatness one must love music more than oneself. First there must be a love of music on my part, and then what is being asked of the players for the love of music must be made convincing to them. Honesty and integrity in performance are matters of artistic morality."[20]

Epilogue

MOST THINGS CHANGE with the passage of time. Severance Hall has changed, having undergone a major renovation in 2000 that brought this landmark triumphantly into the twenty-first century. It now features an underground parking garage, a restaurant, a gift shop, a wine bar, and an escalator. After these improvements, its staff grew to ninety, ten times the number that ran Severance Hall during the Szell years.

Deemed financially necessary, the orchestra's touring schedule has been expanded, and residencies of several weeks each year have been established in Miami, Indiana University, Vienna, and Salzburg. These residencies give the orchestra a wider public and enable the management to present pops ensembles in Severance Hall when the orchestra is absent, thereby enlarging the scope of its presentations.

At Blossom, the pavilion's enormous roof has been reshingled with slate, as architect van Dijk originally specified. But new loudspeakers now hang from the rim of the roof, their black shapes marring its pure outline and dismaying van Dijk, whose original design for the speakers had situated them invisibly within the eaves of the roof. It is generally conceded that the pops groups appearing at Blossom between orchestra concerts are what keep the summer season in the black and finance the upkeep of the pavilion and grounds.

The changes in classical music audiences are a microcosm of changes in the population of the country. The people now frequenting Severance Hall and Blossom are a different, more casual, breed than the audiences of the early and middle 1900s that thought listening to classical music in a beautiful hall called for elegant clothes and careful grooming.

The orchestra's musicians have changed too. Within weeks of Szell's death, several men sprouted beards and ponytails that would have made Szell apoplectic. Flouting his well-known stance against infidelity and marital disruptions, six or seven musicians began divorce proceedings, a step they'd never have dared while Szell was alive to lecture them on the sanctity of marriage. And miniskirts, formerly grounds for scathing admonishment, at present cause hardly a ripple.

An announcement in the orchestra's program book imploring audiences to turn off their disruptive cellphones was long ignored. But management has since found a clever way to silence cellphones. Prior to the entrance of the conductor, several blasts of amplified ring tones startle everyone into checking their devices. So far, this ploy has been remarkably successful.

In 1918, when Adella Prentiss Hughes founded the Cleveland Orchestra, symphony orchestras could be heard only in person. A bit later, radio broadcasts did much to familiarize people with the sound of symphonic music. People of the era sang in their school choirs, in churches, at picnics, and at patriotic gatherings, and many children played instruments in their elementary and high school bands and orchestras. Also there had been a longstanding tradition of piano playing. Nearly everyone could read music because it was taught in elementary schools, and most schools had orchestras, bands, and choirs.

That musical culture changed with the advent of television and cuts in school budgets. Group singing is now done mostly in church, and the decline of arts education in schools has resulted in a generation of people who can't read music, rarely sing, and don't know what a melody is. Pianos are no longer as common in people's homes.

Although classical music suffers from many other claims on the U.S. public's attention, music conservatories are building new and larger facilities, attracting more musicians and turning out hundreds of players for orchestras, many of which don't pay a living wage. Local and suburban orchestras rehearse in the evening because their players must have day jobs. That's hardly new, however, for it always was difficult to earn a living in symphony orchestras other than in the Big Five.

Noteworthy is the major change in the personnel of all orchestras. Women have been increasingly admitted into formerly all-male ranks and have proved there is no such thing as a feminine instrumental sound. The violin sections in the Cleveland Orchestra are today more than fifty percent female. Women have broken into conducting. Some of them are even managers of orchestras and opera companies. And formerly all-Caucasian orchestras now have many Asians in their ranks. As of this writing, Asians number a third of the thirty-three-member violin section of the Cleveland Orchestra. Other major U.S. orchestras not only have many Asians in their violin sections but also in their woodwind sections.

Another breakthrough is scientists' discovery of the secrets of Stradivarius and Guarnerius violins. Luthiers in Germany and the United States are turning out fabulous stringed instruments that sell for a tenth of the price of the old Italian ones, thereby enabling players to avoid taking on enormous debt.

Radio, recordings, and television have helped bring about an advance in musicians' abilities, and the current level of playing is extraordinary. Many older musicians readily concede that their younger counterparts possess superior techniques.

Serialism and atonalism left a portion of audiences in the dust. Classical music lovers who were accustomed to hearing melody and harmony couldn't understand the contemporary pieces being programmed and began staying away from orchestra concerts that included cerebral and dissonant compositions. In contrast, however, younger audiences, accustomed to unusual sound effects in movies and rock concerts, are more receptive to strange noises emanating from orchestral instruments. Classical concerts frequently include these kinds of pieces, garnering applause from twenty- and thirty-year-olds who are used to nonmelody, nonharmony, and an excess of decibels.

In an effort at relevance, conductors and symphony boards have come up with "community outreach." Free pops concerts in shopping malls and children's concerts in public schools feature music from movies, musicals, television programs, and rock stars' albums. The thing symphony orchestras do best—playing symphonic music by great composers—is frequently relegated to second place in these settings. Orchestra managements have fastened on popular music as a way of capturing audiences. Sometimes it does. But orchestras across the country still go bankrupt, cut back their seasons, and reduce salaries and personnel. Some failures are due to overreaching. Imagining that there is a large audience for their performances, regional and second-tier orchestras expand unrealistically. As a National Endowment for the Arts survey revealed, 85 percent of the nation isn't interested in classical music.

A major problem for orchestras is the changed interests of philanthropists. Those who formerly lavished enormous sums of money on cultural organizations have been replaced by wealthy individuals who are more concerned with disease, poverty, and the rapid deterioration of the planet. Fortunately the Cleveland Orchestra has not fallen victim to a shortage of donors. It has balanced its budget for the last three years and has expanded its activities.

WCLV continues to broadcast classical music and in 2012 celebrated fifty years on the air. In 2004 WCLV became the WCLV Foundation, guaranteeing in perpetuity radio broadcasts of classical music in northeast Ohio.

Optimum reception of WCLV broadcasts depends on good-quality receiving equipment, but few people other than technophiles have the requisite audio components. It therefore remains true that listening to the Cleveland Orchestra live in Severance Hall is the best way for Clevelanders to experience masterpieces of symphonic literature.

Jet travel enables many conductors to hold two or more conducting posts simultaneously, thus dividing their loyalty and attention. Their main concern their own image and career, they rarely forge bonds with their musicians.

Financial expedience leads orchestra managements to replace musicians who leave or retire with substitutes who have no contracts, receive no benefits, and work for less pay than scale players. Theirs is a week-to-week existence, and in many cases they don't audition before being hired.

Finances also dictate fewer rehearsals and more concerts. In contrast with Szell's insistence on five full rehearsals for his Thursday, Friday, and Saturday performances, many conductors now depend on as little as one or two rehearsals to prepare a full evening's concert. This results in mere read-throughs of compositions that are in need of hours of rehearsing, a practice guaranteeing mediocre performances.

While they create a more egalitarian atmosphere, union rules—on how much power a conductor may wield and how much say the musicians have in their working conditions—undermine the authority of the conductor and protect mediocre players to the detriment of the music. In addition, high union-dictated fees for recording have had the unfortunate effect of driving some U.S. record companies to use cheaper European orchestras.

Most orchestral players concede that a symphony orchestra cannot be a democratic organization because it needs an authoritative person at its head. Yet they chafe under such leadership, always seeking more autonomy.

Symphony orchestras struggle to meet the enormous fees demanded by top-notch soloists and conductors. Although it's true that these artists attract the general public, their appearances usually result in heavy financial losses for orchestras.

A fundamental problem must be addressed: as long as our schools short-change the arts, there will be minimal support for cultural activities that inspire, ennoble, and bring a people together.

Proof that the Cleveland Orchestra under George Szell achieved a musical standard rarely reached by other orchestras exists in its recordings made between 1955 and 1970. Out of their extensive discography, Dvořák's *Slavonic Dances* might be cited as one of the most approachable and exciting. Under Szell, the orchestra played these colorful masterpieces with such brilliance and clarity that even the most inexperienced listener can understand them. There is no need for program notes, just as fireworks lighting up the night sky need no explanation. And Szell's recording of the four Schumann symphonies will never be equaled.

There probably will never be another George Szell. Born a prodigy superior to most other prodigies, he grew up in Vienna, the musical center of Europe where, at an early age, he received an advanced musical education, worked in opera houses where he honed his skills, and flourished in a culture that nurtured classical music. Sadly, that milieu has either been diminished or is lost. No longer are there opera houses in every European town providing experience for aspiring conductors.

Even though there may be fine orchestras in the future, it is doubtful there will be truly great ones because musicians' talents are constrained by the absence of supremely endowed conductors. Technical prowess alone is not enough; it must be allied to great dedication. Szell's players knew he cared more for the music than for himself. For that they were willing to endure his tyranny.

There was something visually unusual about Szell that separated him from other people. His autocratic face communicated high intelligence and supreme confidence. When he spoke, he commanded attention; when he stood silently, a space cleared around him. Concertgoers Gretchen and Bob Larson summed up the feelings of many who came in contact with him:

> We attended a big reception in the Severance Hall lobby after a concert and were busy eating and talking. Suddenly we were aware that Szell was standing above on the staircase and looking down at all of us. His arms were folded across his chest and he had a benevolent look on his face. It was an unforget-

table picture. He seemed like a king looking down on his subjects. Of the many times we had seen him, this moment stands out. He always had an aura about him, but on this occasion it was even more pronounced as he stood contemplating the scene. This was his domain. We were his people.

Szell was looking upon his work and finding it good.

Acknowledgments

I MUST FIRST ACKNOWLEDGE the late Felix Kraus, oboist, English hornist, and my husband, who played·in the Cleveland Orchestra from 1963 to 2004 and, over the years, brought home stories about Szell's formidable rehearsals and spectacular concerts. Felix worked with the orchestra's recording engineer Vladimir Maleckar and also was in charge of quality control of the orchestra's radio broadcasts. He edited many of the tapes in the archives that were issued as compact disks by the orchestra. Years earlier, he had been a student of oboist Marcel Tabuteau at the Curtis Institute of Music.

Next I should mention that my student experiences at Tanglewood playing under Leonard Bernstein and Charles Munch and my professional years in the Portland (now Oregon) Symphony and the Washington, D.C., Opera Orchestra helped give me the perspective to write this book. Had I not been an orchestral musician, I doubt I would have realized how extraordinary Szell was.

My decision to write about the Cleveland Orchestra under Szell was initially prompted by the idea that the concert-going public might be interested in a book written from the orchestra musicians' point of view.

There are two musicians whose insights into Szell's achievements were especially helpful: Jerome Rosen, who played and studied under Szell and discussed Szell's wonderful reorchestrations of the four Robert Schumann symphonies, and Robert O'Brien, the present music librarian of the Cleveland Orchestra, who showed me Szell's Schumann scores in the Szell Memorial Library at Severance Hall.

The following are books I consulted often: Donald Rosenberg, *The Cleveland Orchestra Story*; Laila Storch, *Marcel Tabuteau: How Do You Expect to Play the Oboe If You Can't Peel a Mushroom?*; Robert Marsh, *The Cleveland Orchestra*, and Michael Charry, *George Szell: A Life of Music*. The latter is surely the definitive reference work on Szell. In addition, two books, Stefan Zweig, *The World of Yesterday*, and Harold Segel, *The Vienna Coffeehouse Wits: 1890–1938*, gave me knowledge of events in young Szell's life that undoubtedly influenced him.

Conductor Louis Lane's fascinating essay, *Szell: A Partial Memoir*, in the February 1974 issue of *Cleveland* magazine, gave me insights into Szell's personality and character, and editor-journalist Dennis Dooley's articles in *Cleveland* magazine furnished me with facts and dates on Bob Conrad and Peter van Dijk.

Lawrence Angell and Bernette Jaffe's *Tales from the Locker Room* corroborates some of the stories and opinions that I gathered in my many interviews with Cleveland Orchestra musicians.

Two musicians' reminiscences were especially helpful: Robert Zupnik, the orchestra's assistant principal oboist, was a wonderful source of Cleveland Orchestra lore. He seems to have total recall, and we had more than fifty conversations over the last five years. He is one hundred years old as of this writing. And the orchestra's assistant personnel manager, trombonist Al Kofsky, spoke lovingly about the orchestra and his great respect for Szell. Both players said that Szell was most definitely a genius and responsible for the orchestra's greatness. It gave me much pleasure to hear their words. I truly thank both of them for their great contributions to this bok.

John Teltsch's memoir, *Sursum Corda*, yielded a never-before-published photo of George and Helene Szell. Teltsch also gave me a photo of an oil painting of the young, glamorous Helene. I thank him profusely.

For other interviews I am indebted to cellist Diane Mather, principal French hornist Mike Bloom, principal trumpeter Bernard Adelstein, trombonist Ed Anderson, flutist John Rautenberg, principal percussionist and lawyer Richard Wiener, piccolo player William Hebert, principal French hornists Myron Bloom and Richard Solis, oboist Elden Gatwood, bassist Martin Flowerman, violist Yarden Faden, English hornist Cary Ebli, brass instruments technician Peter Cummings, recording technician Arthur Stokes, philosophy professor Robert Sweeney, lawyer William Buss, tailor Peter

Uhlir, oboist and author Laila Storch, French hornist Dr. David Sachs, and member of the board of trustees Clara Rankin.

I especially thank principal keyboardist Joela Jones, one of only two musicians hired by Szell still with the Cleveland Orchestra. In particular her recollections of her childhood years enabled me to understand the great role a parent plays in the development of a prodigy.

Three books about Robert Shaw were most helpful: Robert Blocker, *The Robert Shaw Reader*, Joseph Mussulman, *Dear People: Robert Shaw*, and Keith Burris, *Deep River: The Life and Music of Robert Shaw*. I am especially grateful to Shaw chorus member baritone Gerald Hughes, who granted me an interview and lent me his collection of Shaw letters. I thank also soprano Chris Miles, who spoke so candidly about singing in Shaw's chorus.

Architect of Blossom Pavilion Peter van Dijk consented to interviews at his home in Cleveland Heights, giving me a trove of information about Blossom that included copies of photos taken during Blossom's construction. He patiently explained terms and materials and edited my draft chapters on Blossom. In listening to his words about his youthful making of toys from humble materials at hand, I could understand his subsequent ability to make intricate architectural models. All of us who frequent Blossom are greatly in his debt.

Structural engineer Miklos Peller, whose design of its superstructure made the Blossom pavilion possible, explained the part he played in its creation, gave me photos and drawings, and also edited my Blossom chapters. His account of walking through land mines to escape Soviet reprisals in Hungary was the most astounding thing I heard in the many interviews I conducted. That daring exploit had antecedents: his youthful practice of hanging by one arm out of third-story windows. Undoubtedly his expertise in designing Blossom's superstructure was partially a result of his early fascination with how buildings were constructed, climbing inside and outside of them to learn their secrets. Mr. Peller has my respect verging on awe.

Acoustician Christopher Jaffe, whose work on the Blossom pavilion has caused many to extol its superlative acoustics, granted me a long phone interview just weeks before his death.

Also contributing to the chapters on Blossom were interviewees Laurel Gensert Bishop, Carrol Gensert, and architect William Gould.

Radio announcer Robert Conrad acquainted me with facts about FM radio broadcasts and the state of classical music in the United States and corrected one of the drafts of my manuscript. He has my sincerest thanks.

Recording engineer Vladimir Maleckar was a valuable source of information about the orchestra musicians and Szell. His facts on audio inventor Daniel Flickinger provided me with details of the Blossom sound system that I would otherwise never have known. I am much in his debt.

Washington, D.C., poet Mary Ann Larkin made many valuable corrections to my manuscript and gave me emotional support. I am very grateful for her help and our long friendship.

Deborah Hefling, archivist of the Cleveland Orchestra, was helpful in producing various photos and documents.

Viennese émigrés Trudi and Paul Eisinger and Elsa, Karl, and Felix Kraus and Lisa Kraus Brinner gave me valuable background on Vienna.

The following people were also helpful: Pat Miller, Nancy Reynolds, Marilyn Zupnik, Sam Denov, Dwight Robinson, Dr. Scott Inkley, Vaclav Benkovic, Lois Glove, Isabel Trautwein, Barbara Green, and Gianni Rosset. I thank them all.

Scientist and oboist Maryanne Pendergast was most helpful when I had computer problems. She shared oboe lore and read through one of my manuscript drafts. I am very grateful to her.

Mr. and Mrs. James Diener provided a photograph of the Szell home in Shaker Heights and gave me an extensive tour of it, describing how it was furnished when they purchased it from Helene Szell in 1970. They have my grateful thanks.

Laurie Matheson, director of acquisitions at University of Illinois Press and a musician herself, surprised me by accepting my book proposal, thereby setting me on a several years' journey filled with hard work and sleepless nights. She has my sincere thanks.

Among the other helpful people at the University of Illinois Press was copyeditor Geof Garvey, who waded through my prose, insisted on ample documentation, and dispensed encouragement when I bogged down. His question about the youthful Szell's diversions goaded me into further research. Documenting who, what, when, and where was followed by moments of "Oh, so that's why." And such insights led to conviction. Because of Geof this book is more informative now than its previous version.

The Cleveland Heights main library quickly obtained the many books I needed to consult. I always encountered patient helpful librarians and I gratefully thank them.

Finally I must give credit to professor Carl Beecher, my harmony and composition teacher at Portland School of Music in Portland, Oregon. He and my musician husband Felix were the most powerful influences in my life, hence the dedication of this book to their memories.

I never spoke to George Szell. I was simply a fascinated onlooker, gathering up strands to be woven together after more than forty years. There's been joy in the telling.

Notes

Chapter 1. A Prodigy's Apprenticeship

1. Charry, *George Szell*, 5.

2. Gal, *Golden Age of Vienna*, 6: "There is hardly a place in the world so deeply imbued with the spirit of a musical past as Vienna" (9).

3. After Vienna's most famous piano teacher, Theodor Leschetizky, rejected young George, Viennese teacher Richard Robert accepted him. Szell's friendship with Rudolf Serkin dates from their meeting in Robert's class. "Sursum Corda," an unpublished memoir by Helene Szell's son, John Teltsch, which includes facts about George Szell, is in the Cleveland Orchestra Archives.

4. Charry, *George Szell*, 9.

5. Charry, *George Szell*, 6.

6. Page 233 in Clive James's *Cultural Amnesia* notes that "for more than forty years in Vienna, talk was a way of life and then it ended." James here refers to the coming of Nazism.

7. Charry, *George Szell*, 10.

8. Page 10 of Charry's book mentions Szell's therapy with Carl Jung in Switzerland. A fad for psychoanalysis is discussed on page 59 of Lieberman's *Shrinks: The Untold Story of Psychiatry*. Charry's page 20 mentions Szell's wayward teenage period during which he frequented a bookstore owned by his friend Worm.

9. It is very likely that the young Szell frequented coffeehouses. The Vienna of Szell's teen years (1910–15) lacked radio, and so the news came only from newspapers and pamphlets that were disseminated in coffeehouses. Harold Segel in his book *The Vienna Coffeehouse Wits: 1890–1938* says on page 6 that the years 1890–1938

were the Vienna coffeehouses' great age. Pages 55–64 talk of Karl Kraus, the most famous of the Viennese coffeehouse wits. Kraus's years, 1874–1936, dovetail with the heyday of the Viennese coffeehouses and his most famous publication, "Die Fackel" (The Torch) would have been familiar to Szell. Kraus was known for his belligerent espousal of ethics and morality in literature and government. It is conceivable that Szell's phrase "artistic morality" in music performance can be traced to his presence at one or several of Kraus's lectures. On page 61 of Stefan Zweig's *The World of Yesterday* can be found a description of Zweig's youth. In the absence of facts about Szell's diversions in his teen years, Zweig's words would help explain the young Szell's progress from musical prodigy to intellectual being: "It had come on us like a fever; we had to know everything, acquire knowledge of all that was going on in every area of the arts and sciences. We crowded in with the university students in the afternoons to hear lectures, we went to all the art exhibitions, we went to the lecture theatres of the Department of Anatomy to watch dissections. Our curious nostrils sniffed at everything and anything. We stole into the rehearsals of the Philharmonic Orchestra, we rummaged around the second-hand bookshops, we looked at the booksellers' display windows every day for instant information on what had just been published. And most of all we read; we read everything we could lay hands on. We borrowed books from all the public libraries, and lent anything we could find to one another. But our best cultural source for all novelty was the coffee house." Zweig goes on to say that "the Viennese coffee house of the better sort took all the Viennese newspapers available, and not only those but the newspapers of the entire German Reich, as well as the French, British, Italian and American papers, and all the major literary and artistic international magazines." Zweig, page 62: "Perhaps nothing contributed so much to the intellectual mobility and international orientation of Austrians as the fact that they could inform themselves so extensively at the coffee house of all that was going on in the world, and at the same time could discuss it with a circle of friends." Zweig lived from 1881 to 1942.

10. Szell's youthful conducting of Strauss's *Don Juan* is on Charry's pages 14–15.

11. Page 238 of Rosenberg's *Cleveland Orchestra Story*; page 11 of Charry.

12. Hans Gal's recollections of Szell are on pages 6, 10, 12, and 20 of Charry. Gal, a friend of Szell and pupil of Robert, became a composer and musicologist. He was also a friend of Austrian conductor Erich Kleiber.

13. Szell's unsuccessful attempts with the French horn are in Charry, page 22. They also are mentioned on page 70 in Angell and Jaffe's book.

14. Szell's great powers of observation and his wonderful hearing enabled him to assess what was going on in his string sections. And his collaborations with violinist Henri Temianka, begun during his conductorship of the Scottish National Orchestra in Glasgow, where Temianka was concertmaster, gave him a fund of knowledge about string instruments, particularly violins. Temianka, who had studied violin and conducting at Curtis Institute of Music, was a virtuoso, and the two played

many violin and piano recitals together. Szell's habit of writing in the bowings for his violin sections was probably based on Temianka's bowing choices. Temianka became known for his beautiful tone quality and great technique. Szell could hardly have found a better violinist from whom to learn violin fingerings. Temianka later founded the internationally famous Paganini Quartet, founded and conducted the California Chamber Symphony, and wrote *Facing the Music*. But Szell had no similar relationship with the great oboist and teacher Marcel Tabuteau, who taught at Curtis Institute of Music and played principal oboe in the Philadelphia Orchestra under Leopold Stokowski. Consequently Tabuteau's oboist innovations would have come only partially, if at all, to Szell through the remarks of his principal oboist Marc Lifschey. Szell probably knew little to nothing about Tabuteau's numbers system for teaching phrasing.

15. Szell's marital problems are discussed on pages 19–20 in Charry.

16. Page 261 of Charry quotes a review in the *London Observer:* "At the Aeolian Hall on Tuesday, Mr. Temianka played the violin neatly and Mr. Szell at the pianoforte noisily."

17. Szell's interactions with violinist Temianka are mentioned on pages 91–92 in Temianka, *Facing the Music.*

18. Evelyn Rothwell Barbirolli's book *Life with Glorious John* on pages 46 and 47 mentions Szell's little-known failed courtship of her.

19. Helene's portrait is mentioned on Charry's page 288. A color photocopy of this painting was given to the author by Helene's son, John Teltsch, who owns it. Painted in 1923 by Austrian artist Victor Tischler, it depicts a fetchingly posed stylish young woman with cropped dark hair and large expressive eyes. The swimming pool incident is on page 44 of Charry. It also mentions a newspaper article that described Szell's action as "caveman tactics." The swimming pool incident was typical of Szell. His sense of humor can be found in his many letters to his friends and their statements about him. Szell's fondness for horseplay is documented on pages 92–93 of his friend Temianka's book *Facing the Music.* Temianka writes of himself and Szell gleefully playing the Mendelssohn Violin Concerto for friends, Szell wielding the bow and Temianka fingering the instrument. Szell's fondness for such horseplay started in his childhood years.

20. Clara Rankin, in her interview with the author on March 19, 2014.

21. Rosenberg's book on page 241 discusses the marriage of George and Helene and their sentimental nicknames for each other. Charry's book page xxi gives the date of their marriage in Glasgow as 1939. Page 241 of Rosenberg's book gives their marriage date as 1938. Charry's page 36 contains a newspaper article detailing what the Szells wore at their wedding.

22. Charry on page 58 quotes composition student George Rochberg saying that Szell's piano transcription of *Der Rosenkavalier* was like "a blinding light."

23. In his April 8, 1969, interview with John Culshaw for BBC television, Szell

mentions his feuds with Metropolitan Opera Manager Rudolf Bing and Bing's famous rejoinder, "Not while I'm alive." This phrase appears on Charry's pages 102–4.

24. Pages 73 and 74 in Charry.

25. Noticed by Vladimir Maleckar, November 26, 2011, interview. Page 104 in Fleisher and Midgette's *My Nine Lives* also mentions the scars behind Szell's ears as a result of mastoiditis operations.

Chapter 2. The Orchestra's Beginnings

1. For Cleveland's beginnings: *A Dictionary of Cleveland History*, edited by David Tassel and John Grabowski; *Euclid Avenue: Cleveland's Sophisticated Lady: 1920–1970*, by Richard F. Karberg and James A. Toman; and *Showplace of America: Cleveland's Euclid Avenue: 1850–1910*, by Jan Cigliano. The exodus from Millionaires' Row to suburban Shaker Heights is pictorially documented in Richard Campen's *Distinguished Homes of Shaker Heights*. A photo of Millionaires' Row taken in 1880 is on page 89 of Cigliano's book. Her page 95 gives a partial list of the wealthy businessmen—Jeptha Wade, Charles Hickox, Louis C. Severance, Samuel Mather, Charles Brush, and John D. Rockefeller—who built mansions on Euclid Avenue.

2. Pages 227–28 in Stuart Isacoff's *Temperament* lists the many piano makers in the United States and Europe and states, "As the twentieth century began, Americans were buying more than 350,000 pianos a year." Arthur Loesser's *Men, Women and Pianos* states that in 1920 the U.S. population of 105 million owned about 7 million pianofortes.

3. Adella Prentiss Hughes's memoir *Music Is My Life* relates on pages 27–40 her beginnings, musical education, and concert managerial activities. Page 45 in Robert Marsh's *Cleveland Orchestra*, page 7, shows a young Adella around 1895. Rosenberg, between pages 160 and 161, depicts a handsome Adella captioned "Adella Prentiss Hughes thrives as manager of the Symphony Orchestra Concerts series, which brings the finest American orchestras to Cleveland for two decades starting in 1901." Rosenberg's page 33 mentions Hughes's "charming and highly selective autobiography." His page 41 notes "Within a year, Hughes would begin to develop something that the city thus far had been unable to sustain, and that would transform Cleveland's cultural life: the belated, but swift, birth of its own permanent orchestra." Hughes's powers of persuasion enabled her to enlist several civic leaders as presidents of her board of trustees: D. Z. Norton (1915–21), John L. Severance (1921–36), Dudley S. Blossom (1936–38), Thomas L. Sidlo (1939–53). It should be noted that Hughes was able to attract these men because of her family's social ties to the wealthy and cultured civic leaders in Cleveland. Her overbearing personality, however, was a major factor in her eventual sidelining by the board of trustees (Charry page 84: "They forced the orchestra's founder, Adella Prentiss Hughes, to retire from full board status and assume the title 'honorary vice president.'") Her managerial position was partially taken over by Carl Vosburgh. Rosenberg page 266: "Hughes had not been directly involved in orchestra affairs since her forced retirement in 1943.") She died in 1950.

4. Pages 30–43 in Robert Marsh's *Cleveland Orchestra* contain information and pictures of the building of Severance Hall, including a brief description of the huge light console backstage, which could be programmed for four thousand lighting combinations. A photo of the console is on page 42 of Marsh's book. He states that much of the equipment was replaced in 1958 when the stage was reconstructed. Marsh's book also contains pictures of John L. Severance and his wife Elizabeth De Witt Severance. Theirs was the original gift of a million dollars for the building of a new concert hall for the Cleveland Orchestra.

5. Cleveland Orchestra oboist Robert Zupnik, in one of his many interviews from 2011 to 2016, told of seeing Mrs. Hughes greeting audience members at the entrance to Severance Hall. The Green Room's original decorations and furnishings were still in place when the author viewed them in 1963. Subsequent refurbishings have included replacing the original silk-velvet drapes, which water had damaged.

6. Oboist Robert Zupnik, in another interview, discussed Rodzinski's tenure with the Cleveland Orchestra and recalled the New York newspaper's article "A Gale Blows in from Lake Erie," which mentioned Rodzinski's excessively fast conducting during the Syracuse concert. Zupnik also said that most of the Cleveland Orchestra musicians knew Rodzinski carried a pistol.

7. On page 189, Rosenberg mentions Rodzinski's stepladder gambit in the orchestra's boardroom. Robert Zupnik, in one of his many telephone conversations with the author, recalled hearing that Rodzinski's words on that occasion were "You can't fire somebody you have to look up to."

8. Charry's page 85 notes the groundswell of support for Szell: "'For the first time in the history of the orchestra,' Sidlo said, 'the task of choosing a regular conductor was virtually taken out of our hands and the choice was made for us by audience and public. . . . Cleveland has never before received a conductor with such universal favor.'" The same page quotes Szell's letter to his friend Eric Oldberg: "I discovered that the people in Cleveland had gone completely wild and were prepared to give me everything I wanted on a golden platter."

9. Charry's page 276 includes a portion of a letter to Hughes from artist manager Constance Hope: "Let us conspire together" (to engage Leinsdorf in Cleveland over Szell). Page 198 in Rosenberg's book relates Leinsdorf's words about Hughes's high-handed ways: "She acted as if she *were* the Cleveland Orchestra." Rosenberg's book on page 197 mentions that she lobbied heavily for Leinsdorf and instigated a smear campaign against Szell and two other conductors. His page 226 briefly describes the enthusiasm for Szell: "Now the public was talking, and the Musical Arts Association was listening. Letters poured in suggesting or demanding that Szell be hired."

10. In the absence of archival files documenting the contract negotiations between Szell and the Musical Arts Association, the author has relied on Rosenberg's and Charry's books, which mention the all-important negotiating meeting on January 15, 1946, between Szell and four Cleveland Orchestra officers that established Szell's

total control. On page 227 of Rosenberg's book: "Szell engaged in a shrewd negotiating game with Vosburgh, Sidlo and trustees Percy Brown and Lewis B. Williams at the Cleveland Hotel. The conductor had the upper hand. He would speak with each man only individually before agreeing on a contract." Charry, on page 85, mentions the meeting with the four men "in the presence of a stenographer with a typewriter."

11. The author could not gain access to Szell's contract in the Cleveland Orchestra's archives. But a lawsuit that MAA violinists Bert Siegel and Gino Raffaelli brought against Szell in 1968 produced the contract, which was reviewed by the presiding judge. Because it stated that Szell had absolute power of hiring and firing, the violinists lost their lawsuit. That situation is discussed in chapter 9 of this book.

12. Szell's conditions regarding personnel, programming, scheduling, touring, recording, broadcasting, soloists, guest conductors, and leaves of absence had to be met before he would consider talking salary. Page 86 in Charry's book notes: "Szell's salary was never officially announced. It was $40,000." Page 270 in Rosenberg's book states that Szell's salary in 1953 was $48,000. Years later, addressing the question of Szell's salary, Louis Lane remarked to several orchestra members, including oboist Felix Kraus, "They could never afford to pay him what he's worth."

Chapter 3. Szell's Improvements

1. Page 87 in Charry's book quotes Thomas Sidlo, president of the Musical Arts Association, as saying, "Let us have nothing but the best. Nothing but the best will do." Page 35 in Robert Marsh's *Cleveland Orchestra* notes that "John Severance spared no expense to make this (Severance Hall) the greatest hall of its day." Charry's page 106 says, "Szell replaced sixteen players." These firings received no opposition from the Cleveland Musicians' Union.

2. Walker's *Hans von Bülow* details Bülow's Meiningen Court Orchestra on pages 282–85, 287, 300. Bülow was born in 1830 and died in 1894, three years before Szell was born. Concertizing all over Europe and the United States, Bülow would have been almost a household name in musically sophisticated Vienna. Birkin's *Hans von Bülow* gives Bülow's Beethoven symphony repertoire on pages 291–93. What became known as "The Meiningen Principle" is detailed on page 291: "separating the sections of the orchestra into strings, winds and brasses."

3. Pages 246–50 in Rosenberg's *Cleveland Orchestra Story* include facts about Szell's firing of musicians in his first season.

4. Lane's article "Szell: A Partial Memoir" in the February 1974 issue of *Cleveland* magazine on pages 44–48 speaks of his audition with Szell and his subsequent long association with Szell and the Cleveland Orchestra.

5. Rosenberg's listing of Cleveland Orchestra personnel on page 650 includes Lane's years with the orchestra. He began as an apprentice conductor and was promoted to assistant, then associate, and finally resident conductor. His tenure lasted from 1947 to 1974.

6. Lillian Baldwin's musical rhymes and drawings are on pages 296–98 in Hughes's memoir *Music Is My Life*. Baldwin's ideas are redolent of a bygone era. Szell's spurning of Baldwin's ideas for children's concerts is quoted in Rosenberg's book on page 288: "Why do you play trash for our children? I blush with shame at the concerts you give our children."

7. Harpist Alice Chalifoux, who had joined the orchestra in 1931, remained his principal harpist throughout his tenure. A list of Cleveland Orchestra personnel in Donald Rosenberg's book on pages 637–49 shows that, beginning in 1947 and subsequently, Szell hired thirteen women for the string sections and keyboardist Joela Jones.

8. Leiter's *Musicians and Petrillo* relates the history of the musicians' union and Petrillo's role in it. Pages 94–111 deal with the jurisdiction and operation of each local chapter in the country. More specifically, the author perused the 113 pages in the September 15, 2013, revised *Bylaws of the American Federation of Musicians of the United States and Canada*. Its Article 5, "Locals' Rights and Duties," contains no reference to the presidents and officials of the locals. Therefore, as explained by a staff member at the national AFM headquarters during a lengthy phone interview, officials of each local throughout the country are free to interpret the bylaws as they see fit. (The informant requested anonymity.)

9. Pages 194–95 in Charry's *George Szell* tell of troubles developing with the Cleveland Musicians' Union. Pages 369–71 in Rosenberg's book address the conflict between orchestra musicians and Local 4. "At a negotiating session with management for a new contract in 1967 he [Tony Granata, president of Local 4] remained steadfast in his refusal to allow the musicians' lawyer Bernard A. Berkman to present a contract proposal." The February 1971 issue of *Senza Sordino*, the publication of the International Conference of Symphony and Opera Musicians, lists on page 2 the musicians' grievances with the Cleveland Musicians' Union.

10. Page 644 in Rosenberg's listing of Cleveland Orchestra personnel shows volatility in the principal oboe position: Philip Kirchner 1919–47, Bert Gassman 1947–1949, Emmanuel Tivin 1949–50, Marc Lifschey 1950–1965. Lifschey was the only oboist, up to 1950, who finally found favor with Szell. In contrast, page 637 in Rosenberg's book lists musicians who later voluntarily left the Cleveland Orchestra. They include principal cellist Jules Eskin 1961–64, assistant principal violinist Anshel Brusilow 1955–59, concertmaster Josef Gingold 1946–60, and violinist Sidney Weiss 1955–66. In a YouTube interview, Gingold told of his conversation with Szell about leaving the orchestra (https://www.youtube.com/watch?v=AH7xF129_0c).

11. Szell's insistence on acoustical renovation of the Severance Hall auditorium, undertaken in 1958, is discussed in Charry on pages 177–79. Pages 114–15 and 299–300 in Rosenberg discuss Szell's acoustical renovation, and pages 40–43 in Marsh's *Cleveland Orchestra* and pages 91–97 in Klaus Roy's *Not Responsible for Lost Articles* also include facts about the renovation.

12. Joshua Krisch's article "When Racism Was a Science" in the October 14, 2014, issue of the *New York Times* tells of the Rockefeller family's and the Carnegie Institution's funding of the eugenics movement. The eugenics office was closed in 1939 but eugenics and anti-Semitism lingered on. Adam Cohen's 2016 book *Imbeciles: The Supreme Court* gives a full account of the pseudo-science of eugenics. One of the chief proponents of eugenics was Oliver Wendell Holmes Jr. Many other prominent men of the time also approved of the eugenics movement. Page 279 in Cohen's book: "Eugenics was a movement of people who believed themselves to be inherently superior, and in Holmes it found a fitting judicial standard-bearer." Page 302: "The United States had 'pioneered' eugenic sterilization for the rest of the world. Nazi Germany adopted its *Law for the Prevention of Hereditarily Diseased Offspring* in summer 1933. Germany learned from the United States when it drafted its own sterilization laws. The Nazis also used sterilization against Jews and people of partial Jewish background, Roma, the children of German women and black French soldiers, and other disfavored racial and religious groups. Page 303: "When the Final Solution was adopted, provisions were made for Germans with mixed Aryan and Jewish blood to be sterilized as an alternative to extermination." Page 319: "By the end of the twentieth century, legal eugenic sterilization had come to an end, but the number of Americans who had been involuntarily sterilized between 1907 and 1983 was staggering: between sixty and seventy thousand." Page 303: "The classic 1961 movie *Judgment at Nuremberg* captures in dramatic fashion how the Nazi defendants used the case (*Buck v. Bell*). The Nazi lawyer then states triumphantly that the words 'Three generations of imbeciles are enough' were those of 'that great American jurist, Supreme Court Justice Oliver Wendell Holmes.'" In view of such shameful U.S. history, Szell's concern for his Jewish musicians was more than justified.

13. "In its heyday, Oakwood Country Club catered to Jewish civic and business leaders who socialized and dined in style in the clubhouse." http://www.cleveland.com/metro/index.ssf/2016/04/historic_oakwood_country_clubs.html.

14. Page 59 in Charry's book mentions that one of Szell's composition students at Mannes School of Music, George Rochberg, remembered Szell's Homburg hat and his coat with its fur collar.

15. Page 194 in program annotator Klaus Roy's book contains violinist Kurt Loebel's anecdote about Szell's early naïveté about U.S. popular culture. Rosenberg's page 261 also relates this anecdote. Robert Zupnik, in one of his many interviews and telephone calls, told the ballgame anecdote. This anecdote is part of the Szell lore known to most orchestra members and appears on page 18 in Angell and Jaffe, *Tales from the Locker Room*.

16. Pianist Leon Fleisher mentions this incident on page 106 of Fleisher and Midgette's *My Nine Lives*.

17. Sorenson's *Famous Ford Woodies* is the definitive book on this popular vehicle. Sorenson's page 179 shows the back of a Mercury station wagon and a brief

description of its hauling capabilities. Maleckar's station wagon would have looked much like the 1946 models. Maleckar, in his November 26, 2011, interview with the author, recalled driving Szell in his station wagon during which Szell manifested his fascination with the vehicle.

18. Both Robert Zupnik and Felix Kraus mentioned to the author in personal communications that Szell seemed to think of himself as the musicians' father and acted as if he was always right.

19. Oboist Felix Kraus, who witnessed the Szell-Harrell exchange on an airplane during an orchestra tour, related it to the author. Oboist Felix Kraus also recounted this anecdote in one of his many conversations with the author. This same anecdote is contained in Angell and Jaffe's *Tales from the Locker Room*.

20. Cellist Teddy Baar told oboist Felix Kraus about Szell's insisting he go back to the hotel for his galoshes just before a rehearsal while on tour. (This anecdote was in one of the many conversations Kraus had with the author.)

21. Page 177 in Charry mentions that Szell frequented such resorts as the Dolder Grand Hotel in Zurich and the Kurhotel Montafon in Schrung, Austria. Charry's page 107 states that one of Szell's favorite resorts was Hotel du Golf at Crans-sur-sierre in Valais, Switzerland. Page 182 mentions Szell's stay at the Bircher-Benner Clinic in Zurich for a health regimen.

22. Szell's concern with breathing fresh air was told to the author by Felix Kraus in his interview, who was on the train bearing the orchestra members through the Alps. Page 67 of Angell and Jaffe's book includes a similar quote from a letter written by Marc Lifschey's widow, Paula Lifschey.

23. Trumpeter Dick Smith's experience in a Salzburg restaurant was told to the author by Felix Kraus. Szell's concern with his musicians' diets is related on pages 145 and 146 in Angell and Jaffe's book. This incident was known by most of the orchestra musicians.

24. Oboist Robert Zupnik to the author in one of his many telephone conversations in 2015 and 2016.

25. Szell's parents were killed by the Nazis, and in 1945 he underwent surgery to save his hearing.

26. Violist Abe Skernick's requests to Szell for pay raises were repeated to assistant personnel manager Dave Zauder and then to various members of the orchestra, including Felix Kraus, who repeated it to the author in another of their many conversations. Page 28 in Angell and Jaffe's book also recounts Szell's words to Skernick about his requests for pay raises.

27. The near-military efficiency at Severance Hall was remarked on by the musicians, including Felix Kraus, who told the author about his parking place assignment.

28. Lois Glove, Peggy Glove's niece, told the author in a 2013 telephone call that Szell highly valued Peggy's loyalty and efficiency. Lois Glove still owns the porcelain vase and described its details to the author.

29. Overheard by Vlad Maleckar and related to the author.

30. Klaus Roy's office was occasionally visited by Felix Kraus, who described its cluttered appearance to the author. Page 152 in Rosenberg's book: Roy "cleaned off his stacked desk in the basement of Severance Hall."

31. Oboist Robert Zupnik's conversation with the author during one of his many telephone calls in 2015 and 2016.

32. Although Charry states on page 277 that "Szell was truly fond of Barksdale and their working relationship remained cordial to the end," Rosenberg shows a different aspect of their relationship on his page 386: "For his part, Szell was weary of a manager who, while meticulous and smart, tended to think too long before acting." Rosenberg writes on page 298, "Barksdale would endure this type of ranting (Szell's) throughout his association with the conductor."

33. Oboist Robert Zupnik to the author during a telephone conversation 2015 told of Pitcock's tight running of the box office and his unwillingness to grant favors.

34. Box office manager Larry Pitcock's curt reply to a ticket request was related to the author by Robert Zupnik.

35. Robert Zupnik to the author during a lengthy telephone conversation on November 22, 2013, said that Szell tolerated Pitcock because he valued his efficiency. Felix Kraus to the author in one of their many conversations about Szell's relationship with Pitcock and specifically his hands-off approach to Pitcock's treatment of donors.

36. This anecdote was told to the author by various Cleveland Orchestra musicians, including Robert Zupnik and. Felix Kraus. It was also repeated by various musicians in Angell and Jaffe's book.

37. The incident in Di Vita's grocery store was told to the author by Felix Kraus, who experienced it.

38. Page 241 in Rosenberg: "Helene would learn to deal with her husband's temper, obsession with perfection and bulldozer approach to gourmet cooking (he made a total mess of the kitchen while concocting a fancy dish)."

39. Rombauer's recipe for Hungarian goulash is on pages 464–65. Rombauer wrote, "a knowing friend claims that shinbone meat . . . ," pages 28–31 in Charry. The knowing friend was probably Szell.

40. Szell as wine connoisseur is an anecdote related to the author on March 19, 2014, by Clara Rankin, a member of the Cleveland Orchestra's board of trustees. Szell's fondness for good food and wine is mentioned on page 143 in Chapin's *Musical Chairs*.

41. Szell's inexperience with children is shown in his impatience with Lillian Baldwin's ideas for children's programs of light classics, in which she had wisely taken into account children's short attention spans. Rosenberg's page 288 states, "Szell had never had much input into children's concerts. And, curiously, the programs he objected to—colorful works by Wolf-Ferrari, Vaughn Williams, Coates, Grainger, Sibelius, Lecuona, and Herbert—could hardly have been termed trashy." Also on Rosenberg's

page 288: "When Szell came," recalled harpist Alice Chalifoux, "he wanted the kids to hear Mozart and they didn't give a damn about Mozart. Ringwall (the orchestra's assistant conductor) did things that children understand at age 6, 7 and 8."

Chapter 4. The Woodwind Section

1. Pages 377 and 384 in Laila Storch's *Marcel Tabuteau* show cane bundled and standing upright to age against trees. Cane supply, reed production and cost, gouging machines, and instrument repair facts were related to the author by oboist Felix Kraus, the author's husband. The author also witnessed firsthand the process of production of reeds from 1956 to 2004.

2. The oboist was Harold Gomberg, principal oboist of the New York Philharmonic from 1943 to 1977. His words were told to the author by oboist Felix Kraus. Kraus referred the author to the website damnreeds.com, but the name of the oboist was not mentioned.

3. The New York Symphony was a different entity from the New York Philharmonic.

4. Tabuteau's harsh words at lessons were related to the author by former Tabuteau student Felix Kraus. The predominance of male students was due to Tabuteau's conviction that female oboists couldn't get jobs in predominantly male orchestras. But a shortage of males during World War II caused him to accept women, among them Storch, who became his dedicated student and secretary and was then hired as principal oboe in the Houston Symphony. Her book on Tabuteau is the definitive work on that great musician. To the author she stated that Tabuteau's lessons lasted forty minutes. Laila Storch to the author during a 2015 telephone conversation.

5. Szell's contract had given him carte blanche in the hiring of players. On page 196, Charry's *George Szell* quotes Szell: "a Board of Trustees who have fulfilled every one of my wishes regardless of cost."

6. Robert Zupnik to the author: "Marc played on the softer side and Szell kept the orchestra's volume down to accommodate him."

7. Second oboist Elden Gatwood played in the Cleveland Orchestra from 1953 to 1963. He then became principal oboist of the Pittsburgh Symphony (2014 phone interview with the author).

8. Assistant principal oboist Robert Zupnik to the author during his interview on March 28, 2013.

9. Felix Kraus to the author.

10. Anecdote related to the author in 2014 by Cleveland Orchestra bass clarinetist Linnea Nereim, who had studied with Marcellus. Marcellus's staying up all night listening to music is mentioned in Angell and Jaffe's book on p 161.

11. Felix Kraus spoke to the author about Goslee's wealth and sunny nature.

12. Heard by entire orchestra including Felix Kraus, who related it to the author.

13. Alfred Genovese played in the Cleveland Orchestra from 1959 to 1960. Don-

ald Rosenberg's list of the Cleveland Orchestra personnel is on his pages 637–50. Tabuteau's admiring words to Genovese are part of the Tabuteau lore known to all Tabuteau students. The anecdote was told to the author by Felix Kraus.

14. Szell's words to Lifschey were told to the author by Felix Kraus.

15. Kraus related to the author Szell's words to him at the end of his successful audition in 1963.

16. Szell's words were related to the author by Kraus. Former second oboist Elden Gatwood experienced similar problems with Lifschey and related some of them in his telephone interview with the author. Robert Zupnik asserted to the author: "Lifschey played on the softer side of the sound and Szell had to tone down the orchestral accompaniment during Lifschey's solos." Pages 38 and 39 in Angell and Jaffe's *Tales from the Locker Room* include Gatwood's remark that Szell often asked him to play louder, but Lifschey insisted that he play softer.

17. Lifschey's brazen words to Szell were heard by the entire orchestra and just an hour after the dramatic incident were reported to the author by Felix Kraus, who was sitting next to Lifschey during the incident. Page 341 in Rosenberg's *Cleveland Orchestra Story* reports the incident with slightly different dialogue. The incident also is told differently on pages 219–20 in Charry. Page 68 in Angell and Jaffe's *Tales from the Locker Room* quotes Lifschey's widow Paula: "The line Rosenberg left out of his *The Cleveland Orchestra Story* about Marc's departure from Cleveland was Marc standing up and saying, 'Fourteen years of this s..t' and then walking off stage." Paula Lifschey's letter to Angell and Jaffe directly corroborates Kraus's words. Trombonist Allen Kofsky in his March 1, 2014, interview with the author recalled seeing Marc hold up his reed and snap it in two. The pitch in question was much lower than the standard A = 440 vibrations per second. It is crucial that the principal oboist set the correct pitch, because all instruments tune to it. Deliberately playing out of tune is musical malfeasance.

18. Szell's words were recalled by Felix Kraus and told to the author.

19. Zupnik told the author about Szell's request that he move into Lifschey's vacated seat.

20. The Cleveland Orchestra's planned tour of Soviet Russia, Scandinavia, and Europe is mentioned on page 341 of Rosenberg's book and page 220 of Charry's book.

21. Both Abe Skernick and Mike Bloom told oboist Felix Kraus about their attempt to phone Szell on Lifschey's behalf; Kraus conversation with the author.

22. Lifschey told Felix Kraus and other orchestra players about his failed phone call to Szell; Kraus conversation with the author.

23. Szell's command to assistant first oboist Zupnik to take over as first oboe was related to the author by Zupnik. Szell's reliance on Zupnik in emergencies began years before. Szell's June 29, 1958, thank-you letter to Zupnik reads: "I want to send you my special thanks for your superb pinch-hitting during our Robin Hood Dell engagement. You have distinguished yourself and contributed materially to the

maintenance of the orchestra's prestige and high standards." Zupnik received a box of Whitman's chocolates from Szell after he had substituted for Marc, and on a similar occasion Szell presented him with a wool plaid tie. He also autographed a picture of himself for Zupnik: "To Bob Zupnik in warm appreciation of his consistent and reliable contribution to the growth of the Cleveland Orchestra—and with special thanks for his help in many an emergency. Cordially, George Szell, February 1968." (Zupnik interview with the author on March 28, 2013.) Szell's letter and autographed picture are owned by Zupnik. He showed them to the author and gave the author a copy of the picture.

24. Bartók's *Concerto for Orchestra* was commissioned in 1943 by the Boston Symphony at the behest of its conductor Serge Koussevitzky.

25. Oboist Felix Kraus in conversation with the author.

26. The chicken–crocodile epithet was told to the author by Maryanne Pendergast, who heard it from John Mack, a former student of Tabuteau at Curtis Institute of Music.

27. Oboist Felix Kraus told the author he had been ordered by Szell to coach the newly hired oboist. Szell's hiring of the new oboist without a formal audition or announcement in the International Musicians' newspaper was not the first or last time he would do such a thing. Rosenberg's book states on page 255 that "a formal audition hadn't been necessary in Gingold's case. Szell liked what he heard and closed the deal himself as did other conductors of the time. Before the musicians' unions gained power in the mid-1960s, orchestras' hiring processes were not democratic." Another significant bypassing of union rules occurred in 1969 with the hiring of Daniel Majeske to replace Rafael Druian; page 276 in Charry's book: "Szell directed assistant concertmaster Daniel Majeske to move into the concertmaster's chair, and shortly afterward officially appointed him to the position." Szell also appointed Joela Jones as his first full-time keyboardist without an audition. The position was not announced in the International Musicians' Union newspaper or elsewhere. Jones interviews with the author on April 5, 2012, October 31, 2012, February 21, 2013.

28. Oboist Felix Kraus related Szell's words to the author.

Chapter 5. World Tour

1. The Cleveland Orchestra's 1965 Soviet Union tour is documented on pages 227–31 in Charry's *George Szell* and pages 329–30 and 341–43 in Rosenberg's *Cleveland Orchestra Story*.

2. Felix Kraus to the author.

3. Oboist Felix Kraus related being given an ivory brooch that belonged to a Russian student's grandmother.

4. Trumpeter Bernard Adelstein to the author in phone interview March 8, 2014.

5. Robert Zupnik to the author in telephone interview February 12, 2012. Felix

Kraus told the author that the Russian food was not attractive unless one liked chicken Kiev.

6. In his August 31, 2013, telephone interview, flutist Bill Hebert told the author about the hidden microphone in his room. Al Kofsky in his March 1, 2014, interview stated that he and his colleagues were aware of electronic surveillance in some hotels in Russia and that they were usually followed by members of the KGB.

7. Bernard Adelstein in his March 10, 2014, telephone interview told the author about Al Kofsky's finding his Remington shaver taken apart by suspicious Soviets.

8. Page 345 in Rosenberg's book: "He was called back to the stage 16 times in Bratislava where Cleveland became the first American orchestra ever to pay a visit." Czech violinist Vaclav Benkovic heard the Cleveland Orchestra in Bratislava and described to the author, during an August 2013 conversation at the home of a mutual friend, the great impression the orchestra had made: "Szell came onstage like a god. It was the world's greatest orchestra for sure." Benkovic vowed to leave the USSR and get to Cleveland. He eventually made it and played in the Cleveland Orchestra from 1975 to 2009. His membership in the orchestra is documented on Rosenberg's page 639.

9. Oboist Felix Kraus to the author.

10. Lawyer Robert Larson in a January 22, 2014, interview told the author of his presence on the 1965 Soviet Union-Scandinavian-European tour and how he diplomatically tried to deal with the trombonist's disruptive behavior. Page 393 of Rosenberg's book mentions the same trombonist's drunkenness in Anchorage five years later in 1970. The scandalous behavior of the trombonist at the Soviet banquet also was related to the author by Felix Kraus.

11. The wrong note played by the newly hired oboist was recalled by Felix Kraus, Robert Zupnik, and other orchestra players who were on the tour. The incident was first told to the author by Kraus. The young oboist was benched upon the orchestra's arrival back in Cleveland. His two-year contract had another year to run, so he remained in Cleveland, sitting unoccupied in the musicians' locker room.

12. Felix Kraus, who spoke German, brought home several of the 1965 German and Austrian newspaper articles about the Cleveland Orchestra and translated them for the author. The clippings have not survived.

13. Oboists Robert Zupnik and Felix Kraus and trombonist Al Kofsky, in their many interviews and conversations with the author, were in agreement about Lifschey's great artistry and prima donna behavior. They said that their opinions on Lifschey were shared by their colleagues. Zupnik stated that Lifschey "was not a team player."

14. Charry's book on page 233 mentions Szell's European vacations: "As in 1957, the Szells stayed in Europe after the tour and did not take part in the welcoming festivities staged by the city of Cleveland. Ten busloads of families and friends came out to meet the orchestra, and were joined by a crowd of 5,500 fans headed by Cleveland mayor Frank S. Locher. . . . Each member of the orchestra walked down the steps

from the plane onto the red carpet to introductions and cheers from the crowd." The author witnessed this triumphant homecoming.

Chapter 6. Szell's Dictates

1. Oboist John Mack stated to the author on several occasions that he regarded the symphony orchestra as one of mankind's greatest inventions. Felix Kraus told the author that Mack would frequently, while playing a composition from the standard orchestra repertoire, close his music to show that he knew the piece from memory. As far as Kraus knew, Mack missed only one concert (owing to a blizzard in Washington, D.C.) in the years he played in the Cleveland Orchestra. Mack frequently insisted on a half-hour rehearsal with Kraus at Kraus's home before the ten o'clock orchestral rehearsal at Severance Hall. These private rehearsals many times involved playing Mozart piano concertos and symphonies in which the first and second oboes play together in thirds or sixths. They both knew that Mozart was Szell's favorite composer, hence the extra effort. Mack's student Maryanne Pendergast frequently alluded to Mack's teaching methods and quoted one of his oft-spoken phrases: "Never take no from an inanimate object." This was in reference to intractable gouging machines, cane, and oboes.

2. Szell's words to Bob Zupnik about Mack were related to the author by Zupnik. John Oboe Mack was the Cleveland Orchestra's principal oboist from 1965 to 2001. Mack's Tabuteau anecdotes were recalled by Felix Kraus. Mack employed teaching methods copied from Tabuteau, whose numbers system for teaching phrasing is widely known by U.S. oboists, including oboist-author Laila Storch. Storch's *Marcel Tabuteau* mentions Mack on numerous pages, for example, 68, 70, 114, and 202. Szell knew Mack's playing for several years before he actually hired him. The latest private audition took place in an empty church in Spain at a Casals festival. The principal oboe opening was not announced in the musicians' union paper or elsewhere. The particulars of the audition and Szell's arrival at the festival, apparently for the sole purpose of hearing Mack once more (he had played for Szell twice before that) were told to the author by Mack's student Maryanne Pendergast.

3. Oboist Kraus told the author that his request to Szell for a smile once in a while was finally granted by Szell's very fake smile during a rehearsal. This anecdote is similarly recounted on page 147 of Angell and Jaffe's *Tales from the Locker Room*. Among the pages of photos in Charry's book is one showing Szell backstage rehearsing John Mack and Lynn Harrell before a Seattle concert.

4. According to Rosenberg's personnel listing on page 640, Tom Brennand joined the orchestra as principal violist in 1937, became its music librarian in 1942 while still playing in the viola section, and retired in 1965. Bob O'Brien, current librarian of the Cleveland Orchestra, spoke of his responsibilities during his July 27, 2016, interview with the author in the George Szell Library at Severance Hall. He stated that graffiti on the players' parts was "a thing of the past."

5. Page 341 of Rosenberg's *Cleveland Orchestra Story* recounts Szell compelling Barksdale to send a memo to the orchestra's male players: "Both Mr. Szell and I have had unfavorable comments from subscribers regarding the short socks worn by some of the men," the manager wrote. "May I remind you once more that you should wear socks of sufficient length to completely cover the exposed part of the leg. The 'over-the-calf' type is preferable."

6. Szell's complaining letter to manager Barksdale about miniskirts at Severance Hall is on page 273 of Charry's *George Szell*.

7. A contrast between Mack's large tone and Lifschey's smaller one was commented on by Bob Zupnik in his April 2, 2014, phone interview with the author. "Marc did not play loudly. He played on the softer side. When he played his solos Szell had to tone down the orchestral accompaniment especially for him so he could be heard."

Chapter 7. The String Section

1. Cleveland Orchestra violinist Isabel Trautwein to the author in a 2015 telephone conversation.

2. Cellist Beverly LeBeck to the author. LeBeck attended Curtis in 1946, a student of Felix Salmond. She is listed in the Curtis Institute of Music 1975 Alumni directory.

3. Cellist-author speaking from her own experience.

4. Cleveland Orchestra bassist Marty Flowerman in his April 23, 2015, interview with the author.

5. Flowerman's remarks are similar to the lengthy footnote on page 283 in Steinberg's *The Symphony*, which points out that Mahler meant the bass solo in Mahler's *Symphony No. 1* to be parodic, and most bass players, striving for beauty of tone and interpretation, undermine Mahler's intent.

6. Oboist Betty Camus, who joined the Cleveland Orchestra in 1979, told the author about Szell's remark. She had heard it from an older member of the orchestra.

7. Michael Cooper's April 25, 2014, *New York Times* article mentions the $45 million asking price for a Stradivarius viola. His article also says, "Even fine modern instruments, whose prices have not been inflated by avid collectors who see them as investments, can cost tens of thousands of dollars, putting them out of reach of young players saddled with conservatory debt."

8. Douglas Quenqua's February 17, 2015, *New York Times* article on prized old Italian violins mentions one of the reasons for those violins' beautiful tone quality: "Using technical drawings, X rays and CT scans to determine the air flow through the f-shaped holes, scientists . . . found that the length of the holes, not the width, and the strength of the back plate had the biggest effect on sound quality." Guarnerius violins had the largest f-holes and emitted the strongest sounds.

9. Page 23 of *Duino Elegies* by Rainer Maria Rilke.

10. Jascha Heifetz's 1952 RCA Victor recording of J. S. Bach's *Sonatas and Partitas* is hailed by many violinists and critics as the definitive one.

11. Cleveland Orchestra violinist Kurt Loebbel told Felix Kraus about Heifetz's bland disregard of Szell's request. Loebbel played in the orchestra from 1947 to 1997.

12. Composer-music critic Thomson's famous epithet on Heifetz's encores is on pages 220 and 221 in his *Music Chronicles*.

13. Violinist Sidney Weiss played in the Cleveland Orchestra from 1956 to 1966. He told Felix Kraus about playing an audition for Szell using a violin he had made. Weiss left the orchestra for the concertmaster position in the Los Angeles Philharmonic. The anecdote about him and his violin is also on page 75 of Angell and Jaffe's *Tales from the Locker Room*.

14. Weiss, in conversation with Felix Kraus, spoke of selling his Stradivarius violin.

15. Gingold played in the Cleveland Orchestra from 1947 to 1960. In a YouTube interview he spoke of Szell's encouraging him to accept the Indiana University position. Friendly relations between him and Szell are mentioned on page 254 in Rosenberg.

16. According to Rosenberg page 256, one player lost his job after Szell noticed that he had purchased a new car instead of a fine instrument. The player's name is not mentioned.

17. Felix Kraus to the author. Kraus's fear of being late to a rehearsal or concert was shared by the other orchestra members. Orchestra members were fined for lateness.

18. Szell had a healthy sense of humor and, like most Viennese of his generation, would have enjoyed jokes about bodily functions. But decorum dictated that certain types of off-color jokes weren't told in mixed company. Chalifoux's ribaldry was certain to embarrass him. Chalifoux joined the Cleveland Orchestra in 1931 and was at the time the only woman in the orchestra. Her greatness as a teacher resulted in her students Lisa Wellbaum and then Trina Struble inheriting her position as principal harpist. Thus Chalifoux's impact on the Cleveland Orchestra's harp section extended from 1931 to the present as of this writing.

19. Harpist Chalifoux's uninhibited personality was described to the author by Al Kofsky in his February 12, 2014, interview. He surmised that Alice picked up her salty language from the men in the orchestra and that her bold personality was a way of protecting herself in an all-male environment.

20. Chalifoux's spat with Szell was related to the author by lawyer Bob Larson in a January 22, 2014, interview.

21. Recollections of quartet sessions with Cleveland Orchestra string players are the author's.

22. Cathleen Dalschaert told the author what she said to Szell.

23. The recollection of Szeryng's rehearsal flirtations was told to the author by a Cleveland Orchestra violinist who requested anonymity.

24. Szell's ruination of Szeryng's performance in Carnegie Hall is recounted by

Arnold Steinhardt on page 91 in Angell and Jaffe's book. Steinhardt said that maybe it was the best conducting technically Szell ever did, managing to get the orchestra at sixes and sevens with the soloist. Page 91 in Angell and Jaffe's *Tales from the Locker Room* mentions Szell's ruining Szeryng's performance in the New York concert.

25. Rosenberg's pages 321–22 recount the Szeryng–Szell standoff, including Louis Lane's comment that Szeryng's ego was "intergalactic in scope."

26. Page 322 in Rosenberg states that "when Milstein and Szell disagreed, they fought it out on a more visceral basis: They screamed at each other in German." Pages 9–10 in Angell and Jaffe includes harpist Chalifoux's recollection that Szell's constant correction of Curzon during a rehearsal caused an exasperated Curzon to finally explode "Get someone else to play your damn concerto" and walk off stage.

Chapter 8. The Brass Section

1. Page 236 in Michael Kennedy's *Richard Strauss* quotes a slight variation on Strauss's words. "Never look encouragingly at the brass" and "If you think the brass is not blowing hard enough, tone it down another shade or two."

2. Felix Kraus to the author. Tubist Ronald Bishop joined the Cleveland Orchestra in 1967.

3. The source for this long quote is trombonist Al Kofsky in his telephone interview with the author on May 22, 2014. Kofsky was a member of the Cleveland Orchestra from 1961 to 2000.

4. Trumpeter Dick Smith was principal trumpet in the orchestra from 1958 to 1960. He remained in the orchestra as a section player up to and including 1967.

5. Bernard Adelstein was principal trumpet in the orchestra from 1960 to 1988.

6. Adelstein to the author in a telephone interview on March 5, 2014.

7. Adelstein to the author in a telephone interview on March 8, 2014.

8. Adelstein to the author in a telephone interview on March 10, 2014.

9. Adelstein to the author. This anecdote is also on page 129 in Angell and Jaffe's *Tales from the Locker Room*.

10. The Fleisher anecdote was told to the author by Adelstein. Fleisher's hand problem had begun to affect his playing. Fleisher and Midgette's book *My Nine Lives,* recounts Fleisher's struggles with focal dystonia. Fleisher is also mentioned in Charry's *George Szell* on page 222: "Fleisher's problem with his right hand is now well known, but at the time just beginning and sadly obvious." Szell's playing for Fleisher is also related on page 129 in Angell and Jaffe's *Tales from the Locker Room*.

11. Adelstein to the author.

12. Adelstein to the author in his telephone interview on March 5, 2014.

13. Adelstein to the author in his March 8, 2014, telephone interview.

14. Adelstein to the author in his March 5, 2014, telephone interview.

15. Adelstein to the author in his March 5, 2014, telephone interview.

16. French hornist Ernani Angelucci played in the Cleveland Orchestra from 1937

to 1944. He left to play in the Philadelphia Orchestra for a year and returned to play in the Cleveland Orchestra from 1946 to 1980. Angelucci's personality and playing were described to the author by Dr. David Sachs, who, as a teenager, had studied horn with Angelucci. Dr. Sachs's conversation with the author took place in a Cleveland restaurant in June 2013. Al Kofsky corroborated his statements about Angelucci during a March 1, 2014, interview with the author.

17. Trombonist Al Kofsky stated that in Szell's eyes Angelucci could do no wrong. Angelucci's mischievous pranks were commented on by Kraus, Zupnik, and Kofsky in their conversations and interviews with the author.

18. Cellist Diane Mather to the author during her December 29, 2011, interview with the author.

19. Page 281 in Rosenberg: "Bloom considered Szell his musical father, especially after one incident when the conductor consoled him after the pressure of playing principal horn became unbearable." "That's what the damned thing does," Martin Morris remarked to Kraus, who then related his comment to the author.

20. Principal hornist Myron Bloom played in the Cleveland Orchestra from 1954 to 1977. In his March 15 and March 29, 2013, phone interviews with the author, Bloom discussed his years with the Cleveland Orchestra and his tremendous admiration for George Szell.

21. Hornist Martin Morris to Felix Kraus (who echoed the same sentiments in conversations with the author). Kraus told the author and several friends that he, too, if he didn't need the money, would have gladly played in the Cleveland Orchestra without pay.

22. Trombonist Al Kofsky to the author in his June 2015 interview.

Chapter 9. Auditions and Mavericks

1. Al Kofsky to the author in his March 1, 2014, interview.

2. Oboist Felix Kraus told the author of Menga's behavior during a 1968 Szell concert. Student violinist Lorentz Ottzen also related to the author a story about Menga's dramatic tantrum at one of young Menga's violin lessons. During this incident involving Menga's tantrum and partial destruction of his teacher's studio, Menga's father had looked on approvingly, apparently considering his son's behavior justified because of Menga's "genius."

3. Menga's virtuosic recital at the Cleveland Institute of Music in 1967 was witnessed by Kraus, the author, and various Cleveland Orchestra players.

4. Donald Rosenberg's *Cleveland Orchestra Story* lists the orchestra's personnel on pages 637–50. Menga's membership in the orchestra was 1967–68. Oboist Felix Kraus commented on Menga and his recital: "Crazy as a loon but could he play!" Violinist Rosen in a June 12, 2016, telephone interview with the author also stated that Menga was crazy.

5. During a 1964 string quartet session with the author, Strawn related the details

of her audition for the Cleveland Orchestra including Louis Lane's repeated words of Szell's. Strawn found her audition experience and Szell's words funny.

6. Strawn to the author in 1964.

7. Rosemary Brown was interviewed by David Frost on his September 23, 1971, television program.

8. John Mack in a conversation with Felix Kraus and the author.

9. Kraus told the author in one of their many conversations that some of his colleagues enjoyed misbehaving when guest conductors were on the podium. Their actions were especially egregious when Robert Shaw conducted them, and Louis Lane sometimes had to endure their attitudes also.

10. Russian-born concertmaster Josef Gingold can be heard on a YouTube interview speaking admiringly of George Szell and the Cleveland Orchestra (https://www .youtube.com/watch?v=4vA8QEyQKjE).

11. The musician who overheard Szell and Druian arguing was Felix Kraus, who had been onstage fixing a reed.

12. Druian's firing is mentioned on pages 275–76 in Charry, *George Szell*, and on page 384 in Rosenberg's book about the Cleveland Orchestra.

13. Majeske laughingly told many of his colleagues, including Felix Kraus, what Szell had said.

14. Bob Larson was the lawyer employed by MAA in the lawsuit instigated by violinists Gino Raffaelli and Bert Siegel. The year they spent in the second violin section is documented in the pages 638–39 list of orchestra personnel in Rosenberg's book. During his January 22, 2014, interview with the author, Larson spoke of his role in the lawsuit.

15. The Cleveland Orchestra musicians constantly conjectured about Szell's motives and actions, and oboist Kraus told the author of the conversations he heard in the musicians' locker room.

16. Cellist Harry Fuchs gleefully told recording engineer Vladimir Maleckar about his deliberate actions with Szell's lawn, and Maleckar repeated the conversation to the author during his November 26, 2011, interview.

17. Vladimir Maleckar to the author during his December 19, 2011, telephone interview.

18. Szell's mistreatment of principal cellist Lynn Harrell was related to the author by Al Kofsky, Joela Jones, and Bernard Adelstein during their interviews. And Felix Kraus told the author about Szell's treatment of Harrell, whom Kraus regarded as a great cellist.

19. Cellist Diane Mather to the author during her December 9, 2011, interview. A version of this anecdote is also on page 101 of Angell and Jaffe's *Tales from the Locker Room*.

20. Oboist Kraus heard Mather's words about playing every note when the two were leaving the stage after a performance of Strauss's Don Juan. He told the au-

thor what she had said during a conversation with the author immediately after the concert.

21. Harrell told Kraus about his refusing to give back his contract with the orchestra, and Kraus repeated the incident to the author during one of their many conversations.

22. Cellist Diane Mather to the author in her December 9, 2011, interview.

23. In the author's interviews with Cleveland Orchestra members, many mentioned Szell's threatening light blue eyes that were magnified by his thick-lensed glasses. Oboist Kraus tried to avoid Szell's eyes by positioning his own glasses far down his nose so that their frames would blot out Szell's eyes. Szell called him on the carpet for doing so and ordered him to get his glasses' frames adjusted.

24. Principal violist Abe Skernick was one of the few players who enjoyed extremely friendly relations with Szell. He had gone through a famous battle in World War II and thereafter took mere surveillance from Szell calmly. Skernick's players, knowing he could successfully intercede for them, were not as worried as players in other sections of the orchestra. The author has observed that viola players in general aren't as high-strung as the other string players, perhaps owing to fewer demands on their techniques. Composers of orchestral music usually give the brilliant and difficult passages to the violin sections.

25. Al Kofsky told the author about Zauder's recruitment to assistant personnel manager. Kofsky himself later assumed that position.

26. Zauder to Felix Kraus, who then related Zauder's words to the author.

27. Cellist Don White was hired by Szell in 1957, a fact noted in a Cleveland *Plain Dealer* headline: "Orchestra Here Signs First Negro" and quoted on page 298 of Rosenberg's book. Charry's book on pages 173–74 also tells of the Birmingham incident.

28. Cellist Diane Mather to the author during her December 9, 2011, interview. Szell's acknowledgment of the Kent State shooting is on Charry's page 284 and Rosenberg's page 391. Mather's words are also on page 104 in Angell and Jaffe's book.

Chapter 10. Conductor Wannabes

1. The most famous of such pseudo-conductors is probably financial publisher Gilbert Kaplan, whose performances of Mahler's *Second Symphony* were extensively documented in his January 27, 2016, obituary in the *New York Times*.

2. Danny Kaye's 1978 appearance conducting the Cleveland Orchestra is told on page 469 in Rosenberg's *Cleveland Orchestra Story*. On pages 122–23 of Barbirolli's *Life with Glorious John,* Barbirolli mentions Kaye's friendship with John Barbirolli, saying that Kaye attended many of Barbirolli's rehearsals. "Although Danny was not a trained musician, he was so naturally talented, with such innate rhythmic sense, that he 'conducted' very well."

3. In his April 8, 1969, interview with John Culshaw for BBC television, Szell mentions studying scores at the piano. Pages 41 and 42 in Gal's *Directions for Score-*

Reading discuss piano playing of orchestral scores. Szell and Gal, having studied with the same teacher in Vienna—Richard Robert—would probably have formed similar score-reading techniques.

4. Robert Zupnik to the author during one of his numerous interviews and telephone calls. Zupnik said in several of his interviews, "Szell was one of the geniuses of the twentieth century."

5. During the author's July 27, 2016, interview with current Cleveland Orchestra librarian Robert O'Brien in the Szell Memorial Library at Severance Hall, the author was shown various pages of Szell's scores of the Robert Schumann symphonies. Szell's notations, done in pencil in a neat hand, were on many pages.

6. Oboist Felix Kraus, in his many conversations with the author, spoke of Szell's evolving interpretations that occasioned more rehearsals of compositions "that we knew backwards and forwards. He just couldn't resist tinkering."

7. Beethoven to Marie Bigot (p. 448 in Swafford's *Beethoven*).

8. Because Szell had, in his youth, been a composer of nearly three hundred pieces, he understood the art of music composition more thoroughly than many other conductors who didn't themselves compose. His sense of duty to the score was apparent to his musicians, who said that Szell's few words to them about a composition would often start "We must remember that. . . ." There would then follow a brief and succinct description of the time period of the composition along with remarks on how the musicians of that period may have played the work. Many of the Cleveland Orchestra musicians spoke of Szell's erudition and his constant studying. On page 318 in Irving Kolodin's *The Interior Beethoven,* Kolodin includes an instance of Szell's great memory for musicological facts: "In a conversation with the late George Szell, I hazarded the guess that the lighter strokes represented a hand other than Mozart's, possibly that of a copyist. "No," Szell corrected. "It is probably all in Mozart's handwriting. Don't forget, in those days they made ink by dropping a tablet in a little jar of water. As the ink was used up, more water was added. By the time Mozart had written out the main lines of the four movements and came back to put in the other voices, the ink had become very much diluted. That's why the part that was written in later is lighter in tone." Some of Szell's artistic credo may be found on page 292 of Charry. The author has known this story for some time but could not find the source of the Bartók remark.

9. Stravinsky's famous statement is on page 495 in Vera Stravinsky and Robert Craft's *Stravinsky in Pictures and Documents*.

10. Szell's words about artistic morality are quoted on page 292 in Charry.

11. Robert Zupnik to the author.

12. This anecdote, quoted on page 326 of Rosenberg's book, was known among the orchestra members and told to the author by Felix Kraus. Page 208 of Charry's *George Szell* includes Szell's opinion that the hall was a disaster and they had best tear it down and begin all over again.

13. Maleckar to the author during his November 26, 2011, interview.

14. Andrew Kazdin's overriding of Szell's interpretations was told to the author on November 26, 2011, by recording engineer Vladimir Maleckar. Maleckar also said, "I visited Columbia Records' office in New York and was told that they improved the reverberations on the records they made by using their second-floor stairwell. Somebody there had noticed that it had just the right amount of reverberation time and they could easily enhance the finished product. So that stairwell was partly responsible for the success of Columbia Records."

15. Zupnik to the author.

Chapter 11. The Percussion Section

1. John Mack to the author.

2. A timpanist who wished to remain anonymous stated that most conductors (and indeed other musicians) don't understand percussion instruments, neither their individual properties nor the expertise that goes into playing them.

3. The notorious drum incident is corroborated by musicians of the Szell era who vividly remember it and is included on page 203 of Charry's *George Szell*. Although most of the Szell-era musicians agreed that Szell was fair in his dealings with them, they also said that it was Szell's fault the drummers became too nervous to play the Bartók solo with its designated accents and diminuendo.

4. This anecdote is recounted on page 203 of Charry's book.

5. Weiner to the author in a January 21, 2012, interview.

6. Weiner to the author in his January 21, 2012, interview. Weiner joined the Cleveland Orchestra in 1963 and was appointed principal percussionist by Szell in 1968. Weiner also is a lawyer and his May 21, 2015, e-mail to the author detailed some of his activities on behalf of his colleagues when they agitated for better working conditions in 1967.

7. Weiner to the author in his May 21, 2015, e-mail corrections of the author's text.

8. Weiner to the author in his January 21, 2012, interview. Weiner's auditions and interactions with Szell also are partially recounted on pages 125 and 126 in Angell and Jaffe's *Tales from the Locker Room*.

Chapter 12. Szell's Methods, Touring Travails

1. These events were witnessed by the author. At one particular reception the author saw Louis Lane off in a corner by himself, totally ignored by the fans crowding around Szell.

2. Felix Kraus to the author.

3. Pages 91–93, 183, and 217 in violinist Temianka's *Facing the Music* speak of Temianka's and Szell's great friendship and respect for each other's musicianship.

4. Rautenberg to the author. Rautenberg's deception is also mentioned on pp 36, 37 in Angell and Jaffe's *Tales from the Locker Room*. But the detail "black shoe polish" is incorrect. Rautenberg told the author he used black paint.

5. The incident between Szell and the Chicago Symphony's assistant principal clarinetist, Jerry Stowell, and Szell's subsequent command to Marcellus was related to the author in a January 12, 2013, e-mail from Dwight Robinson. Robinson had studied clarinet with Stowell some years previously.

6. The loss of a cellist because of an endpin malfunction was told to the author by lawyer Robert Larson in his January 22, 2014, interview.

7. The balky calfskin incident was told to the author by Robert Larson in his January 22, 2014, interview.

8. The bus-in-the-snowdrift anecdote and Szell's scolding of the Mount Holyoke audience were related to the author by oboist Zupnik in one of his many telephone conversations.

9. The *Deep Throat* anecdote was told to the author by Felix Kraus. He was more than "somewhat mistaken" in his prediction of the film's failure. In subsequent years *Deep Throat* has grossed more than fifty million dollars worldwide.

10. Page 293 in Rosenberg's *Cleveland Orchestra Story* relates this incident.

11. Page 293 in Rosenberg's book contains Szell's quote.

12. The Szell–Previn story is on page 316 in Rosenberg's book. Angell and Jaffe's *Tales from the Locker Room*, page 74, places the event at Szell's home: a faulty recollection, because Szell owned two pianos, one grand piano in the living room and another upright piano in his second-floor studio. Nathalie and James Diener, present owners of the Szell house, showed the author where the two pianos had been located when they purchased the house from Helene Szell in 1970. It is interesting to note that page 108 in Fleisher and Midgette's *My Nine Lives* relates a similar incident but places it in a hotel room in London with Fleisher at a coffee table. The author also has heard several other versions of this anecdote from the various Cleveland Orchestra members interviewed.

13. Recording engineer Vladimir Maleckar reported the exchange to the author during his November 26, 2011, interview. Maleckar had been following behind Szell and Serkin as they exited Severance Hall after a rehearsal.

Chapter 13. Prodigies, Masterpieces, Boulez

1. Theodore Leschetizky's rejection of young Szell is mentioned on page 5 of Charry's book. Szell's parents then took their son to Richard Robert, a Viennese piano teacher who numbered among his young pupils Rudolf Serkin. In that atmosphere little George flourished.

2. Menuhin's home schooling is mentioned on page 9 in Tony Palmer's *Menuhin: A Family Portrait*: "Marutha, Yehudi's mother, decided they (her three children) would do better at home. A host of private tutors were engaged: tutors in foreign languages, history, and geography. Most of his sister Yaltah's earliest memories are of 'teachers coming and going.'" Page 148: "Yehudi by his own admission had only one day's public education." Toscanini's fascination with Yehudi Menuhin's playing was

first engendered during their time together in 1932 on an ocean liner. Pages 172–173 in Robert Magidoff's *Yehudi Menuhin: The Story of the Man and the Musician* tells of Toscanini's giving the young artist a backrub during the intermission of a Menuhin concert, taking father Menuhin's place, and saying, "Tonight I am Papa." Page 37 in Palmer's book includes a quote by Zamira, Yehudi's only daughter: "My father was never allowed to cross a street by himself. "Yehudi Menuhin's deteriorated playing in his adult years is mentioned on pages 51–52 in Janos Starker's *The World of Music According to Starker:* "A few days later I attended a concert where Yehudi Menuhin played and I was shocked. I had heard him in Budapest when he was about fourteen or fifteen and had been awed, like everyone else. Now his tone was cramped and his breathing was audible at the back of the hall. He was struggling." And Palmer's book says on page 38, "In later years, Yehudi often seems unable to play all the right notes." The author, while playing in the Portland Symphony (now the Oregon Symphony) in 1957, witnessed Menuhin's mediocre playing. But his kind nature and yoga headstand demonstrated during intermission of the rehearsal endeared him to the musicians.

3. Joela Jones interview with the author on April 5, 2012.

4. Joela Jones interview with the author on October 31, 2012.

5. Joela Jones interview on February 21, 2013. Jones was hired by Szell in 1968 to be his principal keyboardist. She is still in the Cleveland Orchestra as of this writing.

6. Oboist Felix Kraus witnessed this scene also and reported it to the author.

7. Joela Jones interview with the author on April 5, 2012.

8. Szell's Teutonic approach to Debussy's *La Mer* and Ravel's *Daphnis and Chloé* was a running joke among the orchestra's musicians: Felix Kraus to the author.

9. Carlos Kleiber's graceful conducting of the Vienna Philharmonic is on the Deutsche Grammophon DVD *New Year's Concert in Vienna.*

10. Szell was the total opposite of Leonard Bernstein in podium style. Bernstein's was unabashed emotion, especially when conducting Mahler symphonies.

11. Szell need not have been ashamed of his inability to conduct Stravinsky's masterpiece. Musicologist Nicolas Slonimsky, on page 69 of his book *Perfect Pitch*, relates that Stravinsky's great composition had Boston Symphony conductor Serge Koussevitzky similarly stumped. He asked Slonimsky for help, and Slonimsky altered much of the score by rebarring it with blue pencil lines. These lines made it visually more understandable and, with less confusing pages in front of him, Koussevitzky got through its performance. Years later, using this same blue-penciled score, his protégé Leonard Bernstein recorded the work with great panache. The rebarred score didn't help the timpanist, however. He still had to doggedly count. And concertmaster of the Philadelphia Orchestra Anshel Brusilow, on page 173 of his book *Shoot the Conductor,* says, "Bill Smith had rewritten it for Ormandy in such a way that it sounded almost like what Stravinsky wrote but was much easier to play." Smith was the assistant conductor of the Philadelphia Orchestra.

12. The family of the now-deceased professional timpanist requested anonymity.

13. The author was accustomed to seeing many empty seats in Severance Hall on the nights contemporary compositions were performed. Audience comments heard by the author after Boulez conducted one of his own compositions: "He's trying to educate us." Another: "I don't like having this stuff crammed down my throat."

Chapter 14. Concert Experiences

1. Robert Conrad during his September 27, 2013, interview with the author.

2. Robert Conrad during his October 29, 2013, interview with the author.

3. Robert Conrad during his December 5, 2013, interview with the author.

4. Robert Conrad's November 17, 2014, e-mail to the author.

5. Szell interview by Conrad, from a tape recording held in the WCLV archives and given to the author by Conrad.

6. Szell's words on a tape in the WCLV archives. A copy CD was given to the author by Conrad.

7. Szell's words to Conrad were repeated to the author by Conrad.

8. Robert Conrad interview with the author on October 29, 2013.

9. Robert Conrad interview with the author on December 5, 2013.

10. Robert Conrad interview with the author on September 27, 2013.

11. Conrad to the author. Pages 190–91 in Charry's *George Szell* and page 305 in Rosenberg's *Cleveland Orchestra Story* mention the Benny concert. The anecdote is also on page 76 in Angell and Jaffe's *Tales from the Locker Room*.

12. McFerrin concert at Severance Hall was witnessed by the author. The orchestra's singing earned a standing ovation from the audience.

13. Conrad to the author during a September 27, 2013, interview.

14. Heller told Felix Kraus about his surreptitious taping of rehearsals at Szell's request. Robert Zupnik recalled the musicians' alarm that they had been spied upon.

15. The Sunday afternoon WCLV broadcasts of the Cleveland Orchestra began in 1965. Most of the players listened to them. The superior recording techniques enabled the musicians to hear how they actually sounded. The author witnessed oboist Felix Kraus listening to and frequently taping these broadcasts so he could closely study them.

Chapter 15. Szell's Haydn and Schumann Interpretations

1. Page 106 in Charry's *George Szell* reports the firings. Page 248 in Rosenberg's *Cleveland Orchestra Story* refers to Szell's firings as "a veritable bloodbath."

2. On page 46 of his article "Szell: A Partial Memoir," published in *Cleveland* magazine in February 1974, Louis Lane wrote of Szell's obsession with eighth notes. "Szell would get dreadfully annoyed and emotionally aroused over someone in the orchestra not placing an eighth note correctly. I can remember vividly an incident when one player with whom Mr. Szell had been on the best personal terms was not, in Szell's opinion, placing an eighth note properly in a phrase. Szell kept stopping

the orchestra and pointing to the player and saying, 'Incorrect! Incorrect! You're placing it late! You're placing it late!' This happened two or three times before the player finally got it right. Still both were quite discomfited because they had been friends. So after the rehearsal the player went into Szell's office and I could hear him saying, 'George, George, are you going to make an issue out of an eighth note? Is an eighth note worth our friendship?' And I could hear Szell reply loudly, very loudly, though his door was closed, 'When it comes to my music it certainly is.' That very fairly represented his view: a friend is a friend and it's wonderful to have one, but an eighth note is more important."

3. This is one of Szell's legendary remarks to the orchestra. Felix Kraus told it to the author. Szell's avoidance of Viennese schmaltz is described in Joseph Wechsberg's Profiles article in the *New Yorker* magazine of May 30, 1970.

4. Szell's recordings of Haydn symphonies are listed in Rosenberg's discography on pages 659 and 660 and Charry's discography on pages 339–40.

5. Robert Zupnik to the author in one of his many interviews and telephone conversations between 2011 and 2016.

6. The Cleveland Orchestra's music librarian, Robert O'Brien, in his July 27, 2016, interview with the author in the Szell Memorial Library at Severance Hall, opened all four of Szell's Schumann symphony scores. As he leafed through the pages, the extent of Szell's penciled-in changes was readily apparent. O'Brien discussed the fact that legally none of the contents of the Szell library can be removed from the room, neither for scanning or photocopying. Any copying of his scores has to be done by hand "although one could take photographs." This partially explains why no other conductor has been able to duplicate or come close to the brilliance of Szell's recordings of these symphonies completed in 1960. O'Brien spoke admiringly of Szell's painstaking preparation for orchestra rehearsals, proof of which can be seen not only in the Schumann symphony scores but also the scores of other compositions in Szell's repertoire. Recordings of the Schumann symphonies are listed on page 346 of Charry's discography and page 667 in Rosenberg's discography. It can be conjectured that Szell used 1959 to work on his reorchestrations of *Symphony No. 3* and *Symphony No. 4* recorded in 1960. The recording dates—chronologically— were *Symphony No. 1*, October 24 and 25, 1958; *Symphony No. 2*, October 24, 1958; *Manfred Overture*, January 21, 1959; *Symphony No. 4*, March 12, 1960; *Symphony No. 3*, October 21, 1960. The preparation and recording of the two-disc set thus took place over a span of three years.

7. Violinist Jerry Rosen during phone interviews on May 28, 2015, and June 12 and 19, 2016. Rosen also edited some of the author's words in a May 29, 2015, e-mail.

8. Rosen, who participated in the Szell recording of Schumann's fourth symphony on March 12, 1960, stated to the author that Szell recorded the twenty-four-and-a-half-minute symphony in one continuous take—the way it was performed, because "the work is not divided into separate movements but, instead, the four sections are

linked." The author's conjecture on the months it took Szell to reorchestrate the four Schumann symphonies might also be supported by two additional facts: the widely spaced recordings from 1958 to 1960 and the need to use concert performances of them at Severance Hall as paid rehearsal time prior to each recording session. Szell, ever conscious of suitable programming for each concert, would have been careful to integrate the Schumann symphonies into the Cleveland Orchestra's regular series at Severance Hall. Regarding Schumann's *Symphony No. 4*, musicologist Hans Gal, in his slender book *Schumann Orchestral Music*, says on page 29, "The Schumann enthusiast has reasons to place this symphony at the top of the four." Gal then goes on to give an analysis of the Fourth Symphony but only briefly mentions the stupendous transition marked "Langsam" (slow). Rosen, however, got it right when he singled out this section and said he got chills from it. Those mere sixteen measures constitute one of the most uncanny moments in the entire symphonic literature. Here Schumann conjures up an unearthly image comparable to the avenging angels blowing trumpets in Michelangelo's painting *The Last Judgment* on the wall of the Sistine Chapel. The two CD album of the four Schumann symphonies performed by Szell and the Cleveland Orchestra is on the Epic label and listed as digitally remastered from the original source (Sony Classical Number MH2K62349).

9. Robert O'Brien interview with the author on July 27, 2016.

10. Page 64 in Rosenberg's *Cleveland Orchestra Story* lists the years of Lifschey's membership in the Cleveland Orchestra: 1950–59 and 1960–65. In the one year during which he was absent, oboist Alfred Genovese played the oboe solos in the recording of Schumann's *Symphony No. 4*. His beautiful playing proves that his departure from the Cleveland Orchestra was solely because Szell wanted Lifschey back. The oboe-cello solos in the second movement of Schumann's *Symphony No. 4* were played by Genovese and Jules Eskin, the orchestra's principal cellist from 1961 to 1964. Their matched tone qualities (even similar vibratos) are of great beauty.

Chapter 16. Attire, Duty, Respect, Decorum

1. Philip Kennicott recalls in his September 2, 2013, *New Republic* essay "Strike Down the Band," "When [Mark] Twain recounted his European travels to American audiences, one thing he noted approvingly about the musical experience in Germany was the audiences: they were quiet, well-behaved, and reverential, unlike American audiences which still enjoyed classical music as if in a beer hall." Szell's disgust with U.S. audiences is mentioned on page 137 of Charry. He put his foot in his mouth in a Cleveland interview, comparing the good manners of the Europeans with the "vulgar" ones of the United States.

2. Szell's insistence on proper audience behavior was related to the author by lawyer William Buss in a November 20, 2014, telephone interview.

3. Cleveland Orchestra musicians spoke of Szell's great ability with the standard repertoire, but his inabilities with some contemporary compositions were well known

among them. Szell himself, aware of his lacks in contemporary repertoire, hired Pierre Boulez in 1967 to conduct contemporary compositions. Boulez had previously made his Cleveland Orchestra debut in March 11 and 13, 1965, conducting his own compositions, various French ones, and Stravinsky's *Le Rossignol*. Page 255 in Rosenberg says, "When Szell had lapses in his conducting technique—especially in twentieth century music—Concertmaster Gingold would discreetly lead the ensemble."

4. Szell's words to his musicians were related to the author by recording engineer Vladimir Maleckar during his November 26, 2011, interview.

5. Emmanuelle Polle's *Jean Patou* extensively documents the influence of French couturier Patou, widely considered the most fashionable European man.

6. Oboist Felix Kraus told the author of Szell's stringent dress code. The musicians had to wear dress shirts, suits, and ties, especially on tours involving hotels, buses, trains, and planes.

7. Cellist Jacqueline du Pré performed the Elgar Cello Concerto in E minor. The author witnessed her 1967 performance.

8. Rosen spoke about his relations with Szell in an interview with the author. His treatment by Szell also is included on pages 109–16 in Angell and Jaffe's *Tales from the Locker Room*. On page 110, Rosen admits, "I was a little animal. . . . I didn't know how people talked at society parties and was careless about the way I dressed."

9. Szell's antipathy to bad acoustics and the color blue for concert halls partially dates from the 1958 renovation of Severance Hall. Page 300 in Rosenberg includes Szell's words: "Please make sure that it is not overlooked to change the ghastly blue paint (on the stage shell) back to the color matching the rest of the auditorium." Severance Hall's auditorium ceiling and walls were, and remain, shades of buff and ivory with touches of silver.

10. This tape recording is in the WCLV archives. A copy was given to the author by Conrad.

11. A tape recording of Szell's disgusted words on background music is in the WCLV archives and Conrad gave a CD copy to the author during her October 29, 2013, interview with him at his WCLV office.

12. Tape recording in the WCLV archives; a copy was given to the author.

13. Page 126 in Charry's *George Szell* gives the complete Szell quote: "The Kalliwoda Overture as such, the putrid piece of an utterly imitative, 5th rate composer, is only ridiculous today. But there is *one* excuse to include it and give the public something to think (and chuckle) about: if one puts it in antithesis to the Bartok *Divertimento*, discreetly indicating what 'New Music' was at the Philharmonic's first concert and what it is today."

14. Clara Rankin to the author in her March 19, 2014, interview.

15. Peter Uhlir to the author in his November 13, 2011, interview.

16. A photo of Szell laying out his travel wardrobe on his bed may be seen on the wall of Severance Hall's restaurant.

17. Felix Kraus told the author that Szell was constantly prying into every aspect of the workings at Severance Hall, even including checking up on the toilet paper in the hall's restrooms. He said that his colleagues frequently joked about Szell's fussiness even in nonmusical matters. Kraus told the author about his experience at a local grocery store, where the butcher told him Szell always insisted on cutting the meat himself.

18. Furnishings in the Szell's home were seen by Nathalie Diener in 1970 and described to the author in a June 7, 2013, interview with Nathalie and James Diener at their Shaker Heights home.

19. Page 212 in Matthew Boyden's *Richard Strauss* tells that "Strauss had no choice but to stand by and watch family and friends conform to his wife's increasingly eccentric house rules. Everyone—including Strauss—had to wipe their feet before entering the house (in later years she placed a second mat in front of the first, just in case)." Page 92 in Michael Kennedy's *Richard Strauss* records Pauline Strauss's "fits of rage" over domestic trivialities such as mud on the carpet. Bob Conrad told the author that he was required to remove his shoes before entering the Szell living room when he came to improve Szell's audio system. And Szell himself was in his stocking feet while pacing around the living room with a T-bar antenna.

20. Page 14 in Charry's book tells that the young Szell impressed composer Richard Strauss with his cufflink trick.

21. Witnessed by various orchestra members, including Felix Kraus, who related the incident to the author. This incident was also related by Cleveland Orchestra violinist Alvaro deGranda in Angell and Jaffe's *Tales from the Locker Room*.

22. Overheard by Louis Lane and told to Felix Kraus, who related it to the author.

23. Felix Kraus received these small date books between 1963 and 1969. They are in the author's possession.

24. Felix Kraus told the author that it was only after Szell's death that some of the musicians dared to begin divorce proceedings.

25. In his December 18, 2014, conversation with the author, Robert Sweeney discussed Szell's friendship with Father Dulin. Cleveland Orchestra keyboardist Joela Jones, in her February 21, 2013, conversation with the author, also spoke about Szell's friendship with Father Dulin.

26. Because Catholicism was the official religion in Austria, it was politically and socially expedient to be Catholic. When Szell's Jewish parents moved to Vienna from Budapest in 1900 they converted and had their three-year-old son baptized. There is no record documenting Szell's practicing of Catholicism as an adult. But his close friendship with Catholic priest Father Dulin suggests his sympathy with aspects of Catholicism.

27. Louis Lane mentions Szell's "proprietary and paternal attitude toward the orchestra" on page 46 in his "Szell: A Partial Memoir," published in *Cleveland* magazine's February 1974 issue.

Chapter 17. A New Chorus Conductor

1. The hiring of Robert Shaw in 1955 is mentioned on page 159 of Michael Charry's *George Szell* and on page 289 in Donald Rosenberg's *Cleveland Orchestra Story*.

2. Soprano Chris Miles's August 9, 2012, telephone interview with the author.

3. Soprano Chris Miles's August 9, 2012, telephone interview with the author.

4. Pages 6 and 7 in Keith Burris's *Deep River* recount the details of Shaw's upbringing. *New York Times* music critic James Oestreich, however, in his April 30, 2016, article on Shaw casts doubt on various statements of Burris's.

5. Page 3 in Mussulman's *Dear People . . . Robert Shaw*.

6. Page 12 in Mussulman.

7. Page 55 in Burris.

8. Page 56 in Burris.

9. Szell taught at Mannes School of Music in New York from 1940 to 1944. Shaw attended Mannes for only a short time, taking a mere four lessons with Szell. Szell's ideas about aspiring conductors may be seen in his requirements for apprentice conductors of the Cleveland Orchestra announced in a bulletin on November 21, 1958. They are listed on page 301 in Charry: "Applicants will be asked to play a piano piece of the classical repertory, conduct from memory the first movement of a symphony by Brahms, Beethoven or Mozart (not with orchestra but by humming or singing the leading voice): play an orchestral score on sight; transpose from piano or orchestral score at sight; orchestrate a page of piano music; realize at sight a figured bass; and will be examined in hearing, rhythm, and musical memory." Shaw at the time of his first encounter with Szell could barely play the piano and would certainly not have been able to read a full orchestral score let alone perform a piano reduction of it. So Szell would not have been interested in him at that time.

10. Page 375, n. 9, in Charry includes a June 16, 2002, interview with Louis Lane in which Lane mentions that Szell was suspicious of the musicianship of violinists, which Ormandy also had been, calling them "one-line musicians." Szell favored conductors who were pianists because they play and therefore hear multiple lines, a basic feature of orchestral music.

11. Page 66 in Burris; page 59 in Mussulman.

12. Robert Shaw was hired in 1955 to direct the Cleveland Orchestra Chorus.

13. Baritone Gerald Hughes to the author in his March 26, 2013, interview.

14. Felix Kraus to the author.

15. Both keyboardist Joela Jones and chorister Gerald Hughes mentioned in their interviews that Shaw was a humble person who, though he used profanity when upset by the chorus's mistakes, was not dictatorial and went out of his way to apologize for his own mistakes.

16. Page 19 in Robert Blocker's *Shaw Reader* includes the dagger letter. And page 143 in Mussulman mentions the dagger letter. This letter is virtually a concrete poem

and is in chorister Gerald Hughes's collection of Shaw letters to his chorus, which Hughes lent to the author on March 26, 2013.

17. Joela Jones to the author in her October 31, 2012, interview.

18. Former chorus member soprano Charlene Peterson mentioned her tape recording of Shaw reading a Winnie-the-Pooh story.

19. Felix Kraus told the author about some orchestra members' treatment of Shaw, as did Joela Jones in her October 31, 2012, interview.

20. Marc Lifschey to Felix Kraus and the author in 1964.

21. Joela Jones to the author in her October 31, 2012, interview.

22. Page 290 in Rosenberg.

23. Joela Jones to the author in her February 21, 2013, interview.

24. Joela Jones to the author in her February 21, 2013, interview.

25. Joela Jones to the author in her February 21, 2013, interview.

26. Chorister Gerald Hughes to the author during his March 26, 2013, interview.

27. Felix Kraus to the author.

28. Martin Geck's *Johann Sebastian Bach: Life and Work*, page 32, records that for the *St. Matthew Passion* Bach had apparently bought the most expensive paper available in Athens-on-the-Pleisse to emphasize the solemnity of what he was leaving for posterity. Page 409 adds that Bach "reserves the secco for relating the biblical events only, the words of which are written in red ink in the definitive score."

29. Shaw's words about J. S. Bach are quoted on page 71 of Blocker's *Shaw Reader*.

30. Oboist Felix Kraus to the author during one of their many conversations.

Chapter 18. The Musicians' Insurrection

1. Vaclav Laksar played second bassoon in the Cleveland Orchestra from 1955 to 1981. His hair-trigger temper was attested to by his colleagues Felix Kraus, Diane Mather, and Allen Kofsky. Cellist Diane Mather told the author in her December 9, 2011, interview that several other second-chair woodwind players experienced Szell's abusive language that morning and that Szell was "badgering" Laksar.

2. Felix Kraus to the author.

3. Felix Kraus to the author.

4. Witnessed by the author and Felix Kraus.

5. Charry's book on page 197 tells some of the musicians' objections and court rulings. The protest would last several years with the musicians filing suit against the Cleveland Musicians' Union and also management.

Chapter 19. Picketing and Resolution

1. A partial list: concertmaster Josef Gingold left the orchestra in 1960, assistant concertmaster Arnold Steinhardt left in 1964, violinist Sidney Weiss left in 1966, cellist Michael Grebanier left in 1963, principal cellist Jules Eskin left in 1964, cellist Ronald Leonard left in 1957, principal oboist Marc Lifschey left in 1965, clarinetist

George Silfies left in 1963, hornist Roy Waas left in 1966, cellist Thomas Liberti left in 1966. With the exception of Gingold, Steinhardt, and Lifschey, all these listed players left the Cleveland Orchestra for other orchestras that paid better.

2. Szell to Felix Kraus at his 1963 audition.

3. Szell's 1966 letter to Barksdale stating his wishes for a summer venue for the Cleveland Orchestra is quoted on page 257 of Charry's *George Szell*. A search for the archival document was unsuccessful.

4. Felix Kraus to the author in the days leading up to the strike.

5. Feelings ran high and many musicians made belligerent statements in the locker room and in telephone calls to their colleagues. Some friendships unraveled during this tense period, and several principal players initially sided with management. Kraus spoke of these internal frictions during conversations with the author.

6. Page 249 in Charry's book states that the picketing began on September 11, 1966.

7. Felix Kraus recounted management's lawyer's words to the author.

8. Page 252 in Walter Salmen's *The Social Status of the Professional Musician from the Middle Ages to the 19th Century*: "The orchestral player always thought of himself as an obedient and loyal servant"; page 254: "Beyond this, the musician was still, as he had always been, considered as belonging to a group of unreliable non-serious lazy 'characters'"; page 257: "Yet this also had the effect, in the course of time, of placing him [the orchestral player] beneath the composer, the virtuoso, and finally also the conductor, who were no longer, from an artistic and social point of view, 'his kind.'"

9. Isabel Trautwein to the author in an April 30, 2015, telephone conversation.

10. Felix Kraus to the author.

11. Page 376 in Rosenberg's *Cleveland Orchestra Story*. By one calculation method, these amounts would be around $1400 and $1700 in 2017 dollars.

12. Allen Kofsky to the author during his June 2015 interview.

Chapter 20. A Suitable Summer Site

1. Szell's annual European vacations centered on resorts: Charry's book on page 177 mentions the Dolder Grand Hotel in Zurich and the Kurhotel Montafon in Schrung, Austria. His page 107 states that one of Szell's favorite resorts was the Hotel du Golf at Crans-sur-sierre in Valais, Switzerland. His page 182 mentions Szell's stay at the Bircher-Benner Clinic in Zurich for a health regimen.

2. Page 261 in Charry's *George Szell*.

3. Van Dijk to the author in his November 13, 2011, interview.

4. Buckminster Fuller was an architect, author, and inventor of the geodesic dome. He coined the word *tensegrity*.

5. Van Dijk to the author in his July 18, 2012, interview.

6. Van Dijk interview on August 28, 2012. Page 219 in Leon Fleisher and Anne Midgette's *My Nine Lives* states that Saarinen turned down the Boston Symphony's request for an inexpensive building, saying that for such a small sum all they would

get would be "a shed." A local, unnamed architect designed it instead. This fact is contrary to the popular belief that Saarinen had designed the shed.

7. Acoustician Chris Jaffe to the author during his April 29, 2013, telephone interview. Pages 130–34 in Jaffe's *The Acoustics of Performance Halls* speaks of his role in the acoustics design of Blossom Pavilion. His page 133 includes the statement "I replied that the best-liked orchestral sound could always be found in the upper balconies of these halls and suggested that perhaps we should design the new pavilion for the Cleveland Orchestra as the world's biggest balcony. At first we all laughed at the thought, but as the evening wore on and the idea took shape, Pete and I sketched out a design on the back of a napkin. That sketch evolved into the final design of the facility, and Blossom Music Center stands today as a fine al fresco music pavilion and as the world's biggest balcony."

8. Van Dijk interview with the author on October 12, 2013.

9. Architect William Gould to the author in his January 2015 interview.

10. Van Dijk's words in his April 19, 2013, interview: "I knew they had found the spot." He quoted the words of Renaissance artist-biographer Giorgio Vasari: "*non murato ma veramente nato*" (not built, but rather born; Lotz, page 45). Elation must have seized van Dijk as he viewed the pristine spot. Here would be his creation—a giant shell of perfect symmetry cradled by the welcoming earth.

11. Van Dijk to the author in his September 13, 2013, interview said, "It hadn't been done before." Carol Strickland's *Annotated Arch*—a comprehensive study of arches—contains not a single example of a tilted arch held up by exterior columns. Apparently van Dijk's innovation was truly a first.

12. Although van Dijk's great Blossom design is usually described as an arch holding up a vast roof, van Dijk stated in his August 25, 2015, letter to the Cleveland *Plain Dealer*'s architectural critic Steve Litt, "Blossom's is not an arch at all. As you know, an arch and a vault span a space and transfer the weight of the roof to the foundations. Blossom's pavilion has a very large pie-shaped plan. Overheard, a clear-span roof is about an acre in area. In sections, the roof slopes from 82 feet above the stage to 20 feet at the eave over the rear seats. This heavy roof is supported on 22 trusses of various lengths. One end of each truss bears on one of a pair of big beams that rise from a foundation on the lawn to the top of the pavilion. There they join with a curved section of beam forming a continuous assembly (which looks like a tilted arch). An exterior row of ten leaning columns (my flying buttresses) holds up this beam assembly. All of the exterior structure is of weathering steel called Cor-Ten. (When I was at Saarinen's we were designing the John Deere headquarters building which was the first to use Cor-Ten.) The other end of each roof truss lands on a long beam along the arc of the rear-seating row. This beam is really a series of lintels supported on six small columns. So you see, the roof sits on trusses which sit on beams which sit on columns which sit on footings. No Arch!" But Miklas Peller, in his e-mail to the author on February 13, 2017, stated that "there are 21 main roof

trusses." A scale drawing accompanying the text of his e-mail confirmed the number of trusses. Apparently, van Dijk had forgotten the exact number of trusses, an understandable error after the lapse of forty-seven years.

13. Richard Gensert's many accomplishments—two books, honors, and work with van Dijk—were told to the author by his widow, Carrol Gensert, in her interviews of June 3, 2013, and April 17, 2014. Richard Gensert had frequently attended Cleveland Orchestra concerts and had a huge collection of classical records. In her interview with the author on December 14, 2013, Laurel Gensert Bishop spoke of her father's love of music and his opinion that nature is the best designer.

14. Page 261 in Charry's book mentions that the Cleveland Orchestra's board of trustees hired Belluschi as their architectural advisor. Belluschi's words about van Dijk's design were told to the author by van Dijk.

15. Van Dijk to the author in his August 28, 2012, interview.

16. Van Dijk to the author in his October 12, 2012, interview.

17. The Ford Foundation grant is mentioned on page 258 of Charry's book. Van Dijk told the author that Szell was obviously interested in the model.

18. Jaffe to the author in his April 29, 2013, interview.

19. Page 258 in Charry's book.

20. Robert Zupnik told the author about these events in Humel's life. Zupnik had known Humel when they were both in high school in Cleveland. As teenagers they played chamber music together at Humel's home in Shaker Heights.

21. See page 317 in Rosenberg's *Cleveland Orchestra Story*.

Chapter 21. Blossom's Creators

1. An April 1, 2016, *New York Times* article on the 1956 Soviet repression of the Hungarian uprising: "225 people were executed and more than 10,000 imprisoned."

2. Miklos Peller, in his April 24, 2014, interview with the author, provided details of his participation in the uprising of 1956 that was initiated by Hungarian students and writers. He said that within days of the uprising Soviet tanks and troops returned, banned gatherings on the streets, and arrested the insurgents. Peller, who was in his third year of gymnasium, knew his participation in the uprising doomed him to prison or perhaps even execution. Determined to escape from Hungary, he set out for the Austrian-Hungarian border with no money, food, or belongings so that in case he was apprehended he could claim he was simply walking home. Several days and nights of hiding out and being sheltered by kindly farmers brought him to the border, which was land-mined, lined with a double barbed wire fence, and manned by sentries. Under cover of night Peller pried apart the barbed wire fencing and dared to walk across the mined ground. He then walked several days to Salzburg where there was a camp of 20,000 Hungarian refugees awaiting ships to the United States. The ten-day crossing of the Atlantic on the General Leroy Eltinge ship was marked by severe storms, but the 2,500 seasick immigrants celebrated Christmas

Eve, singing Christmas songs and Hungarian folk songs with Peller at the piano. His first sight of the United States was on New Year's Eve and, as the ship approached land, he saw the Statue of Liberty lit up by fireworks in the harbor. "It looked just the way I had seen it on a postage stamp. It was a fantastic moment." His desperate odyssey had taken him two months, but at last he was safe. Upon landing, he made contact with his uncle in Cleveland. At that time Cleveland had the largest Hungarian settlement outside Budapest.

3. Peller to the author in his August 24, 2014, interview.

4. Peller in his August 24, 2014, interview with the author.

5. Peller interview with the author on August 26, 2014.

6. The Tennessee foundry that fabricated the enormous arch-beam sections delivered them to the Blossom site on flatbed trucks. One of the photos of the construction process depicts one section of the arch-beam with two men standing next to it to show its enormous size. This photograph was given to the author by Peter van Dijk. Turner Construction Company, a national firm, was responsible for the pouring of the concrete foundations and all above- and below-ground construction.

7. Peller to the author during his October 12, 2012, interview.

8. A page of drawings showing the progressive stages of a spider's web was found among Gensert's papers, and a copy was given to the author by his widow, Carrol Gensert, during her April 17, 2014, interviews with the author.

9. Peller to the author during his August 26, 2014, interview.

10. During his August 26, 2014, interview with the author, Peller said that Don Leinweber was responsible for "all of Blossom's substructure" and that he, Peller, designed the superstructure: "Everything that is above ground." The author could not make contact with Leinweber, but several photos of the exposed substructure were given to the author by architect Peter van Dijk. Pages 263–64 in Charry tell of Szell's concern with the musicians' comfort at Blossom; his concerns partially dictated the substructure of Blossom: dressing rooms, lounge area, lighting, and so on. Oboist Felix Kraus told the author of the musicians' surprise and pleasure upon seeing the Blossom underground facilities for the first time. He said that the showers, locker rooms, and lounge area were very impressive and quite superior to those of Severance Hall. The cafeteria was a first for them, as was the spacious lounge area.

11. Van Dijk to the author during his September 13, 2013, interview.

12. These anecdotes are part of the lore about Szell that circulated among the Cleveland Orchestra members. Felix Kraus related both stories to the author. The two anecdotes also are mentioned on page 25 of Angell and Jaffe's *Tales from the Locker Room*.

13. The police officer who stopped Szell was a friend of orchestra violinist Ed Matey, who told Felix Kraus the story.

14. Those who didn't know Szell would not have known that he was insatiably

curious about everything and that his fabulous memory enabled him to retain everything he observed.

15. Szell in his galoshes at the Blossom construction site is pictured in a photograph, a copy of which was given to the author by van Dijk.

16. Sam Jaffe related his conversation with Humel to Felix Kraus and the author during a visit at Jaffe's home.

17. Szell was more than merely curious because he realized that Blossom's amenities directly affected the musicians and hence their performances during what he called Cleveland's "beastly summers." See page 263 in Charry.

18. Van Dijk during his July 18, 2012, interview.

19. Pages 263–64 in Charry's book list some of Szell's requests for Blossom. An archival search for Szell's requests, as mentioned in Charry, was unsuccessful.

20. Van Dijk to the author during his April 19, 2013, interview.

21. Van Dijk September 13, 2013, interview with the author.

22. Van Dijk to the author during his September 19, 2013, interview.

23. Peter van Dijk and Miklos Peller described the various stages of Blossom's planning and construction during their many interviews with the author. They both supplied the author with photos and drawings of some of the plans. The evolution of Blossom's exterior can be seen in the photos of early models of it. Peller gave the author a photocopy of the hinge he designed for the stabilization of the giant supporting girders. Another photo shows Peller himself photographing the hinge.

24. Van Dijk to the author during his September 19, 2013, interview.

25. Peller to the author during his August 26, 2014, interview.

Chapter 22. The Blossom Triumph

1. Van Dijk to the author during his November 13, 2011, interview.

2. Statement by an audience member that was overheard by the author while both stood looking at the Pavilion.

3. In his July 18, 2012, interview with the author, van Dijk mentioned a pizza box that had come to him after the opening Blossom concert. It was signed by several admiring teenagers; he had saved it through all the intervening years.

4. Recording engineer Vladimir Maleckar, during his November 26, 2011, interview and subsequently in his December 19, 2011, and February 2, 2013, telephone conversations with the author. Maleckar recalled his experiences with Daniel Flickinger, emphasizing Flickinger's great expertise coupled with his counterculture persona.

5. Maleckar's recollection that Flickinger's design and components for the Blossom sound system cost $125,000 is different from the figure of $70,000 mentioned in Rosenberg's *Cleveland Orchestra Story*. The Cleveland Orchestra archives contain a single sheet of paper detailing the audio components for the Blossom pavilion. It enumerates each component with its brand—e.g., Yamaha, Spectra Sonics—but

without cost itemization. It is, however, explicit as to placement, connections, and other specifications. This list was obviously generated by an audio engineer, someone with complete knowledge of the subject. It bears a revision date of March 1986. The author could find no mention of Daniel Flickinger in any of the books and articles written about Blossom. Nor is there any mention of Flickinger in the Cleveland Orchestra Archives. But since no one else has been credited as the creator of Blossom's sound system, the author accepts Vladimir Maleckar's statements about Flickinger for inclusion in this book.

6. Recording engineer Vladimir Maleckar during his February 2, 2013, telephone conversation with the author.

7. Wikipedia: Daniel Flickinger.

8. Vladimir Maleckar to the author during his December 19, 2011, telephone conversation with the author.

9. Maleckar to the author during his November 26, 2011, interview.

10. Maleckar to the author during his November 26, 2011, interview.

11. Jaffe, on pages 131–34 of his book *The Acoustics of Performance Halls*, details his design solutions.

12. Schwarzkopf's performance witnessed by the author. Charry's book on page 252 quotes Szell's words on what Schwarzkopf would sing on her two Blossom concerts.

13. Van Dijk to the author during his November 13, 2011, interview. He made clear his reverence for the famous architects of the past, citing Brunelleschi's ingenious solution for the dome of Santa Maria del Fiore in Florence. Throughout his many interviews, van Dijk returned again and again to the idea that good architecture entails looking for the problem and then seeking the solution. He also referred to "starchitects" who design buildings for their own glory and not for usefulness. Van Dijk's term "starchitects" has been widely repeated by architectural critics; the term, however, was not coined by him. Structural engineer Miklos Peller referred to Van Dijk's genial nature in one of his interviews: "Peter was a joy to work with."

14. Van Dijk to the author during his November 13, 2011, interview.

15. Van Dijk to the author during his November 13, 2011, interview.

16. Van Dijk in his September 13, 2013, interview.

17. Peller to the author in his April 24, 2014, interview. Jaffe's page 134, which discusses the boom problem, doesn't tell the complete story of how the Blossom boom was eliminated. Peller's account of the elimination of the boom is the more knowledgeable one. Peller, working with the firm of Warner and Swasey, successfully fixed the problem.

18. Rosenberg's book on page 359 discusses the Blossom boom: "One sound frequently heard at Blossom was not so welcome. Finn put it deftly in 'The Plain Dealer.' At least once during each concert at Blossom Music Center it happens: VA-ROOM! From somewhere backstage comes a loud hollow crash, the sort of noise some giant

door might make slamming in an echo chamber," he reported. Rosenberg continues, "[T]he sound was silenced by the 1971 season."

19. Peller to the author in his August 26, 2014, interview.

20. Peller to the author in his August 26, 2014, interview.

Chapter 23. The Death of the Maestro

1. Page 48 of Louis Lane's article "Szell: A Partial Memoir" tells of Szell's disillusionment with the U.S. government: "During the last three or four years before he died, Szell became increasingly detached from the orchestra and generally disillusioned with life in this country. In a way it started with the assassination of President Kennedy. But the thing that really hit all the orchestra was that we didn't know anything about Vietnam until we toured the Soviet Union in 1965 and there it was all over the newspapers. If you could read any Russian at all there it was on the front page day after day. It was all that the Russians asked us about politically."

2. Page 48 of Lane's "Szell: A Partial Memoir": "He became suspicious of President Johnson—not just of the president, but of the whole process of our government, feeling that it neither really reflected sound, constructive policies from the standpoint of what a logical man would do to govern the country properly nor did it reflect what the people really wanted. He would get terribly upset reading the paper and eventually, towards the end, he stopped reading it altogether."

3. Page 48 of "A Partial Memoir" also relates Szell's disappointment with his players for striking: "A major incident precipitating Mr. Szell's disengagement from the day-to-day affairs of the orchestra came during the players' strike in 1967; after that he turned much of the actual administration of the internal orchestra over to me, though Mr. Szell was still very much in charge of musical policy." "The 1967 strike was unusually bitter." "During the negotiations, for the first time, the orchestra players' committee demanded changes in the contract which reduced the implied authority of Mr. Szell and set up appeal procedures for dismissed players. I think that that was what caused Mr. Szell to withdraw the full power of his will, let us call it, from the orchestra. He felt that the players misunderstood him; that they did not fully appreciate his intentions. Mr. Szell felt that the orchestra should trust that whatever he did was for the orchestra's best interest and that it was not a subject for discussion. Thus, he opposed any appeals procedure. The players were equally determined in demanding them. Eventually a compromise was reached where an appeal mechanism was set up with Mr. Szell as final arbiter. Regardless, Mr. Szell was emotionally alienated from the orchestra by the experience."

4. Vladimir Maleckar to the author during his November 26, 2011, interview.

5. Although Barksdale had resigned his position as manager in 1969 (p. 386 in Rosenberg), he was nevertheless present on the Japanese-Anchorage tour as assistant manager and Szell's loyal friend and helper. Charry says on page 277, "Szell was truly fond of Barksdale and their working and personal relationship remained

cordial to the end." In her January 24, 2017, telephone interview with the author, Gretchen Larson confirmed Barksdale's presence on the tour and said, "Everybody knew that Szell was ill and struggling to carry on." Page 393 in Rosenberg quotes orchestra cellist Michael Haber recalling what happened during Beethoven's "Eroica": "Szell stopped conducting for an instant. 'I felt a chill through my body. . . . I remember thinking something was terribly wrong.'" Page 285 in Charry tells that Szell was energetic on the podium but that when he came offstage Barksdale had to momentarily support him.

6. Felix Kraus told the author about escorting Helene Szell to several shrines in the city where she enjoyed looking at the beautiful gardens. Helene was an avid gardener at the Szell's home in Shaker Heights. In an interview with Natalie and James Diener on June 7, 2013, at their home, which they had purchased from Helene Szell in 1970, Natalie spoke of the sunken garden that Helene had caused to be installed when the Szells took up residence in May 1951. Mrs. Diener also spoke of the oriental screens in the Szell living room which Helene had purchased.

7. Helene Szell usually sat in the Szell box during Szell's concerts at Severance Hall. She was not the kind of conductor's wife who frequent the backstage areas of concert halls. Most of the Cleveland Orchestra musicians interviewed by the author said they rarely saw Helene and certainly had few conversations with her. In Japan she would have followed her usual routine of sitting in a box seat in the various auditoriums. In her January 24, 2017, interview with the author, Gretchen Larson stated that Helene usually "maintained a distance and was aloof with various people." (Robert Larson, as the orchestra's lawyer, accompanied the orchestra on its foreign tours and enjoyed a warm relationship with Szell. His wife Gretchen, who came along with him, had occasion to observe both Szells in a variety of settings.)

8. Charry's book contains a picture of Szell holding the hands of two kimono-clad girls while acknowledging the applause of the audience in Japan in 1970.

9. Elmer Setzer told Felix Kraus, who told the author, about Szell's touching Diane Mather's hair.

10. Page 287 in Charry's book includes Szell's checking into University Hospital on June 10, 1970, immediately upon his return to Cleveland. Rosenberg's *Cleveland Orchestra Story*, page 396, also tells of Szell's critical condition.

11. Lane's "Szell: A Partial Memoir" on page 48: "We spent two or three hours that afternoon talking about the opera."

12. Felix Kraus overheard Lane speaking with two orchestra players and related the conversation to the author.

13. Lane's "Szell: A Partial Memoir." On page 48 Lane says, "We spent two or three hours that afternoon talking about the opera [Don Giovanni]. He was in good form and rather cheerful, rather sarcastic, pointing out that most sopranos committed this musical indiscretion at this point in the opera and most tenors that indiscretion at

that spot and there was a discussion, too, of tempi, articulation—all of the things that concern musicians."

14. Page 48 in Lane's "Szell: A Partial Memoir": "He really had a very good constitution; he was seldom ill and when he was he took very good care of himself so that his illness was kept to as short a duration as possible. Even though he was 73 in 1970, Mr. Szell gave no indication [to his musicians] of expecting to die any time soon."

15. Lane's "Szell: A Partial Memoir," page 48: "Mr. Szell was emotionally alienated from the orchestra by this experience."

16. Page 288 in Charry's book tells of Lane receiving a telephone call at Blossom from the hospital reporting Szell's death on July 30, 1970. Page 397 in Rosenberg's book reports that Szell died at 9:50 PM. from complications of a heart attack he had suffered previously in the hospital. Robert Finn, music critic of the *Plain Dealer*, recounted how the musicians received the news of Szell's death that evening: "The shock of the news left them dumb. They filed out silently to cars and buses, each with his own private thoughts, no one much inclined toward conversation."

17. Joela Jones to the author during her October 31, 2012, interview similarly spoke of the news of Szell's death. "Nobody knew what to say. We were all in shock."

18. The memorial concert for Szell took place on Monday August 3, 1970, in Severance Hall. The orchestra's string section played Bach's "Air on the G String." After various eulogies, the orchestra played other orchestral selections led by Louis Lane.

19. Robert Zupnik to the author during his lengthy November 21, 2013, phone interview. Zupnik's words were similar to those of other musicians who had played under Szell such as trombonist Al Kofsky and oboist Felix Kraus.

20. Szell's foreword is on the unnumbered page at the beginning of Robert Marsh's *The Cleveland Orchestra*. This elegant slip-cased book was published in 1967 by World Publishing. A copy of this book was given to each Cleveland Orchestra member in 1968 on the occasion of the fiftieth anniversary of the first concert by the Cleveland Orchestra.

Bibliography

Ackerman, Jennifer. *The Genius of Birds*. Penguin, 2016.

Agus, Ayke. *Heifetz As I Knew Him*. Amadeus, 2005.

Alexander, Christopher, Christopher Ishikawa, and Murray Silverstein. *A Pattern Language*. Oxford University Press, 1977.

———. *The Nature of Order* (4 vols.). The Center for Environmental Structure, 1980–2005.

Angell, Lawrence, and Bernette Jaffe. *Tales from the Locker Room: An Anecdotal Portrait of George Szell and His Cleveland Orchestra*. ATBOSH Media, 2015.

Auer, Leopold. *My Long Life in Music*. Frederick Stokes, 1923.

Barbirolli, Evelyn. *Life with Glorious John: A Portrait of Sir John Barbirolli*. Robson, 2003.

Birkin, Kenneth. *Hans von Bülow: A Life for Music*. Cambridge University Press, 2011.

Blocker, Robert, ed. *The Robert Shaw Reader*. Yale University Press, 2004.

Boyden, Matthew. *Richard Strauss*. Northeastern University Press, 1999.

Brusilow, Anshel, and Robin Underdahl. *Shoot the Conductor: Too Close to Monteux, Szell, and Ormandy*. University of North Texas Press, 2016.

Burris, Keith. *Deep River: The Life and Music of Robert Shaw*. GIA, 2013.

Campen, Richard N. *Distinguished Homes of Shaker Heights: An Architectural Overview*. West Summit, 1992.

Chapin, Schuyler. *Musical Chairs: A Life in the Arts*. Putnam, 1977.

Charry, Michael. *George Szell: A Life of Music*. University of Illinois Press, 2011.

Cigliano, Jan. *Showplace of America: Cleveland's Euclid Avenue*. Kent State University Press, 1991.

Cohen, Adam. *Imbeciles: The Supreme Court, American Eugenics, and the Sterilization of Carrie Buck.* Penguin, 2016.

Cooper, Michael. "For Sale, Playing a Heady Tune." *New York Times,* March 26, 2014, C1.

Fleisher, Leon, and Anne Midgette. *My Nine Lives: A Memoir of Many Careers in Music.* Doubleday, 2010.

Gal, Hans. *Directions for Score-Reading.* Wiener Philharmonischer, 1924.

———. *The Golden Age of Vienna.* Chanticleer, 1948.

———. *Schumann Orchestral Music.* University of Washington Press, 1979.

Geck, Martin. *Johann Sebastian Bach: Life and Work.* Translated by John Hargraves. Harcourt, 2006.

Hughes, Adella Prentiss. *Music Is My Life.* World, 1947.

Isacoff, Stuart. *Temperament: The Idea That Solved Music's Greatest Riddle.* Knopf, 2001.

Jaffe, J. Christopher. *The Acoustics of Performance Halls: Spaces for Music from Carnegie Hall to the Hollywood Bowl.* W. W. Norton, 2010.

James, Clive, *Cultural Amnesia: Necessary Memories from History and the Arts.* W. W. Norton, 2008.

Karberg, Richard, and James Toman. *Euclid Avenue: Cleveland's Sophisticated Lady, 1920–1970.* Cleveland Landmarks Press, 2002.

Kennedy, Michael. *Richard Strauss: Man, Music, Enigma.* Cambridge University Press, 1999.

Kennicott, Philip. "Strike Down the Band." *New Republic,* 244, no. 14 (September 2, 2013), 46.

Kolodin, Irving. *The Interior Beethoven.* Alfred Knopf, 1975.

Krisch, Joshua. "When Racism Was a Science." *New York Times,* October 14, 2014.

Lane, Louis. "Szell: A Partial Memoir." *Cleveland* magazine, February 1974.

Leiter, Robert. *The Musicians and Petrillo.* Bookman, 1953.

Lieberman, Jeffrey. *Shrinks: The Untold Story of Psychiatry.* Little, Brown, 2015.

Loesser, Arthur. *Men, Women, and Pianos: A Social History.* Dover, 1954.

Lotz, Wolfgang. *Architecture in Italy: 1500–1600.* Yale University Press, 1995.

Magidoff, Robert. *Yehudi Menuhin: The Story of the Man and the Musician.* Doubleday, 1955.

Marsh, Robert. *The Cleveland Orchestra.* World, 1967.

Mussulman, Joseph. *Dear People . . . Robert Shaw.* Himshaw Music, 1996.

Oestreich, James. "Saluting Robert Shaw, a Conductor of Humanist Spirituality." *New York Times,* April 30, 2016, C1.

Palmer, Tony. *Menuhin: A Family Portrait.* Faber & Faber, 1992.

Polle, Emmanuelle. *Jean Patou: A Fashionable Life.* Flammarion, 2013.

Quenqua, Douglas. "Sweetest Violins Explained: Holes Fill In Blanks." *New York Times,* February 16, 2015, D2.

Rilke, Rainer Maria. *Duino Elegies*. Translated by J. B. Leishman and Stephen Spender. Norton, 1939.

Rombauer, Irma, and Marion Rombauer Becker. *The Joy of Cooking*. Bobbs-Merrill, 1975.

Rosenberg, Donald. *The Cleveland Orchestra Story*. Gray, 2000.

Roy, Klaus. *Not Responsible for Lost Articles: Thoughts and Second Thoughts from Severance Hall, 1958–1988*. Cobham and Hatherton, 1993.

Salmen, Walter. *The Social Status of the Professional Musician from the Middle Ages to the 19th Century*. Translated by Herbert Kaufman and Barbara Reisner. Pendragon, 1983.

Segel, Harold. *The Viennese Coffeehouse Wits: 1890–1938*. Purdue University Press, 1993.

Slonimsky, Nicolas. *Perfect Pitch*, edited by Electra Slonimsky Yourke. Schirmer, 2002.

Sorenson, Lorin. *Famous Ford Woodies*. Ten Speed, 2003.

Starker, Janos. *The World of Music according to Starker*. Indiana University Press, 2004.

Steinberg, Michael. *The Symphony: A Listener's Guide*. Oxford University Press, 1995.

Storch, Laila. *Marcel Tabuteau: How Do You Expect to Play the Oboe If You Can't Peel a Mushroom*. Indiana University Press, 2008.

Stravinsky, Vera, and Robert Craft. *Stravinsky in Pictures and Documents*. Simon and Schuster, 1978.

Swafford, Jan. *Beethoven: Anguish and Triumph*. Houghton Mifflin Harcourt, 2014.

Szell, George. Interview with John Culshaw. BBC, April 8, 1969.

Tassel, David, and John Grabowski. *Dictionary of Cleveland Biography*. Indiana University Press, 1996.

Temianka, Henri. *Facing the Music: An Inside View of the Real Concert World*. Alfred, 1980.

Thomson, Virgil. *Virgil Thompson: Musical Chronicles, 1940–1954*, edited by Tim Page. Library of America, 2014.

Walker, Alan. *Hans von Bulow: A Life and Times*. Oxford University Press, 2010.

Wechsberg, Joseph. "Orchestra." Profiles, *New Yorker*, May 30, 1970.

Zweig, Stefan. *The World of Yesterday*. Translated by Anthea Bell. University of Nebraska Press, 2009.

For Further Reading

Axelrod, Herbert R. *Heifetz*. Paganiniana, 1976.

Baker, Nicholson. *Human Smoke: The Beginnings of World War II, the End of Civilization*. Simon and Schuster, 2008.

Barber, Charles. *Corresponding with Carlos: A Biography of Carlos Kleiber*. Scarecrow Press, 2011.

Berman, Bob. *Zoom: How Everything Moves, from Atoms and Galaxies to Blizzards and Bees*. Little, Brown, 2014.

Black, Edwin. *War against the Weak: Eugenics and America's Campaign to Create a Master Race*. Dialog, 2012.

Brand, Stewart. *How Buildings Learn: What Happens after They're Built*. Viking, 1994.

Bremer, Deanna L., and Hugh P. Fisher. *Euclid Golf Neighborhood*. Arcadia, 2004.

Burris-Meyer, Harold, and Edward Cyrus Cole. *Theatres and Auditoriums*. Reinhold, 1949.

Carver, Norman F. Jr. *Italian Hilltowns*. Documan, 1979.

Clausen, Meredith. *Pietro Belluschi: Modern American Architect*. MIT Press, 1994.

Collier, Peter, and David Horowitz. *The Rockefellers: An American Dynasty*. Holt, Rinehart and Winston, 1976.

Dunning, John. *The Encyclopedia of Old-Time Radio*. Oxford University Press, 1998.

Eidam, Klaus. *The True Life of J. S. Bach*. Translated by Hoyt Rogers. Basic Books, 2001.

Feldman, David Henry. *Nature's Gambit: Child Prodigies and the Development of Human Potential*. Teachers College Press, 1991.

Feldman, Ruth Duskin. *Whatever Happened to the Quiz Kids: Profits and Perils of Growing Up Gifted*. Chicago Review, 1982.

Frank, Mortimer H. *Arturo Toscanini: The NBC Years*. Amadeus, 2003.

Fritzsche, Peter. *Life and Death in the Third Reich*. Belknap, 2008.

Geiringer, Karl. *Haydn: A Creative Life in Music*. University of California Press, 1982.

Gladwell, Malcolm. *Outliers: The Story of Success*. Little, Brown, 2008.

Goertzel, Victor, and Mildred. *Cradles of Eminence: Childhoods of More Than 700 Famous Men and Women*. Little, Brown, 1962.

Goldstein, Phyllis. *A Convenient Hatred: The History of Antisemitism*. Facing History and Ourselves National Foundation, 2011.

Gutman, Robert W. *Mozart: A Cultural Biography*. Mariner, 2000.

Hastings, Peter. *Musical Images: Photographs by Peter Hastings of Soloists and Conductors Who Have Performed with the Cleveland Orchestra*. Holly, 1981.

Horowitz, Joseph. *Artists in Exile: How Refugees from Twentieth-Century War and Revolution Transformed the American Performing Arts*. HarperCollins, 2008.

———. *Classical Music in America: A History of Its Rise and Fall*. W. W. Norton, 2005.

Hurd, Michael. *The Orchestra*. Facts on File, 1980.

Johnson, Sarah Anne. *The Art of the Author Interview*. University Press of New England, 2005.

Larick, Roy, Bob Gibbons, and Edward Siplock. *Euclid Creek*. Arcadia, 2005.

Lebrecht, Norman. *The Maestro Myth: Great Conductors in Pursuit of Power*. Citadel, 2001.

Martens, Frederick H. *Violin Mastery: Interviews with Heifetz, Auer, Kreisler and Others*. Dover, 2006.

Morton, Marian J. *Cleveland Heights*. Arcadia, 2005.

———. *Cleveland Heights Congregations*. Arcadia, 2009.

Newhouse, Victoria. *Art and the Power of Placement*. Monacelli, 2005.

———. *Site and Sound: The Architecture and Acoustics of New Opera Houses and Concert Halls*. Monacelli, 2012.

Powell, Kenneth, Ed. *The Great Builders*. Thames and Hudson, 2011.

Ross, Alex. *The Rest Is Noise: Listening to the Twentieth Century*. Picador, 2007.

Ruminski, Dan, and Alan Dutka. *Cleveland in the Gilded Age: A Stroll Down Millionaires' Row*. History Press, 2012.

Saler, Thomas D. *Serving Genius: Carlo Maria Giulini*. University of Illinois Press, 2010.

Schonberg, Harold. *The Great Conductors*. Simon and Schuster, 1967.

Schorske, Carl E. *Fin-de-Siècle Vienna: Politics and Culture*. Vintage, 1981.

Slatkin, Leonard. *Conducting Business: Unveiling the Mystery behind the Maestro*. Amadeus, 2012.

Solomon, Maynard. *Mozart: A Life*. HarperCollins, 1995.

Strickland, Carol. *The Annotated Arch: A Crash Course in the History of Architecture*. Andrews McMeel, 2001.

Tittle, Diana. *The Severances*. Western Reserve Historical Society, 2010.

Weschler-Vered, Artur. *Jascha Heifetz*. Macmillan, 1986.

Index of Names

MARCIA HANSEN KRAUS, a native of Portland, Oregon, attended Lewis and Clark College and Portland School of Music, where she studied cello, harmony, and composition. At Tanglewood, she played under the batons of Leonard Bernstein and Charles Munch.

Kraus joined the Portland (now Oregon) Symphony and was one of twenty cellists selected nationwide to participate in the first Pablo Casals Master Classes at the University of California–Berkeley. Subsequently she played in the Washington, D.C., Opera Orchestra.

Upon coming to Cleveland in 1963, Kraus founded the Hampshire String Quartet with members of the Cleveland Orchestra. Specializing in programs for elementary school students, the quartet performed under the auspices of Young Audiences. A 1976 grant from the Surdna Foundation enabled her to create and direct the ten-program multimedia series "The Good Earth Festival," combining chamber music, poetry, and art. For this series, Kraus created three-dimensional objects to present various poems and also wrote a thirty-foot-long composition, *Bug Piece,* for string quartet, featuring insect sounds.

In 1991, Kraus's *Concerto for English Horn and Orchestra* received its Cleveland Orchestra premiere under conductor Christoph von Dohnányi. Subsequent performances of the concerto include the Chicago Symphony, the Philadelphia Mainline Orchestra, and other U.S. and European orchestras. It is also featured on the CD *Gems for the English Horn.*

Kraus specializes in song cycles and works for double-reed instruments. Her most recent composition is *The Pied Piper Fantasy for English Horn, Narrator, and Orchestra.* She currently resides in Cleveland Heights, Ohio.

Only a Miner: Studies in Recorded Coal-Mining Songs   *Archie Green*
Great Day Coming: Folk Music and the American Left   *R. Serge Denisoff*
John Philip Sousa: A Descriptive Catalog of His Works   *Paul E. Bierley*
The Hell-Bound Train: A Cowboy Songbook   *Glenn Ohrlin*
Oh, Didn't He Ramble: The Life Story of Lee Collins, as Told to Mary Collins
    Edited by Frank J. Gillis and John W. Miner
American Labor Songs of the Nineteenth Century   *Philip S. Foner*
Stars of Country Music: Uncle Dave Macon to Johnny Rodriguez
    Edited by Bill C. Malone and Judith McCulloh
Git Along, Little Dogies: Songs and Songmakers of the American West
    John I. White
A Texas-Mexican *Cancionero*: Folksongs of the Lower Border   *Américo Paredes*
San Antonio Rose: The Life and Music of Bob Wills   *Charles R. Townsend*
Early Downhome Blues: A Musical and Cultural Analysis   *Jeff Todd Titon*
An Ives Celebration: Papers and Panels of the Charles Ives Centennial
    Festival-Conference   *Edited by H. Wiley Hitchcock and Vivian Perlis*
Sinful Tunes and Spirituals: Black Folk Music to the Civil War   *Dena J. Epstein*
Joe Scott, the Woodsman-Songmaker   *Edward D. Ives*
Jimmie Rodgers: The Life and Times of America's Blue Yodeler   *Nolan Porterfield*
Early American Music Engraving and Printing: A History of Music Publishing in
    America from 1787 to 1825, with Commentary on Earlier and Later Practices
    Richard J. Wolfe
Sing a Sad Song: The Life of Hank Williams   *Roger M. Williams*
Long Steel Rail: The Railroad in American Folksong   *Norm Cohen*
Resources of American Music History: A Directory of Source Materials from
    Colonial Times to World War II   *D. W. Krummel, Jean Geil, Doris J. Dyen,
    and Deane L. Root*
Tenement Songs: The Popular Music of the Jewish Immigrants   *Mark Slobin*
Ozark Folksongs   *Vance Randolph; edited and abridged by Norm Cohen*
Oscar Sonneck and American Music   *Edited by William Lichtenwanger*
Bluegrass Breakdown: The Making of the Old Southern Sound   *Robert Cantwell*
Bluegrass: A History   *Neil V. Rosenberg*
Music at the White House: A History of the American Spirit   *Elise K. Kirk*
Red River Blues: The Blues Tradition in the Southeast   *Bruce Bastin*
Good Friends and Bad Enemies: Robert Winslow Gordon and the Study of
    American Folksong   *Debora Kodish*
Fiddlin' Georgia Crazy: Fiddlin' John Carson, His Real World, and the World of
    His Songs   *Gene Wiggins*
America's Music: From the Pilgrims to the Present (rev. 3d ed.)   *Gilbert Chase*
Secular Music in Colonial Annapolis: The Tuesday Club, 1745–56   *John Barry Talley*
Bibliographical Handbook of American Music   *D. W. Krummel*
Goin' to Kansas City   *Nathan W. Pearson Jr.*

Carl Ruggles: Composer, Painter, and Storyteller   *Marilyn Ziffrin*
Never without a Song: The Years and Songs of Jennie Devlin, 1865–1952
   Katharine D. Newman
The Hank Snow Story   *Hank Snow, with Jack Ownbey and Bob Burris*
Milton Brown and the Founding of Western Swing   *Cary Ginell, with special
   assistance from Roy Lee Brown*
Santiago de Murcia's "Códice Saldívar No. 4": A Treasury of Secular Guitar Music
   from Baroque Mexico   *Craig H. Russell*
The Sound of the Dove: Singing in Appalachian Primitive Baptist Churches
   Beverly Bush Patterson
Heartland Excursions: Ethnomusicological Reflections on Schools of Music
   Bruno Nettl
Doowop: The Chicago Scene   *Robert Pruter*
Blue Rhythms: Six Lives in Rhythm and Blues   *Chip Deffaa*
Shoshone Ghost Dance Religion: Poetry Songs and Great Basin Context
   Judith Vander
Go Cat Go! Rockabilly Music and Its Makers   *Craig Morrison*
'Twas Only an Irishman's Dream: The Image of Ireland and the Irish in American
   Popular Song Lyrics, 1800–1920   *William H. A. Williams*
Democracy at the Opera: Music, Theater, and Culture in New York City, 1815–60
   Karen Ahlquist
Fred Waring and the Pennsylvanians   *Virginia Waring*
Woody, Cisco, and Me: Seamen Three in the Merchant Marine   *Jim Longhi*
Behind the Burnt Cork Mask: Early Blackface Minstrelsy and Antebellum American
   Popular Culture   *William J. Mahar*
Going to Cincinnati: A History of the Blues in the Queen City   *Steven C. Tracy*
Pistol Packin' Mama: Aunt Molly Jackson and the Politics of Folksong
   Shelly Romalis
Sixties Rock: Garage, Psychedelic, and Other Satisfactions   *Michael Hicks*
The Late Great Johnny Ace and the Transition from R&B to Rock 'n' Roll
   James M. Salem
Tito Puente and the Making of Latin Music   *Steven Loza*
Juilliard: A History   *Andrea Olmstead*
Understanding Charles Seeger, Pioneer in American Musicology
   Edited by Bell Yung and Helen Rees
Mountains of Music: West Virginia Traditional Music from *Goldenseal*
   Edited by John Lilly
Alice Tully: An Intimate Portrait   *Albert Fuller*
A Blues Life   *Henry Townsend, as told to Bill Greensmith*
Long Steel Rail: The Railroad in American Folksong (2d ed.)   *Norm Cohen*
The Golden Age of Gospel   *Text by Horace Clarence Boyer; photography by
   Lloyd Yearwood*
Aaron Copland: The Life and Work of an Uncommon Man   *Howard Pollack*
Louis Moreau Gottschalk   *S. Frederick Starr*
Race, Rock, and Elvis   *Michael T. Bertrand*

The University of Illinois Press
is a founding member of the
Association of American University Presses.

———————————————————

Composed in 11.5/14 Arno Pro
with Scala Sans Pro display
by Jim Proefrock
at the University of Illinois Press
Cover designed by Dustin J. Hubbart
Cover photo by Oleg Makarov, courtesy of the
Cleveland Orchestra Archives
Manufactured by Sheridan Books, Inc.

University of Illinois Press
1325 South Oak Street
Champaign, IL 61820-6903
www.press.uillinois.edu